The *History* of *Hell*

ALICE K. TURNER

The *History* of *Hell*

Harcourt Brace & Company

NEW YORK   SAN DIEGO   LONDON

Requests for permission to make copies
of any part of the work should be mailed to:
Permissions Department, Harcourt Brace & Company, 8th Floor,
Orlando, Florida 32887.

Library of Congress Cataloging-in-Publication Data
Turner, Alice K.
  The history of hell/by Alice K. Turner.
     p.   cm.
   ISBN 0-15-140934-X
   1. Hell—Comparative studies.   I. Title.
BL545.T87   1993
291.2′3—dc20   93-9909

Designed by Trina Stahl
Printed in the United States of America
First edition
A B C D E

Table of Contents

TABLE OF CONTENTS

Introduction

HUMAN BEINGS ALL OVER THE world believe in life after death, in the survival of the conscious personality after the body has ceased to function. Anthropologists, archaeologists, sociologists, classicists, analysts of the history of comparative religions agree that this is true of all cultures, so far as we know. Some part of us, we believe, continues to exist somewhere. Beyond that simple statement, the particulars of afterlife existence vary from culture to culture, from creed to creed, though not so much as one might think.

The dead can influence the living, we believe, interceding for us with the gods, perhaps, or appearing to us as ghosts to warn or plead or for their own obscure ghostly purposes. And we can influence them, burying or burning their cast-off bodies in approved fashion in order to assure their correct treatment in the afterlife. Our prayers, offerings, or neglect can affect them. Some cultures believe that spirits of the dead are reincarnated into new living bodies, human or animal. Others believe in a perpetual after-death existence in a land of the dead, a gloomy Ananka or Sheol, a sunny Tir na n-Og, a heroic Valhalla, or a whole patchwork of geographic regions as in ancient Egypt. And some believe in eventual physical resurrection of the flesh-and-blood molecules of the body.

Most of us, suspending logic, hold a number of these views at once. A good Christian, even in our secular age, might simultaneously believe that

From a thirteenth-century French Apocalypse, the Hellmouth

Uncle Arthur rests where he is buried in the cemetery; that his soul resides somewhere else, possibly above, courtesy of a merciful God; that his ghost or spirit might be contacted through a medium or spiritualist, or in a significant, perhaps prophetic dream; and that at a future Judgment Day his physical self will be reconstructed in the prime of manhood. A generation or two ago, many Western people believed that a ghost could haunt either a person or a particular venue, and some still believe it or half-believe it. In earlier days, if the departed person were not only Uncle but also King Arthur, he might be thought to be at once buried, in heaven, able to haunt, someday to be resurrected, and also preserved in a sort of permanent twilight sleep, waiting to be summoned by necessity or the Last Trump.

If he were, on the other hand, Saint Arthur, the very skin and bones of his dead body might be held in reverent awe; his body might be torn literally limb from limb, not by enemies but by faithful Christians, and the pieces borne away to shrines to be importuned by the sick and needy. Intercession or miraculous healing could occur, it was widely thought, through the medium of the dead saint's finger bone, or even a piece of his garment.

This book is about Hell, one of the two principal after-death destinations for the soul or surviving personality affirmed by the Christian religion.

Other great world religions have Hells of their own, with surprisingly familiar scenery: Hindus number up to several million of them, while Buddhists count from eight hells to several thousand. None of these hold a soul eternally, however, and no other religion ever raised Hell to such importance as Christianity, under which it became a fantastic underground kingdom of cruelty, surrounded by dense strata of legend, myth, religious creed, and what, from a distance, we might call dubious psychology.

This investigation is geographical rather than theological or psychological. What is Hell thought to be like? How did it come to be thought of in that way? And how did its topography change with the centuries? The pull of the Pit on the creative mind has been extraordinary. Poets and artists have always taken an immoderate interest in Hell, and have explored it in some curious ways. Theologically, Hell is out of favor now, but it still seems more "real" to most people than Fairyland or Atlantis or Valhalla or other much imagined places. This is because of the sheer mass and weight and breadth of ancient tradition, inventive fantasy, analytic argument, dictatorial dogma, and both simple and complex faith employed over a very long time—thousands of years—in the ongoing attempt to map the netherworld. The landscape of Hell is the largest shared construction project in imaginative history, and its chief architects have been creative giants— Homer, Virgil, Plato, Augustine, Dante, Bosch, Michelangelo, Milton, Goethe, Blake, and more.

Heaven is different. The theologians or poets or painters or survivors of "near-death experiences" who have tried to describe it tend to shy away from specifics. (Emanuel Swedenborg, the eighteenth-century spiritualist, was an exception.) The concept of Heaven is instinctively understood as a metaphor, an inadequate attempt to convey the bliss or ecstasy of the soul dwelling in God's grace, rather than a real address with pearly gates, harps, and halos. Hell, the place of punishment for sinners, has always been taken much more literally, perhaps because it is easier to understand. If Heaven is spiritual, Hell is oddly fleshly, with tortures that hurt and an atmosphere that is, particularly during some of Hell's history, excessively gross. But Hell also seems darkly intriguing in a way that Heaven does not. To some people, during some periods of history, it has seemed romantic.

A possibly radical aspect of Hell is what Hollywood might call its "entertainment quotient." Alongside solemn eschatology, there seems always to have been a subversive comic view of the afterlife. The laughter may be nervous, but it is undeniable. Graveyard humor stretches as far back into history as we can reach, to the very first tales of the Land of the Dead left to us from the ancient Near East, and survives today in our taste for horror films and the novels of Stephen King. Humor is not always present—no one would be so misguided as to dub Augustine or Milton a humorist—but it is never far away. Even the most supposedly pious and church-ridden periods of Christian history, the Middle Ages and the Puritan Reformation, offer examples of Merry Hell.

This is not a book about the Devil, except insofar as he is in residence. The subject of the Devil is complex and large, and touches on such serious problems as the existence of evil and suffering. Here, instead of diabology, we have infernology, a simpler subject. Demons and the Devil, either as prince or as principal sinner, are citizens and caretakers of the infernal regions, however, and we will encounter them there, though not without taking note of other underworld rulers, some of them queens rather than princes.

According to a recent Gallup poll, 60 percent of Americans believe in Hell or say they do, up from 52 percent in 1953. Only 4 percent think they're likely to go there. Other than Hitler or the latest serial killer, who *will* go? Among Christians, it is no longer politically correct to send political enemies, dissenters, atheists, or adherents of other religions to Hell, and "sin" in the post-Freudian age is more debatable than it used to be. I myself do not believe in Hell—I could hardly attempt this book if I did—but I have found it, literally, an incredibly interesting place to visit. Hell is viewed here as a human construct, not one fashioned by God or the Devil. This is a real history of an imaginary place.

One of the less savory notions of the early Church was that of the *abominable fancy*, the idea that part of the joy of the saved lay in contemplating the tortures of the damned. In many illustrations, blessed souls, ranged in orderly rows, their eyes lowered demurely toward the fiery chaos beneath, watch Heaven's eternal late-night TV. To follow the history of Hell is sometimes to identify, at least in this regard, with the blessed. There seems to be a kind of staged unreality about the whole business. But one should keep in mind that the idea of Hell has had, for a very long time, for a very large number of people, a fearful reality that has literally shaped their lives.

4

The Great Below

THE FIRST ACCOUNTS OF THE Land of the Dead that we know about were written nearly four thousand years ago on baked clay tablets from the Tigris-Euphrates Valley north of the Persian Gulf in Iraq. Sumer is the earliest name we have for the region, and, until the twentieth century, we knew very little about it. Modern Sumerian scholars have deciphered its non-Indo-European language, and their translations have brought us a new legacy of ancient poetry and myth.

The Sumerians were conquered by the Semitic Akkadians, and the area began to be known as Babylonia, after the principal city, Babylon. The Sumerians, Akkadians, Babylonians, and neighboring Assyrians are frequently grouped as Mesopotamians, and they shared many of the same beliefs and myths, though their gods sometimes went by different names, as did the Greek and Roman deities later on.

These very early, surprisingly sophisticated stories of gods and heroes have been extraordinarily pervasive in later religious thought, myth, literature, and eschatology. In *The Other World*, the medievalist Howard Rollin Patch lists a number of elements that appear in nearly all known accounts of the underworld or the otherworld (which need not be chthonic), Eastern as well as Western. These include: a mountain barrier, a river, a boat and boatman, a bridge, gates and guardians, an important tree. Except for the bridge (the Chinvat Bridge to the Land of the Dead appears in later

Persian literature from the region), all are already present in Mesopotamian mythology.

Four of the existing Mesopotamian stories are set partly in the Kingdom of the Dead. The best known is *Gilgamesh,* the epic tale of the hero-king which appears in the Sumerian, Akkadian, Hittite, and Assyrian languages. The others are worth knowing, however.

Looking back four thousand years, the cosmography seems familiar to anyone acquainted with classical or northern mythology. The gods, a pantheon led by the Sky God, inhabit the Great Above. The most interesting and lively Sumerian tales focus on Inanna, Queen of Heaven and Earth, whom the Akkadians called Ishtar; the Assyrians, Astarte; the Palestinians, Asthoreth. Queen Ereshkigal (Allatu in Assyrian), her sister, rules the dead in the Great Below, the Land of No Return. Mortals live on Earth, but patches of the otherworld adjoin this one. Beyond the Mountains of Mashu is the Earthly Paradise, with Dilmun as the Isle of the Blest, where one privileged mortal and his wife live forever. One thinks of Eden, of the Gardens of the Hesperides, of Atlantis, Avalon, the Land-Under-Wave, the Kingdom of Prester John, all here on earth—but where?

The Harrowing of Hell is a fundamental story that turns up in many guises throughout history. In it, a living person descends voluntarily to brave the dangers of the underworld on a quest that may range from the deeply serious (Orpheus seeks his wife) to the seriously misguided (Theseus and Peirithoos attempt to kidnap Persephone). Technically, it is called the "descent motif." The earliest of all descent stories that we know features Sumerian Inanna.

For obscure reasons, Inanna decides to visit her sister, Ereshkigal: "From the Great Above, she set her mind to the Great Below." Prudently, she informs her vizier, Ninshubur, of her intentions, instructing him as what to do should she not return. Dressed in her most splendid clothes and jewels, she is halted by an officious guardian at the first lapis lazuli gate to the Underworld, and the crown is removed from her head. At each of six following gates, an article of her apparel is taken, till, naked and furious, she confronts Ereshkigal, at whom she "flies." Her sister stops her in midflight, releasing on her the "sixty miseries" (in the Akkadian version) or hanging her from a stake (the Sumerian text). Three days and nights pass or, in the Akkadian version, a season in which "the bull springs not upon the cow, the ass impregnates not the jenny . . . the man lies down in his own chamber, the maiden lies down on her side." The Akkadian version marks this as a fertility myth; the Sumerian version may interest readers looking for parallels to Christ's story—or the story of Attis hung on his tree, or Odin on his.

Alarmed by her absence, the faithful vizier petitions the gods for his mistress's rescue. Reluctantly, Ereshkigal permits Inanna to return to the upper world, provided she can provide a substitute or ransom for herself (this theme will turn up again in a number of guises, one of them important to Christianity). A brace of escort goblins is sent topside to make sure she keeps her word. The ransom she sends is Dumuzi (Tammuz in Akkadian), Inanna's shepherd consort, who incurs the wrath of the goddess by having rather enjoyed her absence. Eventually, a political compromise is reached by requiring Dumuzi to stay below for only six months of the year if his sister will stand in for him during the other six months. (The turn-and-turn-about theme turns up again in the Greek tale of the brothers Castor and Pollux.)

This story is one of those known as dying-vegetation-god myths, many versions of which are known: Tammuz and Ishtar (Akkadian), Telepinus and Kamrusepas (Hittite), Baal and Anath (Ugaritic). Famous later ones are those of Osiris and Isis (Egypt), Attis (or Endymion) and Cybele (Middle East), Persephone and Demeter (Greece), Proserpina and Ceres (Rome), Adonis and Aphrodite or Venus (Greece and Rome). In the New Testament gospels, when the group of women appear at the sepulcher on the spring morning of the Resurrection, there's a clear echo of these old ritual stories of death and rebirth, winter and spring.

What's puzzling in the Inanna-Dumuzi story is that, while the typical fertility-myth goddess rescues and/or mourns her apparently dead consort-son (daughter), Inanna appears to have packed Dumuzi off to the Land of the Dead herself, although, in other Sumerian poetry (which can be graphically erotic), she is passionately attached to him. Perhaps a Dumuzi stand-in was dispatched to the underworld by the high priestess impersonating Inanna each year, after which she welcomed his handsome successor. Or perhaps time has confused two different tales, one with Inanna as the fertility sacrifice going to the Great Below voluntarily (or as a trick; Inanna was a tricky goddess), and one with Dumuzi as a substitute sacrifice.

"How Ereshkigal Found a Husband" is quite another matter. Though it's risky to interpret the intent of a story from a distant age and a strange culture, it is hard to see how the story of Nergal and Ereshkigal could ever have been meant to be taken entirely seriously, except perhaps by earnest doctoral candidates. Its format is classic; it appears to be the very first underground comedy, the *ur* ribald tale of a femme fatale and a hapless male.

It begins with a party. Since the Queen of the Dead cannot leave her underground kingdom to come to a banquet in the Great Above, she sends her vizier up to collect a covered dish of delicacies. The vizier is insulted by the minor god Nergal, and Ereshkigal demands a personal apology. The other gods give Nergal advice on how to survive his journey below; he must refuse bread, meat, beer, water for washing—anything proffered to him underground.

Down he goes, through the seven gates. Ereshkigal, the perfect hostess, offers him bread, meat, beer, and water, all of which he rejects. But when she offers her divine body to him, his resolve weakens. For a delirious week, they lie in bed together. Then, sated, he tries to get away. If she will let him go back to the Great Above to announce their betrothal to the gods, he promises, he will return at once. As all the men and most of the women who have heard versions of this exit line during the past four thousand years know, he is lying.

Ereshkigal is not about to put up with male fickleness, however. She sends a warning to the Great Above: unless Nergal returns to meet his fate,

---

Although this alabaster lady comes from Mesopotamia, she is too recent (c. 300 B.C.) to be a likely Ereshkigal, who, at the time that she flourished might have been portrayed more like the red clay figure on the right.

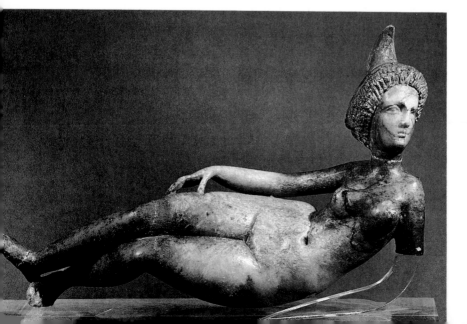

"I will send up the dead that they might devour the living,/ I will make the dead more numerous than the living." When her vizier arrives to fetch him back, Nergal disguises himself as bald, palsied, and lame, but the ruse fails. Down he must go again, giving up possessions at each of the gates, just as Inanna did. (Clearly, he has lost status: he was spared this on his first visit.) The tablet that records this journey breaks off here, but we know the ending: Nergal is listed in mythological dictionaries as Eresh-kigal's consort.*

Gilgamesh is a great and complex poem, but on a certain level it is simply the story of one man's attempt to escape *timor mortis,* the fear of death. When Gilgamesh, the king of Uruk, and his best friend (or lover) Enkidu offend Inanna, the gods decree that one of the offenders must die. In a dream, Enkidu has a dreadful premonition of the dusty, dreary underworld, where mighty kings have been brought low. He falls sick and dies, and Gilgamesh is not only grief-stricken but terrified. He determines to avoid this fate and sets out to find the only man who has ever been granted immortality, the Mesopotamian version of Noah, Utnapishtim (Sumerian: Ziusudra). After a long journey, he passes in total darkness through the magical Mountains of Mashu, guarded by the Scorpion People, and emerges into an enchanted garden of precious stones, through which he proceeds to the edge of the sea. He meets a divine barmaid, then a boatman, both of whom tell him his search is futile. But the boatman agrees to ferry him across the "waters of death" to Dilmun, the enchanted isle. There he meets the immortal sage, who, after relating the story of the Flood, tells Gilgamesh that he should practice conquering death by first conquering sleep. No sooner does Gilgamesh, sleepless since Enkidu died, hear this than "sleep like a wet haze blew over him." He sleeps for seven days and nights, and when he wakes, he knows his quest is vain.

Utnapishtim forbids the boatman ever to bring another mortal to Dilmun, but, at the prompting of his wife, he leads Gilgamesh to a plant that will restore youth, if not grant immortality. But before Gilgamesh can get home, a snake steals the plant; as it flees, it sheds its skin, to appear once again gleaming and youthful. Snakes in the ancient world, because of their skin-shedding ability, often symbolized immortality or eternal youth.

---

*There is another, duller version of this story in which Nergal bullies Ereshkigal out of her kingdom.

A Mesopotamian couple who might well be Inanna and Gilgamesh looking aghast at her huluppu *tree.*

With his return to Uruk, the story of Gilgamesh ends, or should end, at the end of the eleventh tablet. There is a twelfth tablet in *Gilgamesh,* however, and it is certainly confusing—a free-floating dialogue between Gilgamesh and Enkidu about the underworld. In fact, it is the end of *another* story, and how it got tacked onto the end of *Gilgamesh* by one scribe, and then copied by so many others, will remain forever mysterious.

"The Huluppu-Tree" is a different version of the Inanna-Gilgamesh-Enkidu triangle, focusing on death in a very different way. It begins as a sort of Eden myth: Inanna finds a tree (perhaps the First Tree) and plants it in her "holy garden," waiting for it to mature so that she can fashion a throne and a bed out of its wood. To her horror, demons invade the tree—a serpent, the Zu or Anzu bird, and the Lilitu or Lilith, a female demon who would later become important in Jewish tradition as Adam's first wife. Inanna bursts into tears and summons Gilgamesh, here called her brother, for help. The hero routs the intruders with his bronze ax and carves a throne and a bed for Inanna. To reward him, she makes a *pukku* and a *mikku* from the roots and crown of the tree. These offend the women of Uruk, and they fall (are thrown?) down a hole into the Underworld.*

At this point, the twelfth tablet begins, as Enkidu prepares to go and fetch the *pukku* and *mikku*. Gilgamesh gives advice on his conduct: he must wear old clothing and go unoiled and barefoot; he must leave his spear and his staff behind, must not speak or kiss anyone. Naturally, Enkidu, like Nergal, ignores this advice, and Ereshkigal seizes him. Gilgamesh appeals to the gods, and one of them persuades Nergal, the consort, to open a hole so the two friends can communicate. They try to embrace but cannot, for Enkidu's shade is too insubstantial.

Gilgamesh asks what it is like below. Enkidu says that it is so dreadful he cannot talk about it. Vermin are eating his body; it is filled with dirt. Gilgamesh throws himself on the ground in horror, then asks after the fate of a number of people; the news is bad.

The dead spirits in these early stories lead a grim, bleak, dry, and completely egalitarian existence. There is no division yet into privileged or blessed souls versus sinners or common folk. The thought of death terrifies Gilgamesh; in *Gilgamesh*, he accepts it because he has to, but he is reduced to abject, unkingly fright in "The Huluppu-Tree." Shades are literally shadowy, too insubstantial to touch; later Greeks thought a taste of blood might lend them momentary strength.

Other ancient stories tell of heroes who go beyond this world to fight monsters or to speak with their ancestors. The Etruscans had a dark underworld demon named Charun. Illustrations on ancient pottery show him carrying his characteristic weapon, which looks exactly like a polo mallet. His name would be confused with that of Charon, the Greek ferryman of dead souls, and even with Cheiron, a Greek centaur, half man, half horse.

---

*No one knows what a *pukku* and a *mikku* are. Various scholars have proposed a drum and drumstick, a hockey puck and stick, and other items. I think they represent Gilgamesh's penis and testicles and can argue the point, though not here. The reason for bringing it up is that I also believe the entire huluppu-tree sequence, including the last tablet of *Gilgamesh*, to be a sort of bawdy ghost story, a *Merry Wives of Windsor* to the grandeur of *Gilgamesh*. Thus Enkidu's wails from the underworld are exaggerated for effect. This is not, however, an orthodox interpretation.

The Egyptian Book of the Dead

THE OTHER ANCIENT AREA TO leave us a written rec-
ord of its concerns about the world beyond the grave is Egypt. Some
Egyptian hieroglyphic writings date from more than four thousand years
ago, and the ritual spells and incantations recorded in the earliest Book of
the Dead papyruses may have been already in use for centuries before they
were written down. Unlike the Middle East, which seems always to have
been torn by wars and clashing religious beliefs, Egypt has had relative
peace and prosperity throughout most of its very long history. As we know
from the splendid tombs of the pharaohs, the carefully prepared mummies,
the abundance of grave paraphernalia, and from the copiously illustrated
Books of the Dead on papyrus rolls, which contain protective survival
spells to ensure a safe trip through the otherworld, the Egyptians were
deeply concerned with the afterlife.

We also know a great deal about their changing eschatological beliefs;
we can trace these from the Old Kingdom (c. 3000–c. 2200 B.C.) when
only the right-living nobility could expect an afterlife, through the Middle
Kingdom (c. 2130–c. 1570 B.C.), when Osiris emerged as god of the dead,
and so on. But the ancient Egyptian afterlife is not ours. The Jews were
prisoners of the Egyptians before the Exodus, but Egyptian religion seems
to have been too foreign, too exotic, and too complicated to affect them

much. Rich as it was, Egyptian mythology, with the exception of the influential but late Hellenistic Isis cult, failed to travel well.

Some Egyptian ideas do, however, find echoes in Christianity. The figure of the heavenly Jesus owes something to Osiris. Not only was Osiris the judge, king, and god of the dead, he—unlike nearly all other rulers of the dead—was believed to be wholly benign. Like Jesus, he was himself the sacrificed and resurrected god; his divine son Horus ruled the living. The Egyptian dead had a bodily existence, which is also thought to be true of Christians after the Last Judgment. The idea of judgment after death may come from Egypt, if not from Persia. And the Egyptian dead who survived annihilation were often subject to horrendous sudden perils, if not exactly punishments.

To reach the Sekhet Hetepet, your *ka* or vital life-force (which looks exactly like you) and your *ba* or soul (portrayed as a human-headed bird)* would embark in the boat of Ra (the sun) which traverses the river of the sky (the Milky Way) during the day to arrive at the West at night with its cargo of the newly dead. Agen and Mahaf, who has his head turned back to front, are the celestial ferrymen. After disembarking, you must go through seven gates, each with a Gatekeeper, Watcher, and Herald, whose names you will invoke upon consulting your Book of the Dead. Next you must greet the many mysterious portals of the house of Osiris before they will open to let you pass.

Anubis will then escort you to the Hall of Justice, you being correctly "pure and clean and clad in white garments and sandals, painted with black eye-paint and anointed with myrrh." Anubis is usually characterized as the "jackal-headed" god, but anyone who has ever seen a pedigreed pharaoh hound, an animal whose noble Egyptian bloodlines stretch back for millennia, will recognize him immediately. A jackal has sinister connotations, especially when linked with corpses, but Anubis is a faithful dog come to guide you in his role as psychopomp, or leader of the soul.

Much less agreeable is the horrid little monster Ammit, who squats below the Scales of Justice, where you will be given the chance to plead the case for your former and continuing existence. Ibis-headed Thoth, God of Wisdom, acts as a prosecutor. Osiris, the Judge, sits on a throne attended

---

*Other aspects of the self were the *khu* or spiritual intelligence, the *sekhem*, an aspect of power, the *khaibit* or shadow and the *ren* or name. To blot out the name is to destroy the self for eternity. When the metaphysical heart is weighed, *ka*, *ba*, *khu*, and *ren* together make up its weight.

Anubis weighs the heart. In this rendition, Ammit is definitely female; in others she is more beastlike.

by the goddesses Isis and Nephthys. You may be as eloquent and long-winded as you like, but eventually Anubis will place your heart on the scale to weigh against a feather from the headdress of Maat, Goddess of Truth. If your heart sinks low under its burden of sin, Ammit will gobble it up. And that will be the end of you.

Let us suppose you survive and are admitted into the Sekhet Aaru or Field of Rushes, clad in your new body or *sahu*. Your troubles are not yet over. The Book of the Dead has spells to protect you from crocodiles, snakes, giant beetles, suffocation from lack of air, putrefaction, dying again (the *sahu* is not invulnerable), and turning topsy-turvy and being forced to eat feces. Your aim now is to transform yourself (or perhaps your *ba*) into a bird: a golden falcon, a phoenix, a heron, or a swallow. Or perhaps

you would like to be a crocodile or a snake (symbol of renewal and reju-
venation, as we saw in *Gilgamesh*)? Or a lotus.

Or perhaps you would like to be a farmer. The Field of Rushes consists
of fifteen *Aats* or regions, each with its own ruler, some of them inscrutable.
Ikesy, for example, "a region hidden from the gods" is inhabited only by
"that august god who is in his Egg." You wouldn't want to live there;
there is no air and the Egg god is not friendly.

You might find another spot suitable for agricultural activity, however,
which would include plowing, sowing, irrigation, reaping, and so forth,
all to be achieved with the tools and implements placed in your tomb. Your
thoughtful relatives will also have entombed your *shabti*, a figurine who
will be your golem-slave in the afterlife and do the hard work, while you
lead the comfortable life promised in all paradises—wonderful food and
drink, sexual pleasures, good companions, and all the comforts you should
have had at home. King Tut had 414 *shabti*s in his tomb, but as a less grand
personage, you might be content with one or two.

Zoroastrianism

SOMETIME AFTER THE OLD BABYLONIAN period, the Middle East produced a prophet named Zoroaster (Zarathustra) who founded a long-lasting religion adopted by virtually the entire region, stretching up into southern Russia and the eastern Balkans and eastward as far as India. Zoroastrianism persisted until the Muslim invasions of the seventh century A.D., which were followed by severe persecutions, and still survives in India, especially in Bombay (where Zoroastrians are called Parsis: Persians), and, until recently, in Iran.

The art of writing had been lost to the area by the time of the prophet and was religiously forbidden for many centuries afterward, so we know practically nothing about Zoroaster, not even when he lived. Modern scholars speculate that the prophet was raised among the Bronze Age nomads of the south Russian steppes, perhaps as much as a millennium before Christ.

Considering that the Avesta, the sacred book of Zoroastrianism, was not written down until the fifth century A.D.—and then in a special invented sacred language, never used again—and that the only existing manuscript dates from the fourteenth century and is not complete, it is safe to say that what we know of this faith may not be exactly what Zoroaster had in mind—which is probably true of all religions and their founders, even if their sacred books are dictated by God or by the Angel Moroni.

16

Pazuzu, an Assyrian demon who displays many characteristics of later Christian demons

But Zoroastrianism had an enormous influence, directly and indirectly, on the history of Christianity and, specifically, of Hell. It was based on the early Vedic faith, from which Hinduism and Buddhism also developed, but instead of relying on a pantheon of gods, Zoroaster taught a dualistic religion: The divine force of Good, Ahura Mazda ("Wise Lord") or Ohrmazd, who lives above with his seven *anesha spenta* ("Immortal Holy Ones"), or angels, is pitted against Angra Mainyu or Ahriman ("Evil

Spirit"), the Lord of Lies, who dwells in the darkness of Hell under the earth, sending out his *daevas* or devils to torment the world. Law, order, and light oppose darkness, filth, and death. Their conflict is the history of the world, and the object of the conflict is the soul of man.

After death, the soul, which first hovers around the head of its corpse for three days, is judged by Rashnu, the genie, or angel, of justice, and by Mithra—who, in Hellenistic times, embarked on a new career as a soldiers' god. All good deeds are entered in a great ledger as credits, all wicked actions as debts. At the foot of the underworld Chinvat ("Accountant's") Bridge, the reckoning is made. If it is positive, the Daena, a beautiful maiden accompanied by two guardian dogs, escorts the soul across the bridge into the House of Song. If negative, "even if the difference is only three tiny acts of wrongdoing," the soul falls into Hell, ruled by Yima, or Yama, the first man to die. If the balance is even, it passes into a kind of limbo called Hammistagan, quite similar to the old Babylonian underworld, where it will stay until the apocalypse. Neither prayer, sacrifice, nor the grace of Ahriman can influence the legal outcome of the mathematical trial.

A manuscript from about the ninth century A.D. is thought to be a transcription of the much older story of Viraz, the world's best man, who is sent to the otherworld in order to verify the tenets of the faith and there sees many souls in torment. The story is nearly identical in form to many Christian visions of the second through the thirteenth centuries, and it is hard to know which influenced the other. There are differences both in the sins and their punishments from Christian versions. The most Eastern touch is that souls have no contact with one another; in Byzantine art the damned are shown in isolated "boxes," a device not seen in the West, where Hell is characteristically chaotic and crowded.

Eventually, there will be a final cosmic battle between Good and Evil, and Evil will be conquered forever. A savior named Soshyans, born of a virgin impregnated with the seed of Zoroaster, will harrow Hell; penitent sinners will be forgiven; and there will be a universal resurrection of the body, which will reunite with the soul. Hell will be destroyed—burned clean by molten metal—and the kingdom of God on earth will begin.

As any Christian reader should immediately recognize, many of these ancient Zoroastrian ideas had extraordinary staying power. Orthodox Christianity's debt to them is not formally acknowledged, though by bringing the Magi into the Christian nativity story and putting a new star in the

18

East, Matthew, by far the most eschatologically minded of the four Gospel writers, seems to have wanted to make sure his Messiah was firmly linked to the resurrection and immortality promised by Zoroastrianism; similarly, he sent the infant Jesus off to Egypt to imply his connection with ancient wisdom.

Dualistic Christian heresies have cropped up again and again in the last two thousand years, and though the names of the parties change, it is not hard to trace the lines that lead from Zoroastrianism in all its variations to Manichaeism to the Bogomils and Albigensians of the twelfth century. Even now, while Christianity may have won the battle against dualism on the high theological plane, the forces of evil wield considerable strength on the popular level. The same can be said in Islam, where the satanic Iblis or Al-Shaitan has a folkloric importance not admitted in fiercely monotheistic orthodox Muslim theology.

Zoroastrianism links Hinduism, from which Buddhism later derived, to Mithraism, a serious rival of Christianity during the entire period of the Roman Empire, Islam, a later rival, and Christianity itself. The eschatological scenarios of the great religions of Europe and Asia are eerily alike in many regards, which may be due less to Swedenborgian visions of a universal afterlife than to the persistence of trade routes and the relaxed religious determination of armies bound for glory.

Classical Hades

For more than a thousand years before the fifth century A.D., when the whole world changed, the religion of Greece and Rome, with its pantheon of Olympians, was the normal, conservative one for what we still think of as the civilized or "classical" world of the Mediterranean peoples. This was the religion that decent people believed in; anything else was considered archaic, anarchic, exotic, barbaric, or radical. The Greeks fought the Persians, and the thought that the Zoroastrian religion of Darius and Cyrus would ultimately have more effect than their own upon the Mediterranean world would have struck them as irrational. That the peculiar customs of the Jews would carry even more influence would have seemed preposterous.

The Greek writers whose names and works have come down to us wrote poetry, or plays, or history, or philosophy, rather than dutifully recording sacred writ, and they saw no harm in presenting their own opinions. It was a very new kind of writing, allowing for personality, flourishes, and a certain amount of departure, playful or poetic, from orthodoxy. Actually, since poets and artists left the records, it is hard to say just what Greek orthodoxy was. Certainly there was no separation of good and evil as in Zoroastrianism; each Greek god—and there are hundreds of instances in literary tradition to prove it—was capable of both righteous and vindictively destructive behavior.

By tradition, Homer and Hesiod, the first poets to take advantage of the new alphabet borrowed and adapted from the Phoenicians, lived in the eighth century B.C. Hesiod is less read than Homer today, but his *Theogony,* which relates Greek creation myths and legendary history and lists the gods and minor deities, is the essential foundation for an enormous body of literature. Later mythographers, trying to order and institutionalize Greek religious literature, abandoned some of his more fanciful images such as that of the great house of Styx (the river of Hades personified as a goddess) with its silvery pillars reaching to Heaven, but poets, ancient and modern, have always loved and often echoed him.

Hesiod tells us that Erebus and Tartarus, the upper and lower realms of Hades, were born, together with Night and Earth, itself, from the primeval Chasm. He narrates the bloody battles of the gods. First, Uranus, the Sky God, fathered the Cyclops on Mother Earth. When they rebelled, he threw them into Tartarus, a place as far below the earth as the earth is below the sky; an anvil falling from Heaven would reach it in eighteen days. A guarded bronze wall runs around Tartarus, surrounded by Night. Within it is the Abyss, where a man could fall for a year and not touch bottom. The mansion of Hades and "fearful Persephone" is there, guarded by the Hound of Hell.

Homer's *Odyssey* is the earliest well-known story of a visit to the Land of the Dead. It is so well known that most people forget that it never happened. Odysseus and his shipmates, who are told by the witch Circe that they must go to the underworld, never actually get there, though Odysseus does manage to see many of the famous sights of Hades.

Odysseus, the Ithacan soldier-king, after fighting the Trojan War for ten years, has run into serious obstacles in his attempt to get back home. The gods, particularly the implacable Queen Hera, are hostile. The shade of Tiresias, said to have been the wisest of mortals because he lived at varying times as both a man and a woman, may be able to help, if Odysseus is brave enough to consult him.

To do this, Odysseus must sail north to the Grove of Persephone, the Queen of Hades, where the underworld rivers Phlegethon and Cocytus flow into the Acheron. At the mouth of the cave there, he must sacrifice a young ram and a black ewe so that their blood will flow into a trench. Attracted by the smell, ghosts will flock from the cave mouth, but he must hold them off with his sword until Tiresias arrives to taste the blood that will enable him to speak.

The ghosts arrive with "rustling cries," among them Elpenor, a young sailor so newly dead that his shipmates did not yet know he was missing; a memorial is promised for him so that he can reach Hades proper. Tiresias comes to taste the blood and to deliver a dour presentiment of the future. Odysseus sees his mother and asks why she does not acknowledge him. He learns that she cannot speak until the blood has given her temporary strength. She sips, they speak, and he tries to embrace her but, like Gilgamesh reaching for Enkidu, he cannot.

Other famous women draw near, starting a tradition, followed by other poets, of "ladies first" in visits below. Odysseus is shocked to encounter his former commander, Agamemnon, murdered by his own wife after returning home. Other war companions appear, Achilles, Patroclus, Ajax. He attempts to comfort grim Achilles: things are not so bad; why, even here, he is treated like royalty. To which Achilles retorts that he would rather be a wretched farmer's serf than lord it over the "exhausted dead."

Because the souls come up through the mouth of the cave, Odysseus doesn't encounter Cerberus, the famous guard dog, or Charon, the boatman of the Styx. But apparently simply by wishing to see them, he does catch a glimpse of some of the celebrities of Hades: Tantalus tortured by hunger and thirst, Sisyphus rolling his boulder, the Titan Tityus attacked by vultures, the judge Minos, and the happy heroes Orion and Heracles. Fearing that Persephone might send something really unpleasant next, he shouts for his men and they row away as fast as they can.

There is a second journey to Hades (or *nekyia*—hence necropolis, necromancer, and so forth) in *The Odyssey*, near the end, after Odysseus has come home in disguise to find a horde of his wife's suitors despoiling his estate and, after a dramatic battle, has dispatched them to the hereafter. What follows is an interval, a small story within a story. Hermes, the gods' messenger, comes as psychopomp for the souls of the dead suitors. They follow him, "squeaking like bats" in a dark cave, past gray waters and the shores of Dream to the end of the world where the dead inhabit the Fields of Asphodel.

Just lines before this, the suitors seemed close to being thugs, but when they are dead the poet invests their shades with sad nobility. They meet, as equals, the Greek heroes once again discussing their own deaths, which

Led by Hermes in his role as psychopomp, Persephone emerges from the underworld to join Demeter and Hecate. This group of four chthonic figures may indicate that the vase was used in the celebration of the mysteries.

seems to be their endless preoccupation. The souls arrive before they have been buried, countering the Elpenor story earlier. It is a strange interlude that appears to go against what we know of Greek afterlife tradition. As poetry, however, it is extraordinarily effective; for the Greeks, orthodoxy took a second place to poetry.

The story of the rape and abduction of Kore the Maiden, later called Persephone ("Bringer of Destruction"), became the basis for the Eleusinian mysteries, an important religious cult of the Greek and Hellenistic worlds. In the story, a young girl gathering flowers is seized by Hades, the master of Tartarus, and taken below, where she refuses to eat or drink. Her mother Demeter, the corn goddess, wanders the world mourning, neglecting the crops; when at last Kore is found, she turns out to have eaten seven pomegranate seeds, and thus must spend part of each year in the under-world. This is a fertility myth, and long after worship of other Olympians

23

became perfunctory, men and women went through the Eleusinian initi-
ation rites, which are thought to have featured a ritualistic symbolic journey
to the netherworld in imitation of Demeter which ended with the triumph
of spring and rebirth.

Persephone the Queen of Hell is not much like Kore the innocent
maiden; like her Babylonian sister Ereshkigal, she is more fearsome than
her shadowy consort Hades, sometimes called Plouton ("Wealthy One"
—hence plutocrat, and so on) because of his subterranean metallurgical
holdings, the valuable objects often buried with bodies and the wealth of
crops that spring from fertile soil, but also as a euphemism to avoid saying
his other name and thus attracting his attention.

Another important cult centered on Orpheus the harper, who went to
the underworld down a passage at the back of the Taenarus cave to win
back his wife, Eurydice. The Orphic cult lasted for centuries and powerfully
influenced both the Greek and Christian religions. Dionysus, the wine god
with whom Orpheus was often worshiped, was also supposed to have gone
to the underworld to rescue his mother, the demi-goddess Semele; on the
other hand, he is sometimes called Persephone's son by Zeus, the sky god.
The Dionysian-Orphic mystery cult, like the Eleusinian, certainly had to
do with death and resurrection, though Orpheus, like Gilgamesh, *lost* his
heart's desire.

Artists in the Hellenistic period frequently borrowed the attributes of
Orpheus for Jesus Christ. For patrons who wanted to hedge their bets with
the gods, they also borrowed from Egyptian Horus and from Persian
Mithra, but Orpheus-Christos, the Good Shepherd and Harrower of Hell,
was more popular than either.

Other Greek tales of the underworld are not so serious. Theseus was
the first popular Greek hero to attempt to harrow Hell; he failed humili-
atingly. Peirithoos, his boon companion, persuaded Theseus to help him
kidnap the famous Helen, later of Troy but at this point still a child. They
consulted an oracle who said mockingly, "Why not carry off Persephone
instead?" Peirithoos was foolish (and vain) enough to take this seriously,
and off they went down the Taenarus passage. On arrival, their host escorted them to a seat which proved to be the Chair of Forgetfulness—and
they stuck fast to it. For four years, they sat, tormented by serpents, the
Furies, Cerberus's teeth, and the sardonic remarks of Hades.

As befitted his stature as the Greeks' favorite hero, Heracles was bold enough to visit the lower regions twice. The eleventh of his Twelve Labors involved bringing Cerberus to King Eurystheus. Prudently, he went first to Eleusis to be initiated in the Mysteries, with Theseus as his sponsor. Cleansing his considerable burden of sin apparently took four years. Then he too descended by way of the Taenarus cave and terrified Charon into ferrying him across the Styx. Even the ghosts fled from him, though snaky-haired Medusa the Gorgon, apparently forgetting that she was dead and therefore powerless, tried unsuccessfully to turn him to stone, as she had turned so many when she lived.

Finding his old friend Theseus in the unlucky chair, Heracles heaved him up, leaving a significant part of his hinder anatomy behind. Peirithoos would have been next, but Hades interfered. Undeterred, Heracles seized the dog. Grabbing him by all three throats (the number of Cerberus's heads varied, but tradition settled on three), he wrestled the beast down, rolled

Restrained by Heracles, Cerberus the Hell Hound leaps at cowardly King Eurystheus. Greek vase painting from the sixth century B.C.

him up in his lion's skin and dragged him off, with Theseus in indecorous tow. Cerberus was presented to the king, who cowered in a jar until he was removed.

On another journey, Heracles went to rescue Alcestis. This lady had been married to a king named Admetus who was promised death would spare him if he could find someone to substitute for him. His parents, despite their advanced age, refused to do this, but his faithful wife took poison and died for him. Heracles, a boisterous, then apologetic visitor to the household, pursued her and had no trouble winning her freedom, as Persephone considered it outrageous that a wife should be expected to die for her husband. Euripides, the fourth-century playwright, wrote a play called *Alcestis,* but it has no underworld scenes, being concerned, as well it might be, with psychological tensions among members of Admetus's family.

These stories are divorced from any religious element. The Theseus tale is a low take-off on the serious story of Theseus's descent into the Cretan labyrinth (a symbolic Hades) to conquer the Minotaur. The underworld had become, at least sometimes, a place to joke about. So it is not surprising that, in 405 B.C., a few months after the death of Euripides, the comic playwright Aristophanes produced *The Frogs,* a farce about a journey to Hades starring drunken Dionysus, his clownish servant Xanthias, and an oafishly musclebound Heracles posturing in a lion's skin. Instead of fearsome monsters, singing frogs guard the River Styx. The comic trio bargains ineffectually with Charon, then blunders into an Eleusinian ritual (this would have been pointed religious satire at the time), meets a barmaid (as did Gilgamesh), and finally one of the judges of the underworld, to whom they put their demand: There are no more decent poets, give us back Euripides. The dead riot, taking sides between Aeschylus, a senior and graver poet, and Euripides. A poetry contest is held, which Aeschylus wins.

Much later, in the second century A.D., the prolific Lucian of Samosata invented a useful satiric form in the *Dialogues of the Dead*: famous people, safely dead, could speak their minds—really the author's mind—on controversial subjects, including politics and religion. For this he was nicknamed "the blasphemer." The eighteenth century, admiring the sardonic Lucian, revived the form, and it persisted in popular periodicals into the twentieth century.

Obviously, Merry Hell was fair game to the later Greeks; Aristophanes was a popular playwright and in no apparent danger of arrest for blasphemy, though Pythagoras claimed to have seen a vision of the soul of Hesiod bound to a bronze column and that of Homer hanging from a tree surrounded by snakes in payment for all the lies they told about the gods.

BEFORE TACKLING Plato, who complicates the Greek position, we should pause to survey classical Hades and its inhabitants. The few mortals to enter this shadowy underground kingdom go by way of the Taenarus cave, near Marmari in the southern Pelaponnese. The dead emerge at least once by another cave in Persephone's magic grove, on an island inaccessible to ordinary sailors. A newly dead *psyche* or soul is guided by Hermes the psychopomp to the River Styx ("Hated"), which has for its tributaries Acheron ("Woe"), Phlegethon ("Burning"), Cocytus ("Wailing"), Aornis ("Birdless," but actually a mistranslation of Avernus, the Italian equivalent of the Taenarus cave), and Lethe ("Forgetfulness"). The rivers were usually abbreviated to four, not always the same four. Charon is the boatman who must be paid to ferry the soul across the Styx, lest it languish forever on the outer bank. Cerberus is the multi-headed watchdog. Persephone and Hades (or Plouton) preside over Hades, or, more properly, Erebus.

The Titans are chained in lower Tartarus, except for Tityus, one of a handful of imaginatively punished celebrities: for the crime of attacking Leto, mother of Apollo and Artemis, he is pegged out over nine acres of Hades while vultures eat his liver. Because he tried to flimflam his way out of Hades, Sisyphus is condemned forever to roll uphill a rock, which always falls back before it reaches the top. Next to him is Ixion, bound to a fiery wheel for an attempted rape of Hera, Queen of Olympus. Nearby is Tantalus, who served up his own son, stewed, to the gods; now he hangs from a tree over a lake, tormented by hunger and thirst but unable to reach either the water in the lake or the fruit on the tree. Early Greek authors sometimes punished him simply by suspending a stone over his head. Trying vainly to draw water from that lake in sieves are the Danaides, sometimes fifty, sometimes three sisters who murdered their husbands with hairpins.

Monsters and demons live in Hades: dead Medusa; the Alastor, which, like a Christian devil, tempts men toward evil or folly and then punishes them for it; the Erinyes, or Furies, spirits of vengeance who carry whips;

On a Roman sarcophagus, Charon ferries souls across the Styx.

the *keres,* frightening winged death-spirits, one for each living soul; Lamia and the Empusae, vampirish creatures thought to be daughters of Hecate, the witch goddess who is the third aspect of the Kore-Persephone-Hecate trinity—Maiden-Queen-Hag.

Punishment for wrongdoing in the old Greek stories, though it may be supernaturally administered—the Furies, for example, pursue Orestes after he kills his mother—was not generally an after-death affair, except in a few cases of crimes against the gods themselves. The agonies of Oedipus and the famous inherited curse on the House of Atreus that blighted many generations were ordained by the gods for the living, not the dead. It has been suggested that the reason the early Greeks, unlike the Egyptians and Zoroastrians, had no after-death accounting was simply because classical Greece never developed a centralized judicial system.

Nevertheless, by the fifth century B.C., Greeks had taken up Persian or Egyptian ideas: Pindar wrote of an afterlife where bad men endure "toil which is terrible to behold." Plato names the underworld judges in the *Gorgias*: Aeacus, who judges Europeans; Rhadamanthus, who judges Asians; and Minos, who holds the court of appeals. Good souls go to the Elysian Fields, where, as Pindar says, "some delight in horses and athletic contests, some in playing draughts, some with lyres and the whole rich-flowered place blossoms; there are always sacrifices of varied kinds on the altars of the gods mixed with far-shining fire." Bad ones to Tartarus, and the rest of us back to the Fields of Asphodel. The Orphics believed that simple justice requires the souls of the dead to live on in order to receive reward or punishment. The first-century B.C. historian Diodorus cites Egypt as the source of both Orphic and Eleusinian belief and afterworld ritual (Cerberus masks, for instance, which imitated Anubis masks), and also of Homer's use of Hermes as psychopomp in the second *nekyia*.

In the fifth century B.C., we also find for the first time an artist who substantially influenced the history of Hell. For centuries, tourists and pilgrims came to visit the great mural picturing the visit of Odysseus to the realm of the dead that Polygnotus painted for a clubhouse at the Delphic shrine of Apollo. It perished long ago (probably at the hands of Christians), but it was carefully described by the Greek travel writer Pausanias in the second century A.D. His lengthy detail indicates that Polygnotus felt no literal obligation toward *The Odyssey*. Instead, he filled in what he reckoned Homer had forgotten to mention—or what Odysseus might have seen had he been braver and gone below. This included many eclectic mythological characters, among them Orpheus. Also, possibly out of his own head (for Pausanias, so many centuries later, knew nothing of such a myth), Polygnotus created a beast-demon which certainly catches the eye of the infernologist.

> The guides at Delphi say that Eurynomos is one of the *daimones* in Hades, and that he devours the flesh of the dead, leaving them only their bones. Now, the poems of Homer, as well as the *Minyad* and the *Returns* do not know of any *daimon* Eurynomos. Nevertheless, I will describe Eurynomos and the way he has been represented: his complexion is between blue and black, like that of the flies that gather around meat; he shows his teeth, and a vulture's skin is spread for him to sit on.

Eurynomus could have been one of the *keres* or a derivative of Etruscan Charun, who was also dark blue, but Pausanias does not seem to think so. One would like to know if this inquisitive and well-traveled writer, who took great interest in local myths and legends, had encountered tales of the Jews of the Diaspora, which featured Beelzebub, "Lord of the Flies." If not, his simile is quite a coincidence.

Platonic Hell

Pᴌᴀᴛᴏ (ᴄ.428–ᴄ.348 ʙ.ᴄ.), the philosopher and teacher whose influence has been steady for two and a half millennia, provides our best look at what not overly religious Greeks of the fourth century ʙ.ᴄ. actually believed might happen after death. As is usual with Plato, he has it several ways and is joking in some of them, but the theories he puts forward are coherent. The dialogues frequently deal with the destiny of the soul; it is the entire subject of the *Phaedo,* the great and moving deathbed drama of the philosopher Socrates.

Phaedo tells the story, for Plato was rather conspicuously absent. Fifteen of Socrates's friends are with him in his prison cell to share the last hours before he must drink the deadly hemlock. His spirits are excellent, far better than those of his friends, and he jokes that since the soul is the best part of a philosopher, the fact that his is soon to be set free is hardly a cause for mourning. Still, Cebes, a Boeotian, is fearful about the fate of the soul,

> that on the very day of death she may perish and come to an end—immediately on her release from the body, issuing forth disposed like smoke or air and in her flight vanishing away into nothingness.

Socrates immediately undertakes to reassure him, suggesting that this be the subject of his last discourse with his friends, reckoning "no one who heard me now, not even if he were one of my old enemies the Comic poets, could accuse me of talking about matters in which I had no concern!"

The discussion that follows illustrates, among other things, Plato's ideal theory of forms, the idea that any reality we experience is only a corporeal and imperfect image of an ideal. A chair, for instance, is crafted according to a concept, however dimly held, of an ideal chair. This theory has left a deep mark on Western religious beliefs. Plato's writings, reinterpreted by the Neoplatonists of the Hellenistic period, especially the Egyptian Plotinus and the Jewish Egyptian Philo, were carefully read by both Gnostic and orthodox early Christians and profoundly influenced such very un-Greek ideas as those of Original Sin and subsequent salvation. Christians educated in Neoplatonism chose to interpret Jesus in his corporeal form as representing a Platonic ideal of man (those who insisted on his divinity at the expense of his humanity were treated as serious heretics, the Docetists). Later, the Virgin Mary came to represent the ideal in woman. The kingdom of God on earth would be an ideal version of life as early Christians knew it. Leaning on Plato enabled them to escape Persian dualism: they could acknowledge a sinful and corrupt material world, ruled by the "prince of this world," while denying that prince any lasting power.

In the *Phaedo*, Socrates, contending that knowledge is recollection of the already known, proves multiple incarnations of the soul, which, like the ideal form but unlike the body, is eternal and will with good behavior at last pass "to the place of the true Hades, which, like her [the soul], is invisible, and pure, and noble, and on her way to the good and wise God, whither, if God will, my soul is also soon to go."

But what of the souls of the wicked?

Such souls are held fast by the corporeal, says Socrates, and must thus be newly imprisoned in other bodies, each according to the nature of the life it has previously led: a drunkard in a donkey's, a thug in a wolf's. The system seems close to Hinduism or Buddhism. Socrates is not being entirely serious here; he playfully consigns the conformist burghers of Athens to anthills and wasps' nests. A philosopher, on the other hand, is welcomed to the company of the gods.

Later he fancifully describes the "true earth" where the gods dwell: it is a sphere above and encasing our round earth, but from it a vast chasm pierces through to the earth's center; there Tartarus is found. He describes the river Oceanus, which girdles the earth, and the rivers of Tartarus:

31

Acheron, Pyriphlegethon, Cocytus, and the Stygian leading to Lake Styx. Souls of those "who have lived neither well nor ill" are ferried up the Acheron to the Acherusian Lake to be purified of their evil deeds before being rewarded for their good ones and sent back to be reborn as men or animals. But he also shows us how far Hell had developed, even to the point of being eternal for some:

> But those who appear to be incurable by reason of the greatness of their crimes—who have committed many and terrible deeds of sacrilege, murders foul and violent, or the like—such are hurled into Tartarus which is their suitable destiny, and they never come out. Those again who have committed crimes, which, although great, are not irremediable—who in a moment of anger, for example, have done some violence to a father or a mother, and have repented for the remainder of their lives, or, who have taken the life of another under the like extenuating circumstances—these are plunged into Tartarus, the pains of which they are compelled to undergo for a year, but at the end of the year the wave casts them forth—mere homicides by way of Cocytus, parricides and matricides by Pyriphlegethon—and they are borne to the Acherusian Lake, and there they lift up their voices and call upon their victims that they have slain or wronged, to have pity on them, and to be kind to them, and let them come out into the lake. And if they prevail, then they come forth and cease from their troubles; but if not, they are carried back again into Tartarus and thence into the rivers unceasingly, until they obtain mercy from those they have wronged: for that is the sentence inflicted upon them by their judges.

Socrates allows some doubt about this account but "something of the kind" may be true. The *Gorgias* repeats much of the same material. Socrates tells the "very pretty tale" of how the gods divided up their territories, and how the judges of souls were appointed, and how a soul deformed by "license and luxury and insolence and incontinence" is stamped by Rhadamanthus as curable or incurable and dispatched to Tartarus. He adds that the incurable always seem to be public figures. The point, he says, is not whether or not the story is true but that "the best way of life is to practice justice and every virtue in life and death."

In the *Phaedrus* Socrates describes the soul as a winged creature. The perfect soul flies upward while the imperfect one droops and settles to the ground and takes on a mortal body. However poetically Plato may have meant this, it was read painstakingly centuries later by some of the Christian church fathers, especially Origen (c. 185–c. 254), who was also impressed by Plato's account of how reincarnation might work. The image of the winged soul that could move either upward or downward seemed also to prove to him that Hell could not be eternal.

Plato closed *The Republic* with the famous story of Er, a soldier who had what we would now call a "near-death experience." He was left for dead on the battlefield for twelve days before reviving to tell his tale. Er's vision was not of classical Hades: some of it seems to anticipate medieval Christian visions (which it undoubtedly influenced) and some of the imagery seems Eastern. Virtuous souls "ascend by the heavenly way on the right hand," while sinners descend to the left and are met by "wild men of fiery aspect" who drag them off and flay them with scourges and thorns. On the twelfth day, the souls proceed to "the spindle of Necessity," operated by the Fates, to choose how they want to be reincarnated. Plato uses the old mythological heroes to show how—"sad and laughable and strange"—such choices are based not on good sense but on previous experience.

Off they go to drink the waters of Lethe ("Forgetting"), then they burst upward, like shooting stars, to be born again. All except Er, that is, who finds himself lying on his funeral pyre, quite alive.

If an eternal soul is assumed, reincarnation—or metempsychosis, or the transmigration of souls—is logically (if logic applies) a more satisfactory solution to the judicial questions of sin and punishment, inexplicable human suffering, and the worldly triumph of the wicked than a fixed system of eternal after-death reward and punishment. By being morally dynamic and part of the natural order—like the metamorphosis of a butterfly or the cycle of the seasons—rather than static and decreed by inexorable supernatural law, metempsychosis evades some very real difficulties. Many would prefer to believe that sin can eventually be "cured." Monotheists in a static system must wrestle with an evil principle that has to be a part of God if it is not opposed to him. But, though it has always been widely accepted in Eastern religions, metempsychosis was rejected in the West. The Christian doctrine of the resurrection of the physical body (inherited from Zoroaster and also taken up by Islam) made it impossible.

The Roman Empire

Thanks to enterprising merchants and mercenaries and Greek armies having pushed the Persians back to the Middle East, Greek culture became dominant in the Mediterranean from at least the fifth century B.C.; its only real rival was the old and static civilization of Egypt. But when Alexander the Great set out to conquer the world in the fourth century, Greeks quickly formed a network of cities and Greek civilization reached from India to Spain. Alexander placed his agents in power—the Ptolemies in Egypt and the Seleucidae in Syria and Asia Minor. Eventually the Romans, whose culture was heavily influenced by Greece, stepped in, battling barbarians through Gaul to the northwest all the way to Britain, bringing the civilization of the Mediterranean with them.

It has always worked both ways, of course. Soldiers marry native girls and take them home or leave the army to settle down—either brings cross-culturalization. The upper classes in a far-off city aspire to the aristocratic Hellenic ways of their conquerors, while local peasants teach the newly arrived infantry native traditions. Young people or the dissatisfied, presented with previously unimagined choices, want something new. Slaves from Asia, Africa, Scandinavia, and the Slavic countries bring more strange customs with them. The adjective "Hellenistic" supposedly refers to a syncretic amalgam of Greek and Oriental cultures, but over the long period that includes the Roman Empire the cultural blend was even richer than that.

Never in the history of the world before, and never again until the twentieth century, was there such an astonishing cross-fertilization of languages, cultures, customs, and beliefs. The old religions were assaulted by a mosaic of novelties; entirely new gods like the Graeco-Egyptian Serapis were fabricated, while old ones arrived from strange lands: Sabazios, from Asia; Mithra, from Persia; Isis, from Egypt. The statue of Cybele, the Great Mother, was imported from Turkey to Rome, and the Roman Senate, belatedly scandalized by the epicene parades of her castrated priests, forbade citizens to have anything to do with her.

The long cross-cultural period when Hellenism lapsed into the Roman Empire conveniently stretches about four centuries in either direction from the point that we call zero. At one end is Alexander the Great (336–323 B.C.), at the other Constantine (A.D. 306–337), also called the Great. An important man of ideas, including ideas about Hell, also stands at approximately either end: Plato of Athens and Augustine of Hippo.

Romans, though pious, were not much for myth-making. Their native religion was a form of animism quite similar to Japanese Shintoism: groves, streams, even single trees had their own gods, and so did households and courtyards and each function or aspect of daily life. Each man had his *genius* and each woman her *juno,* a concept that passed into Christianity as that of the guardian angel. There were literally thousands of *numina;* virtually everything that had a name had a *numen.* For their more important gods, of the sky, sun, moon, sea, harvest, and hearth, and the concepts of love, war, marriage, wisdom, and so forth, they adopted Greek myths wholesale, efficiently filling in their own gods' names as protagonists of the stories.

Soldiering in foreign parts, they did exactly the same thing as they marched up to the local shrines. A statue of a maiden thus marked the shrine as that of Diana, no matter who the resident Gauls might think she was, and she would be honored accordingly. The practice worked well: since the armies displayed respect and piety, they managed to avoid much religious conflict. Even in the later empire, the Roman attitude was more or less that of the insouciant Mrs. Patrick Campbell: "Anything you like, as long as you don't do it in the road and frighten the horses." Cybele's flagrant priests violated that code, and so did obdurate Christians who would not concede unto Caesar what was by that time his divinity. Their behavior was, by Roman standards, disrespectful and disorderly.

The widespread Hellenistic mystery cults heavily influenced early Christianity. For example, the Seven Deadly Sins, which Christians appropriated both iconographically and geographically in their own views of Hell, were a Mithraic formulation which looked back to Zoroastrianism, which gave mystic significance to the number seven. As the dead soul rises through the gate of Capricorn, the Mithraic story went, it passes through the seven heavenly spheres, shedding in each the appropriate vice: the Sun—Pride, the Moon—Envy, Mars—Anger, Mercury—Greed, Jupiter—Ambition, Venus—Lust, Saturn—Sloth. Mithra also gave us December twenty-fifth as God's birthday, the Chi-Rho sign which Christians appropriated, and, together with other cults, a persisting interest in astrology and numerology.

Latin poets embellished the old Greek stories and contributed a few additions to the underworld anthology: the spectacular set piece from Virgil's *Aeneid*, Virgil's and Ovid's Orpheus stories, Psyche's girlish adventure in Apuleius's *Golden Ass*, Cicero's *Scipio's Dream*, which deals more with the positive than the negative afterlife, and Plutarch's *Vision of Thespesius*, which looks backward to Plato's Er and forward to medieval dream visions. The Romans changed a few names: Plouton or Pluto was sometimes called Dis Pater, Dis being a contraction of Dives—hence "Father Rich Man." Persephone became Proserpine and possibly less formidable than her Greek counterpart; Hermes became Mercury.

The Aeneid, written between 30 and 19 B.C., was thoroughly researched by the poet, then living in Rome. Virgil's model was Homer, though the underworld scenes show that he also knew his Plato. Virgil's is undoubtedly the best-known description of the Land of the Dead, if only because, until a generation or so ago, Virgil was regularly taught in high schools all over Europe and America.

The hero of the epic is Aeneas, a Trojan who fought in the great war. Like Odysseus he is on a journey; he must find a new home since Troy is devastated. He goes to the underworld to seek advice from his dead father, Anchises, on how to avert the wrath of his implacable enemy, Juno, the Roman equivalent of Hera. There is no question of his luring the ghostly dead into the open; Aeneas is prepared for descent. The Cumaean Sibyl, or priestess, is his guide, and his magical protection against the horrors of the Land of the Dead is the sacred golden bough.

As in *The Odyssey,* the crew prepares a blood sacrifice before the cave mouth, this time at Cumae, near modern Naples. This location is specific—Hell is under Italy, not in some otherworldly location. Virgil sets the scene with macabre special effects: howling dogs, clammy caves, noxious fumes, earthquakes, eerie cries. Hollywood owes a lot to Virgil.

Limbo appears for the first time, a place where "pauper souls" must wait for a hundred years or until they have been properly buried—the Romans appreciated correct bureaucratic form. To his dismay, Aeneas recognizes three of them, but the Sibyl promises to use her influence as a priestess to redeem them later. They go past the caves of Sleep (Virgil was attentive to Hesiod and Homer: these are the caves the dead suitors passed; Romantic poets would visit them later), cross the river with curmudgeonly Charon, throw a sop to Cerberus, pass the hall where Minos judges, encounter women, first among them Dido, Aeneas's tragic, suicidal lover, who turns her face away from him. Next, the heroes appear, Trojans this time instead of Greeks, with their own gloomy war stories.

The Sibyl hurries him along the right-hand fork of a divided road, the one that leads past the house of Dis to the Elysian Fields. But Aeneas stops to peer to the left, across a fiery river, at a triple-walled citadel secured by a mighty gate atop which perches one of the Furies. From inside he hears groans, the thud of the lash, the clanking of chains. Rhadamanthus has sent them there, the Sibyl tells him, to be avenged by the "savage sisterhood" and the horrible fifty-headed Hydra before falling into the abyss.

The Sibyl points out the usual celebrities—the Titans, Tityus, Ixion, Peirithoos, Theseus (when poets need him, Theseus returns to his chair). But here are ordinary sinners too, those cruel to their relatives, misers, adulterers, traitors. If the Sibyl had a "throat of iron," she says, she could not relate all their sins.

Virgil's is the first thoroughly graphic description of Hell, and one of the best. Though all the images in it were current and general to the era, vivid art has a way of fixing general ideas into quite specific shapes. Virgil's impact was enormous, not only on later poets and storytellers like Dante, who would invoke him as guide and mentor (and who himself forever changed Hell's map), but on the men who hammered together the early guidelines for Christian cosmology: Clement of Alexandria, Origen, Tertullian, and especially Augustine, who quoted him frequently.

The rest of the underworld visit is anticlimactic, though not to Virgil,

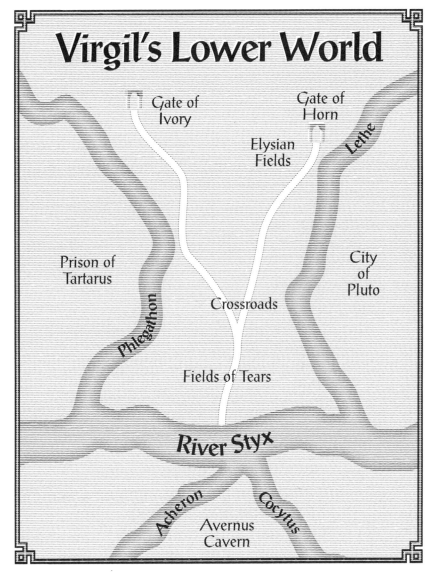

Virgil's Lower World

Gate of Ivory

Gate of Horn

Elysian Fields

Lethe

Prison of Tartarus

City of Pluto

Phlegathon

Crossroads

Fields of Tears

River Styx

Acheron

Cocytus

Avernus Cavern

Map of Virgil's Lower World

whose patriotic point lay in linking royal Roman lineage to the noble house of Troy. Anchises appears and explains how the afterlife works: it is close to Er's description. Then there is the proud parade of Aeneas's descendants, showing off the future glory of Rome. Aeneas is so enthralled by the spectacle of his progeny that he nearly forgets to ask about Juno; he knows now he will live to father a line. Finally, he and the Sibyl pass out, oddly, through the false Gate of Ivory as opposed to the honest Gate of Horn.

PLUTARCH (c. 46–c. 120 A.D.) was actually a Greek, but he lived for some time in Rome. Because of his popularity throughout the Middle Ages, his *Vision of Thespesius* is of considerable interest. Its form is like that of the Er story: a reprobate named Thespesius suffers a severe fall and is left for dead. Three days later as he is about to be buried, he revives and tells of his "near-death" vision. His spirit was borne into the realm of a few bright stars, where he saw the souls of newly dead men and women in fiery bubbles, some of which rose, others fell in disorder, and some seemed uncertain. Rising souls shone purely, others had scaly spots on them, some were entirely covered with these spots. A cleansing punishment was meted out by Dis the judge, but some cases were incurable, and one of the Erinyes chases these from place to place, tormenting them with miseries till they fell into the abyss. Thespesius found his own father in the place of the damned; he confessed that he poisoned some of his guests for their gold. Souls writhed in torment, some with their entrails torn out. Three dreadful lakes were near, one of boiling gold, one of freezing lead, one of iron shards, and demons tossed souls from one to another. The last things Thespesius saw were the souls undergoing "correction," by being hammered and pummeled brutally to get them "in shape" for being sent back to another life. This book looks forward to the Christian era, while Lucius Apuleius's *Golden Ass*, a much sunnier contemporary work, looks backward: pretty Psyche has to go to Hades to fetch a magic box of beauty and, like so many others, disobeys the warnings. Luckily, her adventure ends happily ever after.

Sheol

THE JEWS, JUDGED SOLELY BY the evidence of the
Old Testament, were either the least morbid or the least imaginative
of the Mediterranean peoples. Unlike their neighbors, they had no rela-
tionship with the dead; they did not worship them, sacrifice to them, visit
them, hope to reunite with them in an afterlife, nor anticipate any kind of
interaction with Yahweh after death—quite the contrary:

> I am as a man that hath no strength: Free among the dead, like the slain
> that lie in the grave, whom thou rememberest no more: and they are
> cut off from thy hand. (Ps. 88.4–5)

The dead were, in fact, unclean.

The Hebrew word *Sheol* occurs frequently in the Old Testament; sometimes it is translated as "Hell," sometimes as "the grave," and sometimes
as "the pit," but nowhere does it seem to indicate anything other than the
place in which a body is laid to rest, except when used metaphorically to
indicate depression or despair. At times Sheol is likened to a prison. A
second word sometimes translated as Hell is *Gehenna*, which means simply
the valley of Hinnon, a sort of garbage heap or town dump where, in
addition to refuse, the bodies of criminals and animals were thrown into

40

fires, which burned perpetually for sanitary reasons. Human sacrifices to the pagan god Moloch were said to have taken place there in earlier days. The name Gehenna served as a metaphor for an unpleasant place and also as a curse, for death in such a place would have indicated a life far removed from the laws of Yahweh. Other terms used occasionally were *Abaddon* ("Destruction") and *Bor* ("the pit").

Israelites may have shared with their Mesopotamian neighbors some notion of a dry and dusty underground venue for a shadowy afterlife; it would have been from that place that Samuel's ghost or shade appeared at the summons of the Witch of Endor (1 Sam. 28.7). One short diatribe in which the prophet Isaiah curses the king of Babylon is entirely Babylonian in its imagery:

Hell from beneath is moved for thee to meet thee at thy coming: it stirreth up the dead for thee, even all the chief ones of the earth; it has raised up from their thrones all the kings of the nations. All they shall speak and say unto thee, Art thou also become weak as we? art thou become like unto us? Thy pomp is brought down to the grave, and the noise of thy viols: the worm is spread under thee, and the worms cover thee. How art thou fallen from heaven, O Lucifer, son of the morning! how art thou cut down to the ground which did weaken the nations! For thou has said in thy heart, I will ascend into heaven, I will exalt my throne above the stars of God: I will also sit upon the mount of the congregation, in the sides of the north: I will ascend above the heights of the clouds; I will be like the most High. Yet thou shalt be brought down to hell, to the sides of the pit. (Isa. 14.9–15)

This tricky passage has been cited as a biblical voucher for both the existence of an Israelite Hell and the fall of Lucifer. In context, however, it is quite specifically directed at the king of Babylon. It *alludes* to the story recounted in First Enoch, described on page 45, but only metaphorically. Its message is exactly the same as the one Enkidu reported to Gilgamesh, that great kings are brought low in Ereshkigal's domain. Indeed, in sending a Babylonian king to a Babylonian Hell, the prophet appears to be making a grim joke.

A similar curse, or "lamentation," is directed by Ezekiel against the king of Tyrus (Ezek. 28. 1–23; see page 61).

A few tantalizingly brief passages do hint at an eschatological under-current in Jewish thought. The first are also from Isaiah, dated from the third or fourth century B.C. Speaking of "other lords" than Yahweh "who have had dominion over us," the prophet says:

> They are dead, they shall not live; they are deceased, they shall not rise: therefore has thou visited and destroyed them, and made all their memory to perish. (26.14)

By contrast, it would seem, Yahweh's own people will live.

> Thy dead men shall live, together with my dead body shall they arise. Awake and sing, ye that dwell in dust: for thy dew is as the dew of herbs, and the earth shall cast out the dead. (26.19)

Another is from the Book of Daniel, which has been given the date of 165 B.C. At the time of apocalypse, the archangel Michael will appear, and a period of great distress will ensue before deliverance:

> And many of them that sleep in the dust of the earth shall awake, some to everlasting life and some to shame and everlasting contempt. (Dan. 12.2–3)

These passages are thought to show a progression of Persian influence. In Isaiah, the unworthy do not wake at all; in Daniel, they wake to "shame and everlasting contempt." Note that both passages accept the resurrection of the physical body, an idea that may even have predated Zoroaster.

More Jewish evidence for belief in resurrection comes from Second Maccabees, usually printed in the Apocrypha in the English Bible. Second Maccabees is one of several historical texts that chronicle a courageous and successful Jewish uprising against Syrian encroachment in the second century B.C. The relevant seventh chapter is a gruesome account of the torture and execution of seven pious Jewish brothers and their mother. Their crime was their refusal to eat pork. The dying statements of brothers number three, four, and seven, and also of their mother, all indicate confidence that their mutilated bodies will be resurrected whole by Yahweh—who will also wreak vengeance on their tormentor.

Evidence of more change in Jewish eschatological thinking by the first century A.D. comes from both the New Testament and the Jewish historian Flavius Josephus. They document friction between the Sadducees, conservative aristocrats who rejected the "foreign" concept of resurrection, and the Pharisees, populists who embraced it (Mark 12.18; Matt. 22.23; Luke 20.27; Acts 23.8). The word *Pharisee* is thought to refer to Persia, just as a Bombay Zoroastrian is a Parsi. St. Paul was a Pharisee before his conversion, and so was Josephus; by the time he died, some twenty-five years after the destruction of Jerusalem in A.D. 70, virtually all surviving Jews were Pharisees. Reform Judaism, it should be noted, does not accept resurrection.

Josephus, writing shortly after the Jewish war against Rome of A.D. 66–70, tells us of a third group, the Essenes. These monastic brothers, heavily influenced by Neoplatonism, envisioned an afterlife, not a physical resurrection but a resurrection of the soul separated from the body. *The Jewish War* shows how similar ideas were cross-fertilizing the sects of the Roman Empire.

It is indeed their unshakable conviction that bodies are corruptible and the material composing them impermanent, whereas souls remain immortal forever. Coming forth from the most rarefied ether they are trapped in the prison house of the body as if drawn down by one of nature's spells; but once freed from the bonds of the flesh, as if released after years of slavery, they rejoice and soar aloft. Teaching the same doctrine as the sons of Greece, they declare that for the good souls there waits a home beyond the ocean, a place troubled by neither rain nor snow nor heat, but refreshed by the zephyr that blows ever gentle from the ocean. Bad souls they consign to a darksome, stormy abyss, full of punishments that know no end. I think the Greeks had the same notion when they assigned to their brave men, whom they call heroes or demi-gods, the Islands of the Blest, and to the souls of the wicked the place of the impious in Hades, where according to their stories certain people undergo punishment—Sisyphus and Tantalus, Ixion and Tityus, and the like. They tell these tales firstly because they believe souls to be immortal, and secondly in the hope of encouraging virtue and discouraging vice, since the good become better in their lifetime through the hope of a reward after death, and the propensities of the bad are restrained by the fear that, even if they are not caught in this life, after their dissolution they will undergo eternal punishment.

The first and second centuries, for Jews, are thought of not primarily as Roman or Hellenistic or late antique, and certainly not as Early Christian, but as the time of the destruction of Jerusalem and the beginning of the Diaspora. The Book of Enoch and the Book of the Secrets of Enoch (known as First and Second Enochs, or "Ethiopic" and "Slavonic") date from this period, and are thought to have been written in Egypt by refugees, probably in Greek, as was true of the contemporary New Testament. Though demoted to non-canonical "pseudepigrapha," they have been closely studied by scholars looking for clues to Jewish thought and legend.

In Second Enoch, Yahweh reveals his secrets to Enoch and allows him, in the 365th year of his life, to measure and record the particulars of the whole earth, and the ten heavens, the third of which contains both paradise and Hell. Enoch is speaking:

> And those two men [angels] led me up the north slope and showed me a terrible place. It had all manner of tortures: cruel darkness, dim gloom. There was no light but that of murky fire. It had a fiery river and the whole place is everywhere fire, everywhere frost and ice, thirst and shivering, while the fetters are cruel, and the angels fearful and merciless, bearing sharp weapons and merciless tortures. I said, "How terrible is this place." (2 Enoch 12)

Those who break any of the Ten Commandments go here forever, as well as those who practice greed, lack of charity, child abuse, witchcraft, or magic. Fire and ice are both on hand; ice was not present in the Greek and Roman underworlds. First Enoch gives an entirely different scenario:

> I saw how the winds stretch out the vaults of Heaven and have their station between heaven and earth. These are Heaven's pillars. I saw columns of heavenly fire and among them I saw columns of fire fall, beyond all measure of height and depth. And beyond that abyss I saw a place which had no firmament of the heaven above and no firmly founded place beneath it. There was no water on it and no birds; it was a horrible wasteland. There I saw seven stars like great burning moun-

tains, and when I asked about them the angel told me: "This place is
the end of Heaven and earth. It has become a prison for the stars and
the host of Heaven." And the stars which roll over the fire have trans-
gressed the Lord's commandments in the beginning of their rising, for
they did not appear at their appointed times. And God was angry with
them and bound them for ten thousand years until their guilt was ap-
peased. (1 Enoch 17)

What seems remarkable about this passage is its echo of Hesiod. The col-
umns of fire that reach from Heaven down to the abyss are like the silvery
pillars of the House of Styx; the situation of the imprisoned angels (whom
both books of Enoch identify with the Grigori, or Watchers of Genesis
VI.1–7) is like that of the Titans in Tartarus. The Book of Revelation also
equated fallen angels with falling stars.

The fourth-century Haggadah gives a lively account of Satan's fall—in
this version because he refused to give homage to Adam even after it was
proved that he lacked Adam's great talent, that of beast-naming—and of
Adam's first wife, the feminist demon Lilith. She was sister to that trou-
blesome Babylonian demon, Lilitu; here she rejects Adam because, in sexual
intercourse, he insists on being on top. The Haggadah's Hell is embroidered
in the Oriental fashion with snakes and scorpions but no one is in it, at
least not on the Second Day when it was created. (Paradise was not made
till the Third Day, which may indicate their order of requirement.)

Gnosticism

ANOTHER IDEA OF HELL CURRENT during the overwrought period of late antiquity was that people are in it even as they proceed about their daily life. This pessimistic view is usually labeled Gnostic, though it cropped up over and over again in the widespread Christian heresies of the Middle Ages, and more than a glimpse of it informs orthodox Christianity. Scholars used to separate Gnostics into "Jewish" and "Christian" heretics or freethinkers of the first three or four centuries after Christ, but since the recent discoveries of manuscript libraries at Nag Hammadi and Qumran, they are more cautious. The idea that we live in an inferior shadow of a better world could just as easily be pinned on pagan Plato, who said once that our world "is necessarily haunted by evil."

The most common Gnostic myth goes more or less as follows: An *aeon* or angel named Sophia ("Wisdom") greatly admired the High Unknown or Alien God—again, a Platonic formulation that appealed, as it still does, to people who marvel at the universe but cavil at the concept of a personal god, or a god who permits evil knowingly. Worshipfully but mistakenly, Sophia sought to imitate the self-sufficient asexual creativity of the High God, and this mistake caused her to fall from the clear, light, and pure upper heavens. In her agony and despair, she brought forth a shapeless abortion, which became the Demiurge, or Lower God, the creator of our universe, of the world, of matter, and of human beings. He made all these in total ignorance of the High God and Sophia, his mother; he believed that he was the only god. Hence our world was conceived in ignorance and folly, and so were we, for the god in whose likeness we were created is the Demiurge. Whatever spark of the good or spiritual in nature there is was breathed into us by Sophia, a heavenly exile trying to make amends for her initial error.

Sophia's story was coarsened by a continuing mythology which had her reincarnated in a series of famous women: Eve, Noah's wife, Helen of Troy, and Mary Magdalene, to name four. But where the Gnostic myth caught the imagination was in its interpretation of the incarnation of Jesus Christ. If the world is Hell, or at least a kind of Hades or Limbo, ruled over by an ignorant and ignoble Devil, then the descent of Christ from the heavenly *pleroma* into a body of gross flesh and blood that must breathe the impure air of a world made in error was quite literally a descent into Hell. Its Promethean purpose was to harrow or plunder the unhappy domain of the Demiurge in order to save the souls of mankind by bringing them *gnosis*, or secret knowledge.

Even when the early Church still possessed some of the flexibility of a new, revealed faith, most Gnostic thought, certainly the Sophia story, was unacceptable. The Alien or Unknowable God, while compatible with Neoplatonism (and with Aristotle's Unmoved Mover), was too radically different from the Heavenly Father Jesus had invoked in the Gospels, to merge with the new Christian theology. The Crucifixion and Resurrection lacked meaning if Jesus's only purpose on earth was to bring an esoteric salvation by *gnosis*. And the whole scheme lacked popular appeal, especially as *gnosis* appeared to be limited to the privileged few.

The idea that this world was in the grip of the Devil had many Christian proponents, however, as did the idea that matter, very much including the human body, was inherently evil and gross. References to the Devil or Satan as the god or prince of this world were common, as in the Gospels when Jesus is tempted in the wilderness with "all the kingdoms of this world in their glory" if he will only do homage to the Devil.

Possibly as a counter to perceived Roman decadence, a movement toward asceticism, a kind of disgust with wealth, food, and sexuality, was very much in evidence during late antiquity. This was true for Jews (the Essene monks, for example) and pagans as well as Christians and Gnostics. Until recently, godparents at a Christian baby's baptism promised in its name to renounce "the world, the flesh, and the Devil," an echo of a time when the three concepts were closely linked.

Early Christians and most Gnostics believed the Second Coming and the Last Judgment were close at hand. Christians hoped for Heaven and feared for Hell, while Gnostics aspired to achieve the heavenly *pleroma* by way of their secret knowledge. Since Hell was here and not hereafter, Gnostic punishment lay simply in not being saved. Though most of the human race was doomed, the doom was no more dreadful than the Hell already on earth. In contrast to the lurid imaginings of Christianity as it developed, this fate seems both relatively benign and peculiarly modern.

Manichaeism

MARCION AND MANI ARE LINKED with the Gnostics by tradition, though each would surely have denied the connection. Marcion, a Syrian who lived in Rome in the second century, considered himself a Christian and follower of St. Paul, though he taught that there were two Gods: the capricious and often violent Yahweh of the Old Testament he identified with the Demiurge—not evil exactly, but not good and certainly not omnipotent. Thus he rejected the entire Hebrew Bible and most of the New Testament, retaining only Luke's Gospel and Paul's epistles, both of which he pruned considerably for his flock. Jesus, in Marcion's teaching, was the son of the True God, sent in a spirit of disinterested benevolence as a ransom to the Demiurge who held mankind in captivity but would pass away together with his inferior material universe at the upcoming Last Judgment. Marcion's following flourished well into the fourth century, despite bitter opposition from orthodox Church leaders.

Mani, a Persian born around 215 in a Jewish-Christian community in Assyria, set off on a highly successful mission to preach a new religion when he was only twenty-four. His following was substantial throughout Europe and Asia and lasted for at least a thousand years in the West and much longer in the East, possibly into the twentieth century in China.

Though Mani was executed by orthodox Zoroastrians in about 276, his dualistic system owed much to their religion. In it, too, opposing spirits battle for control of the world. The God of Light is the primal spirit, and his kingdom encompasses the heavens, the virtues, the angels, the beauties of nature, and so on. From the kingdom of Darkness, "Matter," personified and identified with Satan or Ahriman, was born together with demons, fire, smoke, unpleasant weather—and women. Adam was created by Ahriman in his own image, but imbued with "stolen light." Eve, also his creation, was almost completely a creature of the dark; her task was to seduce Adam, and her weapon was lust (this theory would influence Augustine and with him the history of Christianity). Their descendants have varying shades of light and dark, but, in keeping with Eastern tradition, men are always more "enlightened" than women.

Through the suppression of sensuality, right living (including vegetarianism), and adherence to the teachings of Mani, the elect or *perfecti* can gather a larger portion of light unto themselves and will ascend directly to the Kingdom of Light after death. The unredeemed must go through a process of purification in successive lives before eventually being admitted to the light. Unrepentant sinners, at Jesus's Second Coming, will fall into the flames that will consume the entire world for 1,468 years. In a general way, this procedure is not so very different from the one outlined by Socrates in the *Phaedo,* or from the Buddhist one.

Manichaeism was a deliberate attempt to combine and supersede Buddhism, Zoroastrianism, Christianity, and Marcionism, borrowing from the Gnostics as well. In the case of the Gnostics and Marcionites, it succeeded, and most joined the sect. Like them, Manichaeans rejected the Yahweh of the Hebrew Bible as a being to be worshiped. They accepted Adam, Noah, and Abraham as patriarchal figures though, of course, not Moses and the prophets linked specifically with the Jews. They accepted Buddha and Zoroaster, and they accepted Jesus: Mani claimed to be, like Paul, his apostle.

Manichaeism had the advantage of being a rather easy-to-understand system, which explained the struggle of good and evil for control of the spirit, the conflicts in human nature, and the need for and process of salvation more clearly than many religions, including early Christianity, which was in the process of sorting itself out. Manichaeism incorporated a good deal of already familiar mythology, including the final struggle between the forces of good and evil at the end of time, and its asceticism caught the temper of the period. Mani's teachings gained ground quickly in the Roman Empire, reached deep into Asia, and had it not been for severe persecutions following the fifth-century conversion to Christianity of the emperor Constantine, might have been even more persistent than they proved to be in the West. Manichaean monasticism, modeled on Buddhist religious life, strongly influenced Christian practice, as did that of the Essenes. And Augustine, the most influential man in the history of the early Church, was for nine years a Manichaen.

The Early Christians

S AUL OF TARSUS, THE JEWISH Pharisee who con-
verted to become the essential Christian missionary to the Roman
world, is our first witness to early Christian thought. Paul, as he renamed
himself, never met Jesus, but his letters in the New Testament predate the
composition of the earliest Gospel, that of Mark (c. A.D. 70), and were
written more than twenty years before Luke wrote the Acts of the Apostles,
about his own travels with Paul. Paul speaks of Jesus as arriving in flames
at the Last Trump and "everlasting destruction from the presence of the
Lord and from the glory of his power" (2 Thes. 1.9) but goes no further
into after-death prediction.

The Christian doctrine of Hell certainly did not originate with Christianity's first theologian. Paul in three places lists those who will not be
admitted to the kingdom of God: 1 Cor. 6.9–10; Gal. 5.19–21; Eph. 5.5.
They include unrepentant fornicators, idolators, adulterers, homosexuals,
thieves, drunkards, slanderers, swindlers, sorcerers, the envious, the quarrelsome, the indecent, and the greedy. Instead of condemning these wrong-
doers to Hell, he taught that "the wages of sin is death" (Rom. 5.6), and
that is what he meant by "destruction." The good would live, and sinners
would die. Centuries later, this would be called *annihilation theory*. Death
can be avoided through God's grace and baptism in union with Jesus Christ,
and for believers Paul's message was reliably positive: "We do all things,

dearly beloved, for your edifying" (2 Cor. 12.19). Other disciples, Peter (2 Pet. 3) and Jude, did warn of future punishment in their letters, though not of flames.

Mark, who first strung the remembrances and stories of Jesus's life together in a continuous form, probably did not know Jesus but may have known Peter. According to the fourth-century historian Eusebius, "he had only one concern: to leave out nothing of what he had heard nor to include anything false." Mark does speak of "eternal damnation" in store for someone who slanders the Holy Ghost (3.29–30), but he mentions Hell only once. Jesus is speaking to the disciples.

> And if thy hand offend thee, cut it off: it is better for thee to enter into life maimed than having two hands to go into Hell, into the fire that shall never be quenched: Where their worm dieth not and the fire is not quenched. And if thy foot offend thee, cut it off: it is better for thee to enter halt into life than having two feet to be cast into Hell, into the fire that shall never be quenched: Where their worm dieth not and the fire is not quenched. (Mark 9.43–48)

And so on for the offending eye. Given current beliefs, this could be taken as colorfully hyperbolic repetitive rhetoric rather than a direct threat; note that the individual is urged to correct his own transgressions.

Paul's traveling companion Luke, an educated man said to have been a physician, based his own Gospel on Mark's (or on a hypothetical common source sometimes called "Q") and left this passage out. His Jesus urges repentance in order to achieve the kingdom of God rather than to avoid retribution. He does, however, tell the significant story of Dives and Lazarus, related below. And, whether or not the Gospel according to John was written by the same John who was Jesus's disciple, it nowhere mentions Hell. The Book of Revelation, once erroneously credited to John, is something else again.

This leaves Matthew. According to Mark, Matthew was the seventh of Jesus's original twelve disciples, and the Gospel of Matthew lists "Matthew the tax collector." Matthew's Gospel relies heavily on Mark's, however, and there is not much to indicate that it is the work of an eyewitness. It is thought to have been written sometime after A.D. 80, which makes the identification unlikely. But it is on the Gospel of Matthew that much of the Christian proof of Hell's existence and purpose depends.

Matthew's great innovation was to attach eschatological warnings to the parables Mark attributed to Jesus. That this was his own idea is clear when his gospel is compared to that of Luke, who repeats the same stories without the warnings. Eschatology was vitally important to Matthew. He cites Mark's dismissal of bodily parts twice, first at the end of the Sermon on the Mount (5.29–30) and then after the "Suffer the little children to come unto me" sermon (18.89). In neither case do these repetitions sound merely hyperbolic. His Jesus exhorts followers to open the strait gate of righteous living rather than the wide gate that leads to perdition (7.13). He tells them not to fear those who can kill the body but not the soul: "Rather fear him which is able to destroy both soul and body in Hell" (10.28), adding that "whomsoever shall deny me before men, him will I also deny before my Father which is in Heaven" (10.33). Annoyed with an impenitent crowd and claiming that his miracles would have saved Tyre, Sidon, and Sodom had they been performed there, Jesus says, "That it will be more tolerable for the land of Sodom on the day of judgment than for thee" (11.24).

It is at moralizing the parables that Matthew's Jesus excels. He takes time and effort to drive home two points: that salvation is possible only through God represented by his Son, and that not to be saved is desperately perilous. Explaining the parable of the wheat and the chaff, he says that at the end of the world, "The Son of man shall send forth his angels, and they shall gather out of his kingdom all things that offend, and them which do iniquity: And shall cast them into a furnace of fire: there shall be wailing and gnashing of teeth" (13.40–42). And again, good men, like good fish, will be caught in angelic nets, while the angels will throw the worthless "into the furnace of fire: there shall be wailing and gnashing of teeth" (13.50).

In the temple, Matthew's Jesus lays a long and colorful curse on lawyers and Pharisees for their hypocrisy and greed and willingness to corrupt others, crying, "Ye serpents, ye generation of vipers, how can ye escape the damnation of Hell?" (23.33). And finally, on the Mount of Olives, he tells of the Last Days, of the Second Coming, a time of great distress that will herald the birth of a new age. Then he relates a string of parables—the wise servant, the wise and foolish virgins, the ten talents, the sheep and the goats—all of which have a single theme, that the deserving will gain eternal life, while the others will be cast "into outer darkness: there shall be weeping and gnashing of teeth" (25.30) or "everlasting fire that is prepared for the Devil and his angels" (25.41) or "everlasting punishment" (25.46).

Only Matthew stresses these warnings. Mark and Luke do quite well without them, and Paul, who relied on Luke's Gospel to the point of claiming it as his own, would not, we may suspect, have approved.

CURIOUSLY, THE essentially incontrovertible demonstration for early Christians that Hell existed as a *place* of after-death punishment of evildoers came not from the admonitory Matthew, but from the Gospel of Luke. Mark had told the story of the rich man who came to Jesus to ask the secret of eternal life and was dismayed to find it contingent upon giving away everything he had to the poor; this prompted Jesus to offer the analogy of the camel and the needle's eye (Mark 10.17–27). But Luke greatly expanded Jesus's insistence on the social responsibility of the well-to-do toward the less fortunate with a number of parables and cautionary examples on the subject of wealth and property, ending with an address to the Pharisees, who had the reputation of being overly fond of their worldly goods.

"There was a certain rich man, which was clothed in purple and fine linen, and fared sumptuously every day"—he would be called Dives (Greek: "Rich Man"). At his gate lay Lazarus the beggar, whose sores the dogs licked as they all waited vainly for table scraps. Lazarus died "and was carried by the angels into Abraham's bosom." Dives died, too, and went to Hell. Looking up from the flames, he begged Abraham to send Lazarus with a drop of water to cool his tongue, but Abraham reminded him that he had already had "thy good things." Also there was a "great gulf fixed," so that passage was impossible. Dives begged to be allowed to warn his five brothers, but Abraham refused, saying "If they heed not Moses and the prophets, neither will they be persuaded though one rose from the dead" (Matt. 16.19–31).

The parables of Jesus in all the Gospels are rich with metaphoric allusion. Luke's later audience chose to take this particular parable literally, however, using it to scope out the latitudes of Hell more clearly than they could from Matthew's vaguer references to the place of "weeping and gnashing

The story of Dives and Lazarus, from a medieval psalter

of teeth." Hell (it was "Hades" in the original Greek) is a specific fiery
place of torment "afar off" and yet in view of Father Abraham, who held
Lazarus "in his bosom."

Grammatical confusion in translation led to the "bosom" question. The
Latin Vulgate Bible read *in sinu Abrahai*; "sinus" in Latin means the fold
of a garment, hence bosom or lap. In medieval art, Abraham is usually
depicted with what looks like a kind of towel spread across his bosom from
which Lazarus and his privileged peers peep out like children. (Sometimes
an unlettered artist would get the story wrong, understandably confusing
Lazarus the beggar with the other biblical Lazarus, brother of Mary and
Martha, and would portray the beggar rising from the dead, in contrast to

Lazarus and a friend join the elect in Abraham's bosom at the very moment that Dives reaches the hot pot. From a medieval French psalter.

the dire fate of the rich man.) Medieval sages would argue long and earnestly over how many souls were rocked in the bosom of Abraham. Was it just Lazarus? What about Enoch, who "walked with God; and he was not, for God took him"? What about Elijah, who had been swept up in a fiery chariot? And just where was Abraham's bosom anyway?

The difficulty lay in where to place Abraham, who, as a Jew, could not have been admitted to a Heaven that, for the literal-minded, did not exist, or at least was not populated by any save the heavenly host before Jesus's Ascension and was afterward, like a politically incorrect private country club, restricted to Christians. The usual solution to the problem of deserving pre-Christians was Limbo.

57

Limbo ("Borderland," from Latin *limbus* or border) was a region borrowed from the pagans but put to a new use. Christian tradition came to include two Limbos. One was for unbaptized babies whom nobody (yet) was willing to consign to Hell though they could not, without the sacrament, go to Heaven; down the centuries there would be many theological attempts to rescue these innocents. The other was for pre-Christians, particularly Old Testament patriarchs and sometimes such honored pagans as Plato, who were disadvantaged in that they had enjoyed no opportunity to believe in Christ. Abraham would seem to belong in the latter Limbo and his bosom to be a sort of subdivision of it. Yet Jesus's parable made clear that Lazarus was in a paradise of sorts.

In addition to its obvious moral, the story of Dives and Lazarus illustrated the claim that part of the joy of the saved lies in contemplating the torments of the damned. The early Church taught that this view proved God's justice and hatred of sin, and backed it by at least two other scriptural citations—Revelation, 14.9–11, in which the wicked are to be tormented with fire and brimstone in the presence of the Lamb and the angels, and Isaiah 66.23–24, in which the faithful shall go forth and look upon the carcassses of transgressors, "for their worm shall not die neither shall their fire be quenched." Modern churches have quietly abandoned the abominable fancy (so dubbed by the nineteenth-century preacher Dean Farrar), but centuries of artwork endorse it.

THE BOOK of Revelation barely made it into the New Testament canon and finally did only because of a mistake in attribution. Its author is now usually called John of Patmos to distinguish him from the author of the Gospel according to John. It is an apocalyptic work thought to have been written in the latter part of the first century as a protest against Roman dominion, and particularly against the imperial cult of emperor worship. Domitian (81–96), the current emperor, was a cruel and ostentatious man who insisted on always being addressed as *dominus et deus*, "master and god."

The prophetic visions of Revelation probably seem stranger to us now than they did at the time, since the form looked back to traditional Jewish apocalyptic literature, such as the books of Daniel and Ezekiel, often written in response to imposed tyranny. The highly dramatic conflict presented is between cosmic powers of good and evil, evil being represented by the

Roman Empire symbolized by a great red seven-headed dragon. The scene is the end of the world, following scorched earth, the poisoning of both salt and fresh water, volcanic eruptions, plagues of unearthly locusts and horses, the slaughter of two-thirds of mankind, and terrible earthquakes. Seven angels have blown their trumpets and God's "temple in heaven" is laid open, amid thunder, another earthquake, and a hailstorm. See Plate 2.

A pregnant woman "clothed by the sun" appears, and the red dragon tries to devour the son she bears. Instead he is snatched up to God, while Michael and his angel troops attack "that old serpent called the Devil and Satan, which deceived the whole world: he was cast out into the earth, and his angels were cast out with him."

The dragon transfers its power to a grotesque "beast" rising from the sea that is blasphemously worshiped by men. Further calamities overtake the earth, until the Great Whore of Babylon (Jadi or Jeh, a figure from

---

Seven heads identify the beast from the sea, here being worshiped, with the red dragon and the seven hills of Rome. The whore of Babylon, most unusually, has a beast's head here.

Zoroastrian creation mythology) who represents Israel's ancient enemy Babylon as the seven-headed dragon does Rome, the current enemy, is overthrown, and Heaven opens.

> Then I saw an angel coming down from the heaven with the key of the abyss and a great chain in his hands. He seized the dragon, that serpent of old, the Devil or Satan, and chained him up for a thousand years; he threw him into the abyss, shutting and sealing it over him, so that he might seduce the nations no more till the thousand years was over. After that he must be let loose for a short while. (20.1–3)

Then Satan will come out to muster the forces of "Gog and Magog, countless as the sands of the sea." Fire from Heaven will consume them, and the Devil will be flung into the lake of fire and sulphur, together with a "false prophet" to be tormented forever (20.7–10).

At Judgment Day, the sea gives up its dead, and so do Death and Hades. They will be judged on their records. Death and Hades are flung into the lake of fire which represents "the second death" and so are those judged unworthy (20.13–15).

Here, safely in the canon—though not altogether safely: Eusebius reports a third-century bishop, Dionysus, expressing doubts about it—was the approval for the radical Christian fringe, the millenarians, revivalists, ecstatics, mystics, and visionaries who would make use of it. Christianity would have had a much easier time without Revelation, though it would be a less colorful religion.

THE *FALL* is a key metaphor for the Christian faith. Central to it is the Genesis story of the fall of Adam and Eve from a condition of primal innocence and Edenic bliss to a world of pain, loss, suffering, and death. The Jews shared this myth, of course, and many other cultures cite a lapsed golden age, but Christians magnified the meaning and consequence of the original act of disobedience to underscore the significance of redemption and salvation through their own new doctrines and disciplines. Original Sin, Christianity taught, was transmitted to all of mankind from its first parents, creating an atmosphere of corruption so intense that later sins could not be avoided.

The first fall in the Christian creation myth, however, was not Adam's, but Lucifer's. (Some early Christians argued that Lucifer's fall postdated Adam's, but tradition eventually decreed otherwise.) We have seen this once-great fallen figure in the Jewish Second Enoch and, much earlier, referred to in Isaiah's mockery of the king of Babylon. The second biblical reference to a fallen prince comes from the prophet Ezekiel who is laying a long curse upon the king of Tyrus, dictated to him, he says, by Yahweh. The king was once greatly favored:

> Thou sealest up the sum: full of wisdom and perfect in beauty. Thou hast been in Eden, the garden of God; every precious stone was thy covering. . . . Thou art the anointed cherub that covereth; and I have set thee so: thou wast on the holy mountain of God; thou hast walked up and down in the stones of fire. Thou wast perfect in thy ways from the day thou wast created till iniquity was found in thee. (Ezek. 28.12–23)

Most of the curse enumerates the evil in store for the king. Ezekiel compares the wished-for fall to that of a splendid unnamed being, and his lush description of how, before the fall, he glittered with jewels gave rise to the belief that Lucifer had been the most glorious as well as the most favored of the angels. He was even, heretically, called the elder Son of God.

Lucifer ("Fire-bearer") in Hebrew is *Helel ben Sahar,* "Bright Son of the Morning." He is linked to the planet Venus and, somewhat ambiguously, to other fiery falling figures: Hephaestus, Prometheus, Phaethon, Icarus. The pride that made him "sit in the seat of God" led to his fall; this is the Greek *hubris* so often punished by cosmic justice. The final battle of Revelation was also interpreted as a primal battle, the war in Heaven between Lucifer's forces and those of St. Michael at the beginning of time. After the fall, Lucifer, identified with the red dragon, became as hideous as he had been beautiful—that explained the beast—and changed his name to Satan.

The Gospel of Luke reports that Jesus told his followers, "I beheld Satan as lightning fall from heaven" (Luke 10.18). In his second letter to Corinth, Paul warned against false prophets, saying, "Satan himself masquerades as an angel of light" (11.14). By this evidence and that of 2 Enoch,

Satan, the adversary, obstructor, or servant of the Old Testament, evidently became identified with Lucifer, the fallen or fraudulent angel.

In the Hebrew Bible, or Old Testament, *satan* means "adversary" or "opponent," and when the figure named Satan appears, it is always as Yahweh's angelic servant or agent operating against a man or men, certainly not against Yahweh himself, in some less than creditable action. Neil Forsyth in *The Old Enemy* wonderfully calls him "a shady but necessary member of the Politburo." With Yahweh's complicity, he murders Egyptian children (Exod. 12.23), harasses Balaam (Num. 22.22–35), incites treachery against a prince of Israel (Judg. 9.22–23), prompts King Saul to dishonorable behavior (1 Sam. 16.14–16; 18.10–11; 19.9–10), sends plague to Israel (2 Sam. 24.13–16 and 1 Chron. 21.1–30), entices Ahab into military

---

This is thought to be the earliest known portrayal of the fall of Lucifer, c. 500 A.D. The red dragon is metamorphosed into a still-handsome fallen angel—the beastly Satan was yet to come. Up on the left is St. Michael. See also Plate 2.

disaster (2 Chron. 18.18–22), and torments Job. Scholars believe the character of Satan was often added to earlier manuscripts by editors seeking to save Yahweh's reputation; compare 2 Samuel 24.1–25 with 1 Chronicle 21.1–30, two accounts of the plague sent to punish King David's "sin" in attempting a census. Only once (Zech. 3.2–10) is Satan rebuked by Yahweh for punishing Jerusalem too zealously; only here does he evidence any kind of independent action whatever.

By the first century, when the Gospels were written, Satan appears to have achieved autonomy as "prince of this world" in the Temptation in the wilderness—though here, too, he can arguably be seen as God's agent testing Jesus's mettle. (Unlike the Gnostic Demiurge, the New Testament Satan is never credited with *creating* the world he is prince of.) Later he successfully tempts Judas into betraying Jesus to the authorities, though this also seems to have been preordained in the Passion drama. The older, simpler obstructive meaning of the word persists when Jesus says to Peter, "Get thee behind me, Satan," as Peter attempts to dissuade him from the actions that will lead to his arrest and crucifixion.

Jesus's chief recorded activity, aside from preaching, is exorcism of minor demons. Many other healers, magicians, and exorcists were in business at the time; the difference was that Jesus operated through the power of the Holy Spirit. The word *demon* comes from the Greek *daimon* or *daimonion* and it came to be identified with *diabolos,* a word which, in the New Testament, refers only to Satan himself. By the first century, there was some indication among Jews that ordinary, ubiquitous, trouble- and disease-making demons were subordinated to an arch-demon. Inevitably, as the myth of Satan grew, pagan gods were added to the roster of his lieutenants; one man's god is always another man's devil.

What Revelation did, despite or because of the confusion and incoherence of its text, was to offer plenty of room for synthesis and interpretation of a number of allusions and legends, leading to a new myth. The fallen angel was identified with the red dragon thrown down from Heaven with his angels—"one third of the stars in the sky"—who could now themselves be identified with demons. The dragon was linked to a beast like the fearsome and seemingly supernatural beasts of the Hebrew Bible—Leviathan ("Out of his mouth go burning torches, and sparks of fire leap forth. Out of his nostrils a smoke goeth, as of a seething pot and burning rushes. His breath kindleth coals, and a flame goes forth from his mouth

63

Satan sits on the red dragon identified with him in this twelfth-century floor mosaic from the Cathedral of Otranto.

[Job 40.14–21]); Behemoth ("Lo, now, his strength is in his loins, and his force is in the muscles of his belly. He moveth his tail like a cedar, his bones are as tubes of brass, his limbs are like bars of iron. He is the chief of God's works, made to be a tyrant over his peers" [Job 40.16–19]); and Rahab the sea-dragon.

Next, the angel-dragon-beast was linked with "that serpent of old" responsible for the fall of Adam and Eve from Eden. The Gospels had shown Satan as Jesus's and Judas's tempter; Revelation displayed him as the original seducer and tempter of all mankind, the cause of our subsequent sorrow and even of death itself.

By showing Satan in power with "the forces of Gog and Magog," his position as "prince of this world" was further established, at least until his eventual defeat. The fact that the First Coming had apparently done nothing to diminish Satan's evident power on earth was also vaguely explained.

The Last Judgment following a final cosmic battle between the forces of good and evil, already familiar from Zoroastrian and Mithraic writings and from Jewish apocalyptic literature, confirmed the apocalyptic prophecy in Matthew, and God's adversary was identified as Satan.

Finally, unbelievers (those who worship the beast), the beast itself, and its "false prophet" (the Antichrist) are all to be thrown into the lake of fire. After a long term bound in "the abyss," the Devil or Satan himself (the dragon) joins them and so do Death and Hades, personified pagan death figures. After judgment, so do the sinners among the dead formerly in their keeping. This is a significant grouping of many heretofore disparate figures. By the Middle Ages, the beast, the dragon, Death, and Hades would all have merged into Satan.

Early theologians labored over their difficult "factual" texts, seeking to define the role of the Devil and his relation to God and man. On a simpler story-telling level, the synthesis happened organically. Much of it was in place by the third century, as we will see in the *Gospel of Bartholomew*. Augustine, in the fifth century, put most of the last pieces in place, but not until the Middle Ages did the attributes of Hell or even the name of the Devil become conventionalized.*

---

*Other names: Satanel, Beliar or Belial ("Worthless"); Beelzebub ("Lord of the Flies"); Beelzeboul ("Lord of Excrement"); Mastema ("Enmity"); Azazel ("Wasteland").

The Descent into Hell

FOR MOST OF TWO MILLENNIA, the account of Jesus's descent into Hell between Good Friday and Easter Sunday has been integral to the complete Christian story-cycle of Jesus's life, death, resurrection, and ascension. The New Testament source is, vaguely, Matthew 27.52–53, where, at the moment of Jesus's death, there is an earthquake, graves open, "and many bodies of the saints which slept arose." Peter's first epistle (3:19–20) is more specific, saying that Christ "was being put to death in the flesh, but quickened by the Spirit: By which also he went and preached unto the spirits in prison." The passage goes on in a murky way about Noah, the waters of the Flood, and the waters of baptism, but on it rested the belief that, just after the Crucifixion, Jesus went to preach to the souls of the Old Testament patriarchs who predated Noah, and that these then entered the Holy City, or Heaven. Or perhaps he preached to all the dead, pagan and Jewish, even sinners.

Very quickly a more exciting story began to circulate. In it Jesus descended to the underworld as a militant savior on a mission to rescue the souls of the just. A Jewish version of this adventure, the *Testament of the Twelve Patriarchs,* dating from about 100 B.C., sent the Messiah-to-come into the kingdom of Beliar (or Baal), here the chief of Hell, to rescue his captives. By the third century, the *Teachings of Silvanus* and the *Gospel of Bartholomew* had transferred the story from the still-awaited Jewish mes-

66

A Harrowing from a thirteenth-century psalter. Note Eve's attempt at modesty, and the upper figure diving desperately toward redemption.

siah to Jesus. There are many references to the descent in early Christian writing, but the most complete and influential account is the *Gospel of Nicodemus*. The first known written version is from the fifth century, but it was undoubtedly widely known before that, and it was accepted as canonical for centuries.

There are two connected sections. The first, known as the Acts of Pilate, expands the account of Christ's trial and execution presented by the New Testament Gospels. The second is the Harrowing of Hell, related by two sons of Simeon the high priest, who have temporarily risen from the dead in order to bear witness to the great events following the Crucifixion, which Satan arranged himself, but which backfired disastrously so that Hell had to discharge its inhabitants.

Technically, Jesus harrows not Hell but the Limbo of the patriarchs, presented as a dark underground prison administered by Hades (from Greek tradition) with Satan (from Hebrew tradition) as his worldly agent. It features no tortures beyond what one might expect in an ordinary prison, and the patriarchal prisoners, once they sense the outcome, are downright obstreperous—which is, of course, why *Nicodemus* was loved. When Jesus arrives, he defeats Satan and his demons, and, with important symbolism for Christians, Death itself in the person of Hades.

The Harrowing accounted for a crucial period of time and for proper disposal of the revered figures from the Old Testament, beginning with Adam and Eve and including Abraham, who could now be placed above, wherever he may have been at the time of Dives. It dramatized the Christian promise of resurrection much better than any book in the New Testament.

Furthermore, the Harrowing was vitally important to the Christian image in its portrait of a virile, capable Jesus, not suffering on the cross or preaching to the poor, but battling demons, rescuing prisoners, righting wrongs, and issuing orders like a triumphant warrior-prince. For many people, the story of the great rescue and triumph over death may have been the most attractive and comforting part of the new religion.

The Harrowing story presented difficulties, however. If Satan was defeated and imprisoned by Jesus, how can he still be with us? If his death ensured the patriarchs' freedom from Hades or Limbo, and implicitly the future freedom of all good Christians, to whom was the ransom paid? To the Devil? Some of the early church fathers thought exactly that, but others were outraged by the idea—how could the Devil presume to bargain with God?

Though *Nicodemus* does not exploit it, the device of separating Satan and Hades is a clever literary way to subvert "ransom theory" to "sacrifice theory." If Jesus died not to appease or pay off an important adversary (the Devil or Satan) but as a sacrifice to symbolize, through the resurrection, triumph over death, the second character of an abstracted Hades or Death personified, separate from, and ruler over Satan the tempter/devil, is useful. *Nicodemus* approaches the problem with a folktale version of "hoodwink theory," in which the Devil is tricked into thinking he has eliminated Christ only to find his own downfall. However, since Hades, or Death personified, disappeared from the story, not to return until the end of the Middle Ages, theologians found the argument difficult.

No matter how its meaning was argued, the literal truth of the descent was not in question. The Apostles' Creed, the earliest statement of Christian faith, declares:

The demons simply cannot believe what is happening to them. This painting by Andrea da Firenze is faithful to the spirit of Nicodemus.

He descended into hell;
The third day he rose again from the dead;
He ascended into heaven, and sitteth at the right hand of God the
    Father Almighty;
From thence he shall come to judge the quick and the dead.

Later church creeds (except the Athanasian of the sixth century) excluded the descent passage, which may indicate eventual uneasiness with the Harrowing story at higher intellectual levels. In the sixth century, Gregory of Tours, who began his *History of the Franks* with the creation of the world according to Genesis and included Jesus's life, omitted any account of what happened between the Crucifixion and the Resurrection. On the other hand, an Easter poem he composed for Pope Gregory the Great has the lines:

Jesus has harrowed Hell: He has led captivity captive:
Darkness and chaos and death flee from the face of the light.

Pope Gregory and, even more importantly, Augustine were completely matter-of-fact about the Harrowing, never questioning its historical occurrence and essential value to the Passion sequence. Through medieval times, for nearly everyone, including the great majority of the clergy, the story of the Harrowing was as securely fixed in mind as those of Adam and Eve and the miracle of Bethlehem.

THE ANTICHRIST

Like Matthew, Paul warned of false prophets, one in particular, who would come to be known as the Antichrist, Satan's evil counterpart to Christ himself—we have seen him in the fiery lake in Revelation. The millennium could not come until the Antichrist arrived, so there was much speculation about his identity. The Roman Empire held no shortage of emperors qualified for the role—Domitian, Caligula, Nero—but it was more likely that he would be a spiritual leader and miracle worker. Simon Magus of Samaria, the Gnostic magician who had a run-in with the apostles Peter and Paul, was an early nominee. There were many others, until Reformation Protestants decided the term must refer to the entire papacy, and that they had been living through a millennium of false religion.

The millennium is a confusing term. Strictly speaking, it means the thousand-year period of God's kingdom on earth—the New Jerusalem or the City of God—predicted in Revelation, or else to a negative counterpart, which, in the murk of Revelation, seems equally predicted. This would precede the Last Judgment and the end of history. But the term's meaning has changed, and now it nearly always refers to the Last Day itself. All the earliest Christians were millenarians, and, later, Revelation was invoked to explain why the apocalypse had not yet come though they continued to await it. Millenarianism has been constant in Christian history and remains surprisingly widespread today, despite the lesson of two thousand years of failed hopes.

Artists portrayed the Antichrist in Hell as Satan's son, often sitting on his knee, or, later, leading the forces of Gog and Magog—pagans, unbelievers, heretics, deliberate sinners—in the final battle of Armageddon (named for a real Hebrew battlefield). He is not much of a factor any more except in movies like *Rosemary's Baby.*

The Last Judgment

THE LAST AND MOST COMPLEX of the essential Christian narratives regarding Hell concerns the Last Judgment, *Dies Irae*, the Day of Wrath. The Hebrew Bible is full of references to the "Day of Yahweh," or "Day of the Lord," when justice will finally be done; the apocalyptic books, Enoch, Esdras, and Daniel, and the Jewish Apocrypha look forward to this event, but with an important distinction from the New Testament texts: the judgment is to be of the living, not the dead.

Matthew's twenty-fourth book provides the gospel text for the Christian apocalypse and Last Judgment. On the Mount of Olives, Jesus warns the disciples of the terrible time to come, a time of wars, apostasy, "false Christs and false prophets," and "signs and wonders." The universe itself will fall apart. "This generation shall not pass till all these things be fulfilled," he says, then more evasively (Matthew was reporting this nearly fifty years after Jesus's death), "But of that day and hour knoweth no man, no, not the angels in heaven, but my Father only" (36).

Urging his listeners to repent in due time, he tells warning parables ending with the sheep and the goats, which explains how judgment will come about.

Before him shall be gathered all nations: and he shall separate them one from another, as a shepherd divideth his sheep from the goats: And he shall set the sheep on his right hand, but the goats on the left. . . . Then

shall he say also unto them on the left hand, Depart from me, ye cursed, into everlasting fire, prepared for the devil and his angels. . . . And these shall go away into everlasting punishment: but the righteous into life eternal. (32–33, 41, 46)

Matthew does not indicate that this is to be a judgment of the dead as well as the quick, although Paul had added that essential difference in his widely circulated letters (1 Cor. 15; 2 Thess. 9–12) and the Harrowing story later confirmed it.

In the very early Christian era, when the end was expected any day, there was nothing very complicated about belief in the Last Judgment which, after all, rested on ideas that had been around for centuries. As time went by, questions arose. If judgment was delayed until the Day of the Lord, what happened in the interval between the death of the body and that day? How could the body be resurrected after so much time? Would damned souls be resurrected, or only the blessed?

These questions gave rise to the idea of Particular Judgment, by which the destination of the individual soul was determined at death, as in the Egyptian and Persian systems. The parable of Dives and Lazarus seems to support an immediate resolution, and so does Jesus's promise to the good thief on Golgotha. Still, apocalyptic millenarianism argued against it.

The twelfth- and thirteenth-century mosaic from the Cathedral of Torcello in Venice provides an overview of the complete Last Judgment. On the top level is the Harrowing or "anastasis," where Christ releases the souls of Adam, Eve, David, and Solomon as foretold by John the Baptist, at right. On the next level is the Second Coming, with Christ in a "mandorla" held by the Virgin and John the Baptist, the intercessors, and flanked by the saints and martyrs who have already achieved Heaven. In the center of the next level is the "etimasia," a throne with the Bible and instruments of the Passion. Angels blow the Last Trump and to either side the creatures of the earth and sea give up dead bodies to be resurrected. One level down, just over the door, an angel holds a scale while demons try to weigh it down and Mary, below, pleads for mercy. To the left are the ranks of the blessed, and to the right angels chivy the wicked toward Satan holding Antichrist on his knee. (For a close-up of the wicked, see Plate 9.) On the lowest left are Abraham with a soul in his bosom, the Virgin, John the Baptist, a "covering cherub" guarding the gate of Heaven, Peter, and an angel as psychopomp.

Early church fathers tried to reconcile the ideas. In the second century, Justin said that the souls of the good and the wicked would await the Last Judgment in separate (and decidedly unequal) quarters. Tatian, writing at about the same time, thought souls would sleep until the end of time; many heretical and Protestant sects have agreed, but it is not Roman doctrine.

In the third century, Tertullian consigned all souls—except those of martyrs, who would go straight to Heaven—to wait in separate and unequal underworld limbos. By the fourth century, Hilary of Poitiers warned sinners of immediate after-death punishment, even though eternal determination of the soul would wait until the Last Day. Augustine, in the fifth century, declared two judgments, one immediately after death and one to follow the resurrection. This became the rather loosely defined position of the Western Church until it was refined by the doctrine of Purgatory centuries later.

Because the Last or General Judgment is often mentioned in the scriptures, and Particular Judgment never explicitly (we may take the accounts of Dives and Lazarus and the good thief to be implicit), the church fathers had to determine the difference between them. Ingeniously, in *The City of God*, Augustine tied this difference to the doctrine of the resurrection of the body.

> Souls are judged when they depart from the body, before they come to that judgment which must be passed on them when reunited to the body and are tormented or glorified in that same flesh which they there inhabited.

This could be taken as an enlargement of the separate and unequal Limbo theory: the waiting souls of sinners would at once suffer the dire penalty of loss of God's grace (*poena damni*), but not until they were reunited with their fleshly bodies would the tortures of the flames of Hell begin (*poena sensus*). The waiting souls of the just would dwell in a delightful and refreshing place (*refrigerium*) until admitted to the final bliss of Heaven in their own glorified bodies.

The trouble with this interpretation was that it might give hardened sinners some hope of a recess before the tangible punishments they deserved. Also, it did not conform with the Harrowing story, which admitted the patriarchs to the vision of God immediately at the time of Jesus's death.

A more economical Last Judgment from a French manuscript c. 1510. Old corpses are
transformed into radiant new bodies and rise on the left for judgment while St. Michael
summarily ejects the unworthy on the right.

And it was simply too complicated for ordinary people. Most Christians have always believed that the soul is admitted at once to its reward, even as they also await a Last Judgment, and they do not bother to reconcile differences of time or degree.

Judgment Day was also to settle the fate of the fallen angels, as attested to in letters from Peter—"For God spared not the angels that sinned, but cast them down to Hell, and delivered them into chains of darkness to be reserved unto judgment" (2 Pet. 2.4)—and Jude: "And the angels which kept not their first estate, but left their own habitation, he hath reserved in everlasting chains under darkness unto the judgment of the great day" (6). During the first century, fallen angels were like Titans, still prisoners, not yet demons, prison keepers, torturers, or tempters.

As expectations of an immediate apocalypse receded, the bishops of the early Church were faced with many important questions of doctrine, not the least of which was an official stance on cosmic judgment and punishment. It was difficult to know what line to take. Though some theological ventures—Gnostic speculations, for instance—were clearly suspect, several centuries would pass before the Church would decide which Christian writings were to be considered canonical and which were what we now call apocryphal or pseudepigrapha.

Since Christianity was an apocalyptic religion, the whole point of which rested on death and salvation through resurrection, the negative as well as the positive side of the hereafter was of considerable interest. Who would be saved and who damned became subjects of obsessive speculation. Some of this gave way to simple revenge fantasy. Tertullian (c. 160–230), an African millenarian, could scarcely wait for the great moment:

> What a panorama of spectacle on that day! Which sight shall I turn to first to laugh and applaud? Mighty kings whose ascent to heaven used to be announced publicly groaning now in the depths with Jupiter himself who used to witness that ascent? Governors who persecuted the name of the Lord melting in flames fiercer than those they kindled for brave Christians? Wise philosophers, blushing before their students as they burn together, the followers to whom they taught that the world is no concern of God's, whom they assured that either they had no souls at all or that what souls they had would never return to their former bodies? Poets, trembling not before the judgment seat of Rhad-

amanthus or of Minos, but of Christ—a surprise? Tragic actors bellowing in their own melodramas should be worth hearing! Comedians skipping in the fire will be worth praise! The famous charioteer will toast on his fiery wheel; the athletes will cartwheel not in the gymnasium but in flames. . . . These are things of greater delight, I believe, than a circus, both kinds of theater, and any stadium.

The most radical speculation came from Origen (c. 185–c. 254), a student of Clement of Alexandria (c. 150–c. 220). Clement, a well-educated man, applied Plato's theory of the ideal to the problem of evil and explained it as the absence of good—which is to say nonbeing, since God is perfect goodness. (This would lead to difficulties: that matter was evil was a common Gnostic and Neoplatonist position, but it was awkward to claim that matter was nonbeing, as Augustine would point out.) Also, in Clement's view, the rebellion and fall of the Devil and his angels proved the theory of free will. Predestination would imply that God knowingly created creatures of evil, which was unacceptable.

Origen, following Clement on both free will and the descent of bad angel and sinful soul away from God and into grosser matter, found the idea of an everlasting Hell with an unchanging Devil to be unconvincing.

> Since, as we have often pointed out, the soul is eternal and immortal, it is possible that, in vast and immeasurable spaces, throughout long and various ages, it can descend from the highest good to the lowest evil, or it can be restored from ultimate evil to the greatest good.

If we are free to choose how we live our lives it would follow that we should continue to be free to choose after death as well. Reincarnation, as Plato had suggested, was a way of moving upward or downward on the ladder of being, and Origen inclined toward it, though he did not commit himself to it.

Eventually, Origen proposed, everyone would choose to repent, even the Devil. If Christ died for all, that would include the angels: the Devil was once an angel. If God is infinite, everything will naturally return at the end of time to be part of him—the Devil's negative aspects would be destroyed in the refining fire to leave only his essential angelic self. This theory of universal redemption is called *apocastastasis*.

On a Byzantine ivory, cherubs with six wings guard the gate of Hell while avenging angels hurry the damned toward Satan and the Last Trump blows below. It is typical of Byzantine art to divide the damned into separate boxes. Note the worms in the lower box.

Following Origen's logic, Hell could not persist after the end of time; for it to do so would signal a victory for sin and the Devil. Origen also expressed reasonable doubt about the tangible punishments of Hell, though, like so many after him, he felt that ordinary folk should believe in them as a deterrent to sin and crime.

How closely Origen's image of the immortal-but-apt-to-fall soul followed Plato's can easily be seen in this account of his views by Jerome (c. 340–420), a hostile witness who explained this rising and falling action as a great cycle.

Origen's teaching states that all rational, invisible, noncorporeal creatures [here, angels], if they are careless, little by little slide toward the depths. From the matter toward which they descend, they take on airy, ethereal bodies with human flesh. Meanwhile, if the demons, who by their own decision under the Devil's leadership fell away from the Lord's service, had just barely come to their senses, they would also be dressed in human flesh [as opposed to the grosser, more material flesh which Origen, following Clement, supposed demons to inhabit], so that, each one having done his penance, they would begin to rise in the same circular movement by which they first entered the flesh and would be returned to nearness to God, whereupon they would shed their airy ethereal bodies. And then all things would kneel to the God of the heavens, the earth and the underworld, and God, with us, would be everything.

This is close to Platonic metempsychosis, with a nod to Buddhism. Though Jerome did not subscribe to it, other early church fathers did, among them Ambrose, Gregory of Nyssa, and Gregory of Nazanzus. Eschatology was still a developing field.

Controversy over apocastastasis occupied Christian thinkers from the third century into the fifth, until Augustine (354–430), the great bishop of Hippo (the modern Algerian town of Annaba), put an end to it by effectively "proving" the existence of an eternal and essentially static Hell.

Augustine, a Manichaean for nine years, was anxious to refute the Gnostics (who were, by this time, Manichaeans themselves) with their pernicious view of this earth as a kind of Hell and matter as evil. He stressed the beauty and goodness of created nature, quoting Genesis, "And God looked upon it and saw that it was good." Against this, he placed the doctrine of Original Sin, which he has been accused of inventing, though his biographer Peter Brown points out that the idea that an ancient transgression was responsible for the current misery of mankind was common to both pagans and Christians at the time. Augustine's contribution was to link Original Sin inextricably with sex.

Augustine did not begin as a predestinarian, but his stubborn promotion of Original Sin pushed him into that position as he grew older. It is virtually impossible to defend free will while insisting that a genetic sin linked to the mammalian act by which we reproduce ourselves has disastrously and irrevocably tainted humankind to the point where most of us must suffer eternal punishment. If Augustine found it difficult to reconcile his own views, it is no wonder that conflict over predestination and free will has chronically troubled Christianity.

Though Augustine stressed the goodness and beauty of the created world—he maintained that mortality, not matter, was the consequence of sin—he also affirmed that this world was now ruled by the Devil, just as the Dark Lord ruled the Manichaean world. The Christian Devil was not equal to God, however, and he would be punished. In *The City of God,* Augustine cited scripture to prove that:

> Hell, which is also called a lake of fire and brimstone, will be material fire, and will torment the bodies of the damned, whether men or devils—the solid bodies of the one, and the aerial bodies of the others. Or, if only men have bodies as well as souls, still the evil spirits, even without bodies, will be so connected to the fires as to receive pain without bestowing life. One fire certainly shall be the lot of both.

No one is exempt from punishment "unless delivered by mercy and un-deserved grace." To some degree, his argument was based on the theory that "It is not enough to succeed; others must fail." How would we appreciate grace without the perspective of its opposite—and so much of the opposite? "And many more are left under punishment than are delivered from it, in order that it may thus be shown what was due to all."

Against those who thought that punishment could not be eternal, he cited Matthew, Revelation, and Peter. Against those who prayed to the saints or the angels to intercede for themselves or others, he argued that if Christians cannot pray for the wicked angels, which would be blasphemous, they cannot pray for wicked men either. He quoted Plato and Virgil in proposing a temporary purgatorial place for some few of the not-so-very-wicked after "the first death," but after the second, at Judgment Day, he insisted that reward and punishment would be eternal. He also conjectured that the wickedest of the damned might suffer even more than the others.

Baptism alone would not save evildoers, but it was necessary for salvation. Heretics were doomed. So, alas, were unbaptized babies, to the indignation of Julian of Eclanum, the fiery young gadfly of Augustine's crusty old age, who wrote:

> [God] it is, you say, who judges in this way; he is the persecutor of newborn children; he it is who sends tiny babies to eternal flames. . . . It would be right and proper to treat you as beneath argument: you have come so far from religious feeling, from civilized feeling, so far indeed from mere common sense, in that you think that your Lord God

Just what the artist meant by the lines emanating from St. Augustine's heart is inscrutable, but if he wanted to indicate that Augustine influenced (clockwise from bottom) *peasants, shepherds, forestry, technology, transportation, farming, and Hell itself, he would not have been far wrong.*

is capable of committing a crime against justice such as is hardly conceivable even among the barbarians.

Julian was not alone in his feelings, but his was not the opinion that prevailed. Augustine based his case on the terrible potency of Original Sin—which Julian, heretically, did not accept—and the inscrutability of God: God is just, but God's justice is not human justice. Human moral

81

standards do not apply. Either baptism is a solemn and holy sacrament washing away Original Sin, or it is not; you cannot have it both ways.

Babies continued to be something of an issue, however, while Augustine's proposal of a temporary Purgatory between the "first" and "second" deaths would not be accepted as doctrine until seven hundred years had passed. Still, with regard to Origen and his sympathy for the Devil, Augustine's triumph was complete. When the Christian bishops congregated at the Synod of Constantinople in 543, they decreed that:

> If anyone shall say or think that there is a time limit to the torment of demons and ungodly persons, or that there will ever be an end to it, or that they will ever be pardoned or made whole again, then let him be excommunicated.

And, good as their word, they excommunicated the three-century-dead Origen with fifteen separate charges of anathema. To make sure that he was properly serving his time, subsequent synods in 553, 680, 787, and 869 damned him to eternal flames over and over again.

Nevertheless, Origen's ideas persisted. At the end of the twentieth century, what we now call "universalism" is stronger than ever.

Apocalyptic Tours of Hell

APOCALYPTIC LITERATURE OF THE FIRST few Christian centuries presented previews of Judgment Day and the afterlife to follow. They featured or were purportedly written by apostles, saints, and revered Old Testament figures, and claimed to be authentic. Thus a preface to the *Apocalypse of Paul* claims to have found the manuscript in a box with the shoes of the apostle as bona fides. The forger slipped up, however, by putting the date of his "discovery" as 388, which greatly confused medieval scholars who had discovered references to *Paul* in works of Origen written more than 150 years earlier.

The *Apocalypse of Peter,* the earliest, dates from the mid–second century. The *Apocalypse of Paul,* better written and with more detail, was the best known; there are manuscript copies in every European language, as well as Syrian, Coptic, and Ethiopic. The *Apocalypse of the Virgin,* also early, would become important to the cult of the Virgin in the Middle Ages. Other apocalypses, some now in fragments, featured Thomas, Zephaniah, Baruch, Gorgorios, Ezra, Isaac, Pachomios, and Elijah.

Peter differs from most tours of Hell in having no guide or psychopomp except Christ himself. Though it is crudely drawn, with an unpleasantly vengeful and morbid tone, Dante enthusiasts may be surprised at how far the outline of after-death punishments had already developed 1,200 years before the *Inferno.* The distribution of sinners, however, is quite different.

Peter was obviously written at a time when Christianity had serious competition from other religions. The first candidates offered for judgment and punishment are the "spirits" dwelling in pagan idols and images, which the writer took seriously as demons, though statues of Egyptian beast-gods consigned to a furnace seem relatively lifeless. Satan does not appear. At this early point, Hell was administered by God's just but stern angels, Uriel and Ezrael.

Family values were critical. The vengeance exacted for betrayal is fierce: aborted children blind their mothers with fire; abused children watch their parents mangled by wild beasts; disrespectful children and disobedient slaves are tortured; lapsed virgins are torn to pieces; fornicators are cruelly punished, as are homosexuals. Only the last two categories of sinners appear at all in the *Inferno*, and Dante shows considerable sympathy for both.

In the Middle Ages, Hell was frequently organized around the Seven Deadly Sins, which spread human weaknesses around pretty evenly, but early apocalypses focused on the genital area. The concentration documents

Romanesque cathedrals of the twelfth and thirteenth centuries used tortures as decorative elements. This is a column capital from St. Julien in Tours, France.

like *Peter* brought to sexual behavior, as opposed to, say, crimes of violence, became an early and unique characteristic of Christian Hell. The lurid descriptions of punishments drew an audience; it is not going too far to say that the Hell scenes of early apocalypses are a form of self-righteous pornography.

The author of *Peter* had a voyeuristic, sadistic, and scatological bent that set the tone for later visions. On the other hand, he lived in strange times. Before the second century, the laws of the Roman Empire forbade torture for citizens. Only slaves could be tortured and then technically only when accused of a crime—though practically, since they were considered property, their masters had absolute rights over them. But the civil rights of Roman citizens had recently been eroded in a way that would not have been tolerated a century earlier—as we know from the instructive account of Paul's arrest in Jerusalem in the second half of the first century (Acts 22, 23). Taken into custody for sedition, Paul was to be flogged "for examination" before trial, at which point he invoked his Roman citizenship. The reaction to this claim was grave and immediate and ended with Paul's being sent with no fewer than 270 armed troops (to guard him against the Jews he had enraged with his preaching) to the provincial governor at Caesaria for a proper Roman trial.

In the second century, however, the Roman senate had withdrawn civil rights from many citizens, leaving them liable to interrogation and torture. When "treason" was involved, which could be interpreted as any action opposed to the ruling emperor and his party, anyone could be tortured.

Because Judaism was legal in the Roman Empire, Christianity was safe as long as it was considered merely a breakaway Jewish sect. By A.D. 64, however, Christians were separated out from the Jews by the famously cruel emperor Nero. To practice their religion was now illegal as well as impious and subversive, and they were fair game. The list of early saints and martyrs gives graphic evidence of the consequences. Eusebius writes of a mob attack in 177 with horrible tortures following for six days on end, especially of one poor slave girl named Blandina. The public spectacles are what most people remember. Tertullian said, "If the Tiber floods or the Nile fails to flood, if the sky fails to move or the earth does, if there is famine or sickness the cry is the same—throw the Christians to the lions!" The Romans, particularly at the time of the late empire, loved nothing more than a public bloodbath.

A capital from St. Lazare, Autun

Thus, though we may recoil from *Peter* and regret its wide influence, it may be useful to know that at the time it was written the threat of torture was a new anxiety for Christian citizens. The rack, which distended the joints and muscles of the body, the whip, the rod, and red-hot metal instruments were, from the second to the fifth centuries, increasingly common in interrogation. Capital punishment using these techniques was forbidden, though most of the tortured died anyway. Roman methods of capital punishment included beheading, stoning, clubbing, hurling from a precipice, and live burial. Strangling and poisoning, which the Greeks had used, were prohibited; crucifixion was reserved for slaves and degraded criminals. Death by lion was too expensive to be commonplace.

The Hell of the *Apocalypse of Paul* has rivers of fire in addition to pits of fire, snow, and blood, and even more worms, beasts, and avenging angels with instruments of torture than *Peter.* Tartaruchus is the angel of torments, who will preside until the Day of Judgment. Each soul, before judgment, has its own angel which kept a written account of its deeds in the Persian style; when one offers to recount a soul's deeds from the age of fifteen, God replies that he is interested only in the previous five years.*

---

*God very rarely makes a speaking appearance in either appearance in either apocalyptic or vision literature. Considering how widely *Paul* was read, it's interesting that the five-year term for sins never caught on.

On the north side of Hell is a narrow, stinking, fiery pit reserved for unbelievers, and in it is "the worm that does not sleep," several of them in fact, each with two heads. Teeth gnash and chatter because of the extreme cold of the pit despite the fires.

What is innovative about *Paul* is the idea of refreshment or *refrigerium*. After viewing their torments, Paul weeps for the fate of the sinners, though he is chided for doing so (this rebuke is another theme Dante would pick up), but as a consequence Michael the archangel descends with his heavenly host. (Michael, in addition to having routed the rebel angels, is frequently charged with separating sheep from goats on Judgment Day and seeing to their proper distribution.) The voice of Jesus decrees that, because of Paul's pity, on Easter day henceforth torment will be suspended for "a day and a night." This popular folk theme persisted through the Middle Ages when the intercessor was most frequently the Virgin Mary.

An unusual and rather entertaining apocalypse is the third-century *Gospel of Bartholomew*. This features a conversation with Beliar ("Worthless") the beast, whose name used to be Satan. He has been brought up from the abyss by Jesus as a curiosity to show a band of monkish visitors and is

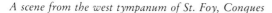

A scene from the west tympanum of St. Foy, Conques

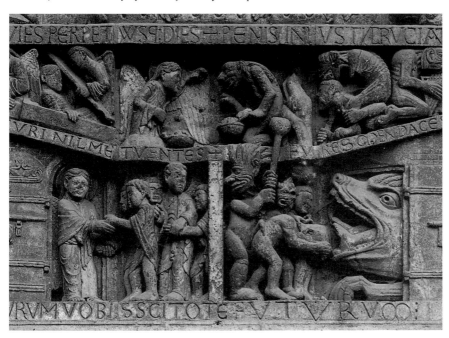

Last Judgment from the west tympanum of St. Foy, Conques. The hanging figure is Judas.

1,600 yards long and 40 yards broad with 8-yard wings, bound by fiery chains and held by 660 angels. The apostle Bartholomew interviews him while treading on his neck, a familiar image in art. Beliar tells the whole story: how he was the first angel to be created, how he refused to worship Adam and fell with his followers (only 600 of them here), how he wandered to and fro in the world, how he seduced Eve (his method was unusual; she drank his sweat mixed with water), how he punishes the souls of men and is punished himself, how he sends his minion demons out into the world to tempt.

Bartholomew also contains an early account of the Harrowing of Hell, told (unusually) from Jesus's point of view, and, even more remarkably at this early date, a first glimpse of the Virgin Mary as Queen of Hell. Beliar/Satan is still separate from the Devil—here, Beelzebub—and from Hades, the keeper of the underworld of dead souls. Avenging angels administer the punishments to Beliar himself, but Beliar's troops tempt and chastise men.

The Middle Ages

T HE RICHEST PERIOD IN THE history of Hell is the
millennium that followed the fall of Rome, the middle period between
the classical world and the one that began with the Renaissance or rebirth
of the classical approach to learning. All the foundations of Hell were
already in place when Rome fell, but what we might call the general land-
scaping of the project was vastly elaborated during the Middle Ages.

Medieval theologians continued to refine doctrine made by the church
fathers, but except for one crucial event—the adoption of the doctrine of
Purgatory in 1253—there were no real advances in intellectual thought on
Hell. Only one major figure, Johannes Scotus Erigena (c. 815–c. 877),
doubted a literal Hell, and he was accused of heresy—in fact, he is said to
have been stabbed to death by his own students with their pens. Peter
Lombard (c. 1100–c. 1160) and Thomas Aquinas (c. 1226–1274) followed
Augustine in insisting on a real fiery Hell with physical torments added to
those of the mind and spirit. Aquinas particularly emphasized the pleasures
of the abominable fancy.

What seems astonishing now is the literal bent theologians brought to
matters that do not lend themselves to the literal. Intelligent, educated men,
who, if they had been born centuries later, might have explained the inef-
fable or metaphorical in terms of quarks and black holes in space, instead
turned their attention to such considerations as whether food consumed
during a lifetime would be part of the body at the resurrection. (Yes, was

the answer, but then interesting questions of cannibalism arose.) "How many angels can dance on the head of a pin?" is the question theologians are supposed to have pondered, but they counted devils too and tried to calculate the size of Hell and where it was—under the earth or somewhere in the ether.

In the new universities that Charlemagne had encouraged, the teachers and thinkers known as Scholastics continued to debate the central problems of Christian salvation, trying to integrate them not with Platonism but with the rediscovered and much admired writings of Aristotle, using Greek rationalist logic to reconcile theological points—a difficult business. But during the Middle Ages higher theology had far less effect on the concept of Hell than what can only be called popular enthusiasm.

The vernacular sermon was developed fairly early as a way of communicating with parishioners increasingly baffled by the mysteries of the Latin mass. In a village or small town, that weekly sermon might be the chief, even the only entertainment for the populace. "Hellfire" sermons drew crowds for complex reasons and have continued to do so almost until the present. The splendid example in James Joyce's *Portrait of the Artist as a Young Man* is supposedly based almost verbatim on a sermon Joyce heard during his student days in Dublin, which would have been about the turn of the twentieth century. Medieval preachers were given aids to help them prepare sermons and take confessions; these included homilies, anecdotal exempla, pulpit manuals, and books of penances. The dire consequence of sin was a favorite subject in all of them, as it was in the inventive sculptures, reliefs, mosaics, frescoes, and paintings made for churches and cathedrals.

Since we have no records of reaction to these sermons and paraphernalia, we must infer their fame from their survival. There is no question, however, about the popularity of Hell in the medieval theater. Mystery plays, like sermons and artworks, were first seen as a way to teach the Bible to parishioners, but they soon escaped their beginnings. The Hell scenes of these plays, with their devilish pratfalls, firecrackers, and crude toilet doggerel, became beloved popular theater—the *only* popular theater—and when, after many centuries, they were eventually banned, they mutated into forms that persist today.

Medieval plays were not "literary," but an astonishing percentage of the high literary tradition also focused on Hell—in the late Middle Ages,

1. An angel fastens the Jaws of Hell. From the twelfth-century Winchester Psalter.

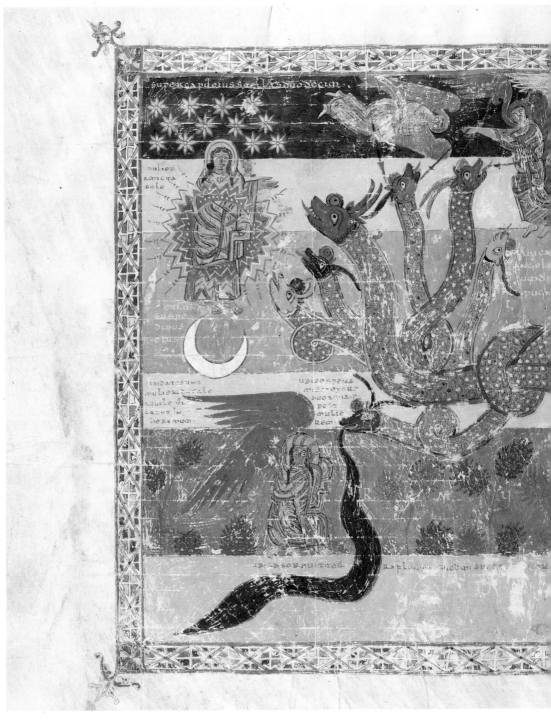

2. Beatus of Liebana, an eighth-century Spanish monk, wrote a text on the Apocalypse of Revelation that influenced manuscript copiers for five hundred years. This thirteenth-century French copy of a ninth-century original is typical. The woman clothed by the sun at the upper left is pursued by the red dragon being attacked by angels as his tail sweeps down

one-third of the stars in heaven, a metaphor for angels. We see them falling as angels, then splashing, naked and childlike, into the lake of fire where Satan, already bestial, lies. Vandalism of Satan's head is, unfortunately, common. This fine Beatus is from the Pierpont Morgan Library.

3–4. These gorgeous and unusual miniatures were painted by the three Limbourg brothers c.1416 for the *Très Riches Heures*, a Book of Hours made for the Duke of Berry. Note Lucifer's beauty as he falls. Above, the Hell is quite specifically Tundal's Hell, though the Devil has the conventional number of arms and legs. Compare with Simon Marmion's version of Tundal on the next three pages.

ample ouuerte et moult
obscure cestt vallee estoit
tree parfonde plaine de
charbons ardans Et sur
icelle vallee auoit vng
couuercle de fer en ronde
tout autour moult grant

nee qui estoient illecq
buslees et artes et sunt
couslees et passees parmy
cestuy auant couuercle en
la maniere que len passe
vne faulse parmy legram
ne et ainsi de la cheoient

5. His guardian angel takes young Tundal on a tour of Hell. First they see the burning Valley
of the Homicides.

6. The Beast Acheron swallows up the miserly and avaricious.

que bien y entruissent de
front a vne fois dix mille
cheualliers armez tous
a cheual. Celle horrible
beste auoit en sa gueule
deux grans diables tres
hideulx et cruelz a veoir
dont lun auoit fichee sa

estoient ces deux diables
en la gueule de celle beste
ensement comme deux cou
lombes Et faisoient en
icelle gueule trois portes
Vng merueillenx feu en
grandeur qui iamais ne
pouoit estaindre ysloit de

7. Tundal must lead his cow across the nail-studded bridge from which thieves and robbers tumble. Compare with the cow in Bosch's *Hay-Wain*, Plate 26.

8. They arrive at the House of Phristinus for gluttons and fornicators. Tundal gets a taste of punishment here.

9. The horrible creature that eats and excretes unchaste priests and nuns. Compare with the bird in Bosch's *Garden of Earthly Delights*, Plate 27.

10. The last alarming sight in Hell is Lucifer, with as many arms and legs as a centipede and his attendant demons around him. Compare with the Limbourg version of the same scene, Plate 4.

all kinds of Hell, some of it thrillingly attractive. Writers blocked by the frightful picture presented by the Church from the ancient theme of the underworld quest inventively managed to displace Hell with eclectic underworld regions taken from classical and Norse mythology, folklore, feudal fantasy, and poetry, where Hell could strangely merge with Fairyland and allegorical knights would go adventuring.

Perhaps most intriguing of all is the thousand-year accumulation of "vision literature"—very different in style from the old apocalypses—which evolved into a genuine mass-market genre. In hundreds of manuscript copies of more than sixty surviving visions, someone is taken by a supernatural guide to the infernal regions, then (sometimes) to Purgatory, and then to Heaven. Though visions were written down by the literate clergy, they were often experienced by quite ordinary people, who certainly believed in them. Their modern equivalents might be reports of UFO abduction. It should be remembered that this was an age of obsessive piety, self-imposed fasting and flagellation, no antibiotics for fevers, and that people were educated to believe in visions. They *wanted* visions. Some accounts, on the other hand, especially late ones, were undoubtedly concocted by born storytellers for the astonishment of the pious and credulous.

AUGUSTINE, WHO had so much to do with the blossoming of Christianity into an imperial religion after the failure of the short-lived pagan revival under the emperor Julian in the 360s, lived to see the Roman Empire fall. The Visigoths sacked the city in 410, barbarians swarmed over Roman territories, and the Vandals broke into Augustine's Africa in 429. The old man died the following year with Hippo under siege and the world he had always known in shards around him.

To say that the fall of the Roman Empire signaled the end of the world is not to exaggerate by much. Civilization as it had been known for many centuries around the Mediterranean and up into Europe collapsed as the tribes from the North and West, the Goths, Visigoths, Ostrogoths, Franks, Saxons, Alemanni, Suevi, and the Huns from the east swarmed over the old territories until the final capitulation in 476 (though Rome was not actually physically destroyed till the next century—and then by Byzantines, not barbarians). Byzantium preserved itself, its currency, military defense, and trading systems, for the next thousand years, and the West went into a Dark Age which can be said to have lasted at least until the reign of Charlemagne (742–814).

The collapse of unified civil power together with the loss of the state-supported system of schools and universities gave the Church, the only large collective body that remained, an opportunity to take charge. And largely because of the vision, administrative capability, and practical common sense of a remarkable pope, Gregory the Great (c. 540–604), it moved quickly into a leadership position.

Gregory, son of a wealthy Roman lawyer, was elected pope in 590. As the first monk to hold the office, he was in a unique position to appreciate the enormous administrative potential in his elite corps of Benedictine monks, whose discipline was equal to that of any military troop and whose education and intellect were considerably sharper. He trained his Benedictines in law and business administration, encouraged their interest in art and literature, and sent them off as missionaries to the barbarians, many of whom were already somewhat Christianized.

In addition to founding monasteries as cultural and theological centers, the Benedictines helped illiterate local leaders develop written laws based on the Roman legal system, keep accounts, collect taxes, administer legacies, and formulate their own history—in short, they made themselves indispensable. The monks became great farmers and vintners, setting an example for the barbarians in the efficient management of estates, which became increasingly enormous as land was deeded to monasteries to escape civil taxation.

Gregory inherited the pragmatic tolerance that had made Roman soldiers such effective foreign campaigners. He warned his "soldiers of Christ" that they would run into many curious and distasteful forms of heathen superstition in Germanic and Frankish Europe and would have to accommodate themselves to these. Conversion would come but could not be forced. Gregory was later heavily criticized for this approach, but a more stringent attitude would never have worked with a tough group like the Merovingians.

Gregory encouraged his missionaries to pay attention to local customs partly because they intrigued him. Before being elected pope, he had hoped to go to Britain himself; he is remembered for exclaiming, on seeing some blond, blue-eyed boy slaves, "They are not Angles but angels!" He appreciated folklore and a good story as much as he did music—the beautiful

92

Gregorian liturgical chants are named for him—and it is appropriate that the first Christian visions in the Western style were recorded by his pen.

There are several of them, set down without embellishment as curiosities in the *Dialogues* written about 590. The first was hearsay, told to Gregory by a fellow monk of a third monk, Peter of Spain, who "died" of an illness, saw "innumerable" places in Hell with notables of this world hanging in flames, and then was restored to life by an angel who warned him to mend his ways. A nobleman, Reparatus, in what seems to have been a dream, saw a huge bonfire being prepared for a sinful priest named Tiburtius; upon awakening, he sent a messenger to warn him, but Tiburtius died before the message reached him. Another priest named Severus, unable to reach a dying man's bedside in time to absolve him, lamented, and the man came back to life. "Disgusting people" emitting flames from their mouths and noses had been dragging him off to a dark place when a "handsome youth" intervened: heeding Severus's prayer, God was temporarily releasing the dead sinner. He died again, absolved, a week later.

Another vision was related directly to Gregory by Stephen, a merchant who fell ill in Constantinople, died, saw things in Hell that he had heard of but never believed in, and escaped because of an error of mistaken identity: another Stephen, a blacksmith, was meant to have died instead. Stephen the narrator was then immediately restored to life. He died of plague three years later at the same time that a local soldier also "died" and experienced a vision of Hell—in which he saw the merchant Stephen!

The soldier's story is the first to report some of the topographical features that would become so familiar in Western visions. He saw a bridge over a black, smoky river that had a "filthy and intolerable smell." Across the river were pleasant meadows and shining mansions, one of gold, but only the sinless, like a priest the soldier saw, could cross over. On this side of the bridge, a sadistic church steward (whom Gregory had actually known) was bound with iron chains in "a most filthy place," and here also was poor Stephen, laboring to cross the bridge. He slipped, and "terrible creatures rose from the river to pull him down by the legs." At the same time, beautiful white beings pulled him up by the arms. At this point, the soldier returned to life, and no one ever knew whether Stephen eventually made his way to the golden mansion.

Gregory's somewhat banal comment on these odd stories was that visions of the afterlife must occur sometimes for the benefit of those who

93

experience them and sometimes as a "witness for others" who, hearing about them, will try harder to avoid sinning. He thought that the mansions with their unfortunate riverside location might be those of basically decent people who had sinned in the flesh.

Contemporary with Pope Gregory was Gregory of Tours (539–594), a fine example of the provincial bishop who was also an able educator, administrator, and diplomat. He was one of the first writers to record miracle stories of the saints, but he is best known for his valuable *History of the Franks.* Two visions are transcribed in it, those of Salvius and of Sunniulf. Salvius was lucky enough to see a glimpse of Heaven before he returned to consciousness, but Sunniulf, the abbot of Randau, was led to a fiery river at which people "gathered like bees at a beehive." Over the river was a bridge so narrow that there was scarcely room to put one foot on it, and on the other side of the river was a white house. Clerics who had been careless of their flocks fell into the river where they were submerged, some to the waist, some to the armpits, some to the chin; conscientious clerics passed over. Gregory the Great would have called this a cautionary vision.

The Venerable Bede (673–735) was an English monk whose *Ecclesiastical History of England* (731) is a classic source for later historians. In it, he recorded two visions of Hell at greater length than his predecessors. Bede was a talented writer with an eye for detail, and he had certainly read the works of both Gregorys as well as some of the apocalyptic literature, so he knew what kind of material he was dealing with and how to make the most of it. Moreover, the stories were not told to him directly—he had read that of Furseus in a previous book, now lost—so he felt free to embroider them.

Furseus's vision is dated to 633 by Bede. Like William Blake, Furseus had a tendency toward visions. He was an Irish preacher who had established a mission in East Anglia as a consequence of his first vision and had heard angelic choirs in another. His third vision was much more frightening. In it, he was born aloft by angels over a dark valley, then saw four fires in the air. The angels told him that these punished respectively liars, the covetous, creators of strife and discord, and the pitiless and fraudulent. Then the four flames joined together in one big flame, in which he saw devils flying. One demon threw a tortured sinner at him, a man from whom Furseus had inherited some money. When Furseus was restored to his body, he carried a burn mark from this experience on his jaw and shoulder for

A wonderful view of the bridge common to so many medieval visions. Sadly, the Hell scene of this anonymous fifteenth-century fresco in Sta. Maria in Piano, Italy, has been completely vandalized; it would have been interesting to see a Hell from a painter so influenced by vision literature.

the rest of his life. And Bede tells us that a very old monk of his acquaintance had known a man who had actually met Furseus and had heard this story told in the dead of winter—yet Furseus was sitting in a thin garment and sweating as though it were a midsummer day.

The second of Bede's stories, which he dates 696, is that of a Northumbrian householder named Drythelm. Drythelm died at nightfall and suddenly came to life again at dawn, terrifying his family. That very day he divided his goods into three parts, one for his wife, one for his children, and one for charity, and soon thereafter took orders at the Melrose monastery.

What had happened to him was this: An angel appeared who silently led him northeast to "a valley of great breadth and depth, but of infinite length." Flames spewed from one side of it, and on the other violent hail and snow flew in all directions. In both, deformed spirits were tormented,

95

but the guide said to Drythelm, "No, this is not what you think, it is not Hell." At the far end of the valley, it grew dark, and suddenly he saw great globes of black flames rising out of a stinking pit and falling back into it again. Each of these was full of human souls. Behind him he heard piteous lamentation coupled with loud, coarse laughter. A gang of evil spirits was dragging souls toward the darkness—among them Drythelm spotted a clergyman, a layman, and a woman. Seeing him, some of the spirits rushed at him with their burning tongs, but before they could reach him, his guide, bright as a star in the murk, reappeared and frightened them away.

The angel showed him a sort of Elysian Field which "is not the kingdom of Heaven, as you think," then Heaven itself. He explained that the valley was a purgatorial place "to try and punish the souls of those who put off confession and repentance till their deathbeds," but at the Day of Judgment they would be saved, though the prayers of the living could hasten the process. Those in the pit, of course, were doomed. And again, Bede invokes an eyewitness, the monk Hemgils, who affirmed that in later years Brother

This imaginative thirteenth-century fresco from the Church of St. Peter and St. Paul in Surrey shows many visionary elements: Jacob's ladder to Heaven, from which demons pluck sinners; the fiery caldron; the bridge of nails; the instruments of torture. Note the serpent twined in the Eden tree.

Drythelm used to stand up to his neck in icy water, saying to those who marveled at such austerity, "I have seen greater cold."

These three widely read and revered writers established and developed the legitimacy of the western vision. All of their visions sound "authentic," like genuine dreams or fever dreams in which half-remembered stories take on vivid colors. Bede's more developed accounts engender suspicion that a manuscript of *Thespesius,* with its burning globes that rise and fall, had reached Britain. His authentication of Furseus's burn and both his subjects' tolerance of extreme cold follow the convention of miracle stories.

Bede also repeated a vision of a dying soldier who had seen good and bad spirits bring account books of his earthly deeds; Gregory the Great had related the same story, but with less detail. Bede started a grand tradition: though examples of vision literature survive from all over Europe, those that came from Britain and Ireland are by far the richest and most imaginative.

The most popular was *The Vision of Tundal,* written in 1149 by an Irish monk. Nearly 250 hand-lettered manuscripts in at least fifteen languages survive, and one is fully illustrated by Simon Marmion, including eleven scenes of Hell (see Plates 5–8). Nothing else like it exists for vision literature, though there is another miniature of Tundal's Hell in the most famous of all medieval breviaries, *Les Très Riches Heures* commissioned by Jean, Duke of Berry, from the Limbourg brothers in about 1413 (Plate 4).

Why was Tundal's adventure so popular? Critically speaking, it was a superior technical example of its genre, and there is no question that by the twelfth century this was a genuine literary or subliterary genre among both clerics and laypeople. After the Bible, the first book translated into Old Norse was *Tundal.* The sameness of vision stories—which can seem numbing to a modern reader—did not trouble medieval readers and listeners, who came to them one at a time. Still, *Tundal* had more scenery, more monsters, and more charm than most of its fellows. Its hero, a handsome Irish knight, was a likable scoundrel: instead of giving money to the Church, he spent it on good times with "clowns, jesters and minstrels." Unlike many duller visitors to the infernal regions, he actually had to go through sensational punishments.

The story begins at the dinner table, where, under the pressure of trying to suppress his anger at a friend, he suffers what appears to be a stroke. For two days he lies in a rigid coma with only the slightest sign of life.

What happens to the soul that leaves his body during that period is terrifying. First a crowd of dreadful fiends screech an appalling parody of his favorite songs, gnash him with their teeth, tear their own cheeks with their talons and scream, "Where are the good times now? Where are the pretty girls? Where's your pride?" Tundal's soul is rigid with terror, until suddenly an angel appears. This turns out to be his guardian angel to whom he has never paid the least attention, but who now proposes to show him what lies in store for him if he does not repent. Meanwhile, he will be protected from the demons, who, thwarted, fall to fighting raucously among themselves.

Tundal is shown murderers sizzling over an iron grate laid across a whole valleyful of stinking coals, then a mountain with fire on one side, ice and snow on the other, and hailstorms in between, where fiends with iron hooks and forks chivy unbelievers and heretics (spies and traitors in another version) from one torture to another.

Next is a deep noxious valley spanned by a plank a thousand feet long and only one foot wide from which the proud and ungenerous tumble. With the angel's help, Tundal's fearful soul is able to cross it, and then to climb the path leading to the enormous beast Acheron with flaming eyes and two great devils in his mouth like pillars. Inside the beast's belly are the greedy—and inside it too, for a moment, is Tundal! His angelic protector disappears and waiting fiends fling him in to be bitten by frenzied lions, mad dogs, and serpents, burned by fire, bitten by cold, suffocated by stench, and clubbed by devils until the angel reappears. Tundal is understandably too weak to continue till the angel proffers a healing touch.

The next ordeal is a two-mile bridge across a lake filled with ravening beasts, only as wide as the palm of a hand, and studded with sharp nails. Thieves and robbers must cross it, and so must Tundal himself, leading a wild cow. "Remember," says the angel, "you stole a cow from one of your friends?" "But I gave it back," Tundal cries. "Only because you couldn't keep it," is the answer, "but because you did, you won't suffer too much."

Tundal has a bad moment on the bridge when he meets a soul going the other way, but he survives, has his torn feet cured by the angel, and sets off for the round oven-shaped house of the cruel Phristinus who punishes gluttons and fornicators (including clergymen); because of Tundal's former ways, the angel lets him have a taste of this too.

Next comes a great bird with an iron beak that eats unchaste nuns and priests and defecates them into a frozen lake where both men and women proceed to give birth to serpents.* Tundal has to go through this too, though, thankfully, we don't hear about it in much detail.

After a difficult climb comes the Valley of Fires, where fiends seize Tundal with burning forceps, throw him into a furnace until he is red-hot, then hammer him on an anvil with twenty or thirty other sinful souls into one mass, tossing this in the air till the angel rescues him. The two proceed downward toward Hell proper.

Excitable demons "like bees" sing "the song of death" around a huge cistern. In the depths is Lucifer himself, once "the first, the most beautiful, the most powerful creature God made." Now he is:

> blacker than a crow and shaped like a man except that it had a beak and a spiky tail and thousands of hands, each of which had twenty fingers with fingernails longer than knights' lances, with feet and toenails much the same, and all of them squeezing unhappy souls. He lay bound with chains on an iron gridiron above a bed of fiery coals. Around him were a great throng of demons. And whenever he exhaled he ejected the squeezed unhappy souls upward into Hell's torments. And when he inhaled, he sucked them back in to chew them up again.

Among these unhappy souls are several of Tundal's friends and relations.

Simon Marmion tried to convey this unusual Satan in his final Hell illustration, with mixed success. The Limbourg brothers showed the scene faithfully but jibed at all the arms and legs. Theirs is a conventional devil with horns and claws, who appears to be basking in what is surely the most spa-like of all pictorial Hells.

Tundal moves on to a meadowlike purgatorial area where the bad-but-not-very-bad suffer from hunger and thirst and the elements, and the good-but-not-very-good are dryer and happier. Heaven waits for these people behind a silver wall, which Tundal and the angel visit, though comparatively briefly. After this, Tundal "felt himself clothed in his body."

---

*This bird, wearing a cooking pot on its head, is in the Hell of Bosch's *Garden of Earthly Delights* triptych; Tundal's cow crossing the bridge is in at least two of Bosch's hells, and fiery forges, some oven-shaped, are a general feature. See Plates 24–27.

And with that, he opens his eyes, asks for Communion, gives all he has to the poor, orders the sign of the Cross sewn on his clothes, and begins to preach the word of God.

Some visions had a political slant. Charles the Fat, a ninth-century king of Swabia, found the religious advisors of his father and uncles dunked in boiling pitch (for giving bad advice), then his father undergoing purgation in order to join his uncle and cousin in paradise. Two deep casks bubbled away for Charles himself, should they be needed. He assured his people that they would not.

Hincmar of Rheims (c. 806–882) told the story of Bernold, who saw, in addition to a good many suffering bishops, King Charles the Bald in a pitiful condition simply because he had not heeded the excellent advice of Archbishop Hincmar. Hincmar was apparently blessed in his informants, for another of them, Eucherius, saw Charles Martel, Charlemagne's grandfather, being tortured; he too should have heeded better advice—like Hincmar's.* Charlemagne himself appears in Hell in the *Vision of Wetti* (824)—but he is in paradise in the contemporary *Vision of Rotcharius*.

Other visions hinted at literary influence. In the *Vision of Thurkill* (1206), an Englishman saw spirits with black-and-white spots (*Thespesius*, again), the usual fires, swamps, spiky bridge, ovenlike furnaces, the pit, and a weighted scale. But he also saw an arena with tiered seats, where a "multitude" sat bound with white-hot iron hoops and nails. In other seats, devils sat as if at the theater, beaming with pleasure as one torture after another was administered for their entertainment. Standing on a wall on a nearby mountain, the saints were also watching the spectacle. Thurkill was supposed to have been a peasant, but his vision seems suspiciously canny and colorful. At the very least, someone must have been reading (or preaching) Tertullian to him.

The *Vision of Alberic* is one that Dante is thought to have read. Alberic of Settefrati was a monk at the famous monastery of Monte Cassino. After an illness that left him in a coma for nine days, he dictated his vision to a fellow monk, Guidone, some time around 1115. Ten or fifteen years later, he rewrote it with the help of another monk, Pietro Diacono. For his trip, Alberic had no fewer than three guides—Saint Peter and the angels Emmanuel and Eligius, not to mention a dove that flew off with his soul. He

---

*Dante put Charles Martel in his Third Heaven, that of Venus. He will turn up again in Hell.

saw the standard sights with some emphasis on the fate of children being purged in flaming gas; also a frozen valley, a thorny wood, serpents, a red-hot ladder, a cauldron of pitch, a sulfurous oven, a lake of blood, a basin of boiling metal, a lake of fire, a river of fire, the narrow bridge. Novelties are an enormous chained dragon near the pit that holds Judas, Ananias, Caiaphas, Herod, and others of the worst sinners, and also a great bird that first drops an old monk into the pit, then plucks him out.

During the later Middle Ages, some vision literature was turned into (sometimes satiric) literary allegory. In *Le Songe d'Enfer* ("Dream of Hell"), written around 1215 by Raoul de Houdenc, the dreaming pilgrim travels through an allegorized landscape, passing spots like the river of Gloutonie to Mount Désespérance ("Despair"). Here he sits with Pilate and Beelzebub to dine on roast heretic and wrestlers with garlic sauce, after which he reads aloud to the king of Hell from a book about wicked minstrels.

Dining on roast heretic in the mouth of Hell. From The Hours of Catherine of Cleves, *c. 1440.*

101

The Flemish poet Jehan de le Mote's more serious *La Voie d'Enfer et de Paradis* ("The Way to Hell and Paradise") dates from 1340, and the English *Weye to Paradys* from about 150 years later. William Langland's *Piers Plowman*, probably the best-known allegorical dream-poem, retells the Harrowing.

One doesn't have to be a psychoanalyst or a literary critic to recognize that the proliferation and popularity of vision literature from the fourth to the fourteenth century was a result of the same appetite that today demands horror movies. But the visions illuminate other points, too. Although debate about Particular Judgment and General Judgment may have occupied intellectuals, they demonstrate that ordinary people—including bishops and kings—believed whatever was going to happen to you after death happened right away: these were not visions of the future, and there wasn't a hint of the idea of going to sleep until resurrection at the Last Trump.

Similarly, although Purgatory was not recognized by the Church until the middle of the thirteenth century, visions from as early as Bede's seventh-century *Drythelm* indicate that the concept of a temporary purifying after-death punishment was common not only to visionaries but to their more educated amanuenses. Charles the Fat's father was definitely on his way upward, just as soon as he had worked off his penance. By Tundal's and Alberic's time, purgatorial areas even had spacious separate quarters.

Considering that Purgatory was not accredited till the thirteenth century, it is significant that one twelfth-century story concentrated solely on it. Technically, *Saint Patrick's Purgatory* is not a vision, since the Irish knight Owen supposedly made his journey in the flesh, like Aeneas or Orpheus or Theseus. Sins were on his conscience, particularly the theft of Church property, and he volunteered to go to Saint Patrick's Purgatory at the monastery founded in the fifth century on Station Island in Lough Derg, in County Donegal. A cave on the island (still visited by tourists) is supposed to be an entrance to Purgatory.* Owen spent the night there, encountered demons and horrors, including an infernal wheel that spun almost too quickly to see the flames. He held off the demons by invoking the name of Jesus. On emerging, he embarked on a life of good works and made a pilgrimage to the Holy Land. Ramon de Perelhos traveled to Lough

---

*Ireland and Sicily are the two places most often cited as holding gateways to the underworld. In Sicily, Mount Etna was specifically the entrance; "sailing to Sicily" was a euphemism for going to Hell.

Derg all the way from Catalonia in about 1398 to have similar adventures, or at least he said he did.

Saint Brendan's Voyage sends a saint on what the Irish call an *imram*, a Christianized series of Sinbad-the-Sailor-like adventures.* The real Brendan lived during the fifth and sixth centuries but the romance (which survives in at least 116 manuscripts in many languages) dates from the tenth century. In it a boatload of Irish monks go adventuring in the Atlantic. On an island, they encounter a demon disguised as a little black boy who possesses a monk; on another, a flock of birds representing souls are working off a penance related to Lucifer's fall; on a third volcanic island, demonic blacksmiths fling fiery coals at the monks; another group of demons carry off a monk to Hell; and finally they find Judas Iscariot sitting atop a bare rock in mid-ocean, enjoying his Sunday respite. Six days of the week he spends in Hell, but he has certain Sundays off—and Saint Brendan wins him an extra holiday, to the great annoyance of the demons. In the French romance *Huon de Bordeaux,* Judas is also encountered in mid-ocean, this time in a canvas boat near the Gulf of Hell. Another French poem, *Bauduin de Sebourc,* sends Saracen voyagers to the location of Brendan's islands.

Most visions, even the *imram*s and romances, seem oddly distanced. The tortures don't really hurt and aren't nearly as nasty as in the old apocalypses; they're just part of the story. Occasionally one of the more ecstatic saints moved in closer, like Saint Brigit of Sweden (c. 1303–1373):

> The fire of the furnace boiled upward under the feet of the soul like water rising through a pipe to the point where it bursts in an overhead geyser, so that its veins seems to flow with the blaze. The ears were like a smith's bellows blasting through the brain. The eyes seemed reversed, looking to the back of the head. The mouth hung open and the tongue was drawn through the nostrils and hung down to the lips. The teeth had been driven like nails into the palate. The arms were stretched down to the feet, and both hands held flaming pitch. The skin seemed like a hide covering the body and like a linen garment spattered with semen; it was icy cold and exuded a discharge like that which oozes from an infected ulcer, with a stench worse than anything in this world.

---

*Many readers have encountered an *imram*: C. S. Lewis, a famous medievalist, turned *The Voyage of the Dawn Treader,* the third book in his Narnia series for children, into a fine one.

OLD ENGLISH was the earliest European language to have a literature of its own, and it should surprise no reader to find that a large percentage of its earliest surviving works are about the subject at hand. *Genesis A* and *Genesis B*, together with *Christ and Satan*, present Lucifer/Satan's biography, and there is a very early verse translation of *Nicodemus*. These poems are said to be of the "school of Caedmon," since Caedmon, a seventh-century peasant lay brother who acquired his poetic gifts by way of an angelic vision, is the earliest poet's name known to us. *Beowulf* has been co-opted into Christian mythology by some critics, but it was hardly known in its own day; its elevation to the canon is entirely modern.

Genesis B is inserted into the more conventional *Genesis A* to fill out the story of the fall of Lucifer and the rebel angels. The account is the familiar one, but with more detail and a distinctly feudal approach. The rebellious and vainglorious vassal raises his own throne in the north of Heaven; God, angry, prepares Hell and flings him down with his retainers. All become demons. Satan, still very much the leader, delivers a speech to his followers: not only is God entirely unjust in his condemnation, he is planning something even more unfair, the creation of a usurping pair of contemptible earth creatures in a brand-new world. Satan himself is bound in Hell, but a subordinate is conscripted to subvert God's plan. Which he does—but not quite in the usual way; like any proper knight, he approaches Adam, the head of the household, first. Rebuffed, he pays court to Eve with the most flattering of lies. The strategy works, and he goes on his way rejoicing demonically.*

Christ and Satan continues Satan's story in three chapters, "The Lament of the Fallen Angels," "The Harrowing of Hell," and "The Temptation in the Desert." The first backtracks to sum up the events of *Genesis*, then segues into original material. Satan, dejected, laments the fate that put them all in this horrid place. The demons complain vociferously. What about this son of Satan who was supposed to rule mankind? It looks as though God's son is grabbing all the glory. (Christ, rather than Michael, leads the war in Heaven here.) And indeed the section ends with a view of Christ in glory.

---

*Milton is believed to have read the unpublished *Genesis* manuscripts before he went blind.

"The Harrowing" follows *Nicodemus*. In "The Temptation," Satan, whose escape from Hell is not remarked upon, lifts Christ up on his shoulders to show and offer him the whole world and its riches—he even offers him Heaven, not that he has any right to it—in exchange for fealty. Christ mocks him and orders him back to Hell to measure its length and breadth with his own hands; it turns out to be 100,000 miles in each direction.

These poems may date from the early ninth century, and the other *Nicodemus*, translated as a canonical New Testament gospel, might be even earlier. In the tenth century, Aelfric the abbot of Eynsham (c. 950–c. 1020), told the whole Satan story again, and for good measure threw in the Antichrist and the end of the world. In the fourteenth century, William Langland retold the Harrowing, with allegorical variations, in *Piers Plowman*. Langland differentiated between Satan and Lucifer, blaming the latter for the Eden temptation ("In lyknesse of lizard with a lady's visage") and identifying Satan as the Devil. A new version of the war in Heaven called *Christ's Victorie and Triumph in Heaven and Earth*, by Giles Fletcher, appeared in 1610.

Milton's notebooks tell us that when he was casting about for a subject for his masterwork he considered a "British Trag," and, in the end, it appears that his subject matter could not have been more British.

THE MANY tribes of northwestern Europe fell into three general groupings: the Celts or Gauls, the Germans or Teutons, and the Scandinavians or Vikings or Norsemen. These are Roman classifications, which meant nothing to the tribes of nomadic warriors, farmers, and seamen so categorized, but we have retained the names for convenience and to differentiate language groups. Generally speaking, the Celts were west of the Rhine; Germania was the area between the Rhine and the Danube, reaching east to the Polish Vistula and up to include Denmark and southern Norway and Sweden; the Vikings were farther north. Because the Vikings were the last group to be converted to Christianity (in about A.D. 1000), we know much more about their religious beliefs than the others, but those of the Germans and Celts seem to have been rather similar, with some local variation.

By Gregory the Great's mandate, the Christian missionary monks sent north and west often managed to subsume rather than combat the beliefs they encountered. Thus Hel was originally the name of the Scandinavian death goddess, and the word came to refer also to her realm, just as Hades meant both the god and the place in Greece. Hellia was Hel's name in Germania. In the north, the word replaced the Latin Infernus (still used in variations in all romance-language countries), which had in its turn replaced the Greek Hades.

The Viking Hell was also called Niflheim. It was thought to be the northernmost land beneath the roots of Yggdrasil, the World Tree. To the east was Jotunheim, the land of the giants, and to the south, across the great void Ginnungagap, was Muspell, a fiery region ruled by the giant Surt. Midgard, or Middle Earth, was our own world. According to the Icelandic poet Snorri Sturluson of the twelfth century *Prose Edda*, Niflheim was the lowest part of Hel, as Tartarus was of Erebus or Hades, and, exactly like Tartarus, it was a place of utter darkness, stagnation, and sterility. Both Hel and Niflheim were considered to be cold, dark, and dreary lands of shadows, not places of punishment. Nastrond, on the other hand, a hall on the Strand of Corpses whose doors faced north and whose roof was formed of venomous snakes, seems to have been a place of after-death torment, very probably reserved for enemies rather than sinners. Dragons, especially the Nidhogg ("Corpse-eater"), are also associated with Hel and with the buried treasure of the dead.

Contrasted with these unpleasant places were Valhalla, Odin's banquet hall, where Valkyrie maidens escorted the souls of brave warriors so that they could feast on pork and mead and continue to battle one another ferociously forever (a concept of Heaven that illustrates why Vikings were so feared), and Glasisvellir, like the Celtic Tir na n-Og ("Land of the Young") or the Welsh Annwn, a paradise but also an uncanny and some-what menacing fairyland. Valhalla was not the only paradise that provided escort services for its male clientele: the Celts had a Land of Women, medieval Germans had the ambiguous Venusberg, and of course the dark-eyed *houris* of the medieval Muslim paradise are famous.*

The best known visit to Hel was that of the messenger Hermod, who galloped Odin's eight-legged horse Sleipnir from Asgard, home of the gods, through dark valleys and high mountains and across deep rivers for nine days till he reached the river Gjall, which he crossed on the Gjallarbru

---

*Valhalla may have housed some women. Wives, mistresses, and slave girls were strangled or voluntarily hanged themselves to join their men on the funeral pyre and presumably in the afterlife. There is a discussion of this depressing practice in *Gods and Myths of Northern Europe*, by H. R. Ellis Davidson.

A Viking picture-stone from Larbro, Sweden, portrays a dead warrior on the back of Sleipnir, Odin's eight-legged horse.

("Echoing Bridge") which was guarded by the skeletal maiden Modgud. He continued north and downward through the Iron Wood, where the trees are black with leaves of sharp metal, a vivid image which found its way into vision literature and into Dante.

Sleipnir leaped over the gate Valgrind of the high-walled city of Hel, guarded by the hound Garm of the bloody breast. Inside, the great cauldron Hvengelmir boils the wicked (or, more likely, enemies) before they are fed to the Nidhogg serpent. From a well guarded by the giant Mimir flow strange rivers: the icy Slith is filled with knives and swords (an image Bosch used). Other tales use other images and other names. Even the Balder story varies; in one account it is Odin himself, posing as Vegtam the Wanderer, who goes to Hel to find him; in another, it is his actual killer, Hoder, who goes to find a magic murder weapon.

The goddess Hel, half black (or rotting) and half flesh-colored, is the daughter of Loki, an elusive figure who has been compared to both Satan and Prometheus. Like Prometheus, Loki is not exactly a god but is represented as a giant. He is not entirely wicked, either; Christians are thought

107

to have blackened his reputation. Originally, he was a trickster, comedian, thief, and sex-change artist: in his female form he was "mother" not only to Hel, but to Fenrir the wolf, the horse Sleipnir, and the great Midgard serpent coiled around the world.

Loki was responsible for the death of Balder, the Norse equivalent of Attis or Dumuzi (he whom Hermod sought in Niflheim, unsuccessfully). Like Satan and Prometheus, Loki was bound after his crime.* Like Satan, he will break free in the Last Days when he will unleash the fury of Ragnarok, the final battle of gods and giants.

Ragnarok has obvious parallels to the Christian Final Battle, and the *Muspilli*, a ninth-century fragment of Christian apocalyptic poetry in Old High German, combines the two. Here Fenrir the wolf allies himself with the Antichrist and Satan on the battlefield. Elias (Elijah) leads the forces of good, but falls. Surt and the sons of Muspell overwhelm the earth just as they did in pre-Christian days, though they are not overtly personified.

A thirteenth-century Norse poem, the *Draumkvaede*, is typical of vision literature (which was frequently turned into verse) except that its imagery is Northern. The usual bridge over the stinking mire is explicitly the Gjallarbru, "decked with red and gold pinnacles," fitted with sharp hooks and guarded by a serpent (or dragon), a dog, and a bull. Otherwise, the narrator's experience is routine.

Celtic eschatological mythology is far from clear, but it seems to have been unusually positive and to have included reincarnation. Romans commented that the reason Celts were so reckless in battle was that they were not afraid to die. One underworld god was called Donn, but not much information about him survives, nor about a triad of enigmatic Germanic underworld goddesses called "the Mothers," whom Goethe would use centuries later in his kaleidoscope of Hell.

The otherworlds of most cultures are far away or inaccessible, but the Celts and Germans believed in a parallel world of earth spirits more or less superimposed on our own; many tales survive of encounters with giants, ogres, trolls, elves, dwarves, goblins, brownies, fairies, pixies, nixies, the Irish *sidh*, leprechauns, werewolves or werebears, and vampires in either their version of the world or our own. These creatures more or less survived

---

* Like Satan, but unlike Prometheus, he is both bound and not bound; he turns up to make trouble despite his chains.

Christianity. To a degree, they became Christian demons, which led, in some cases, to a reduction in demonic status to that of "imp," a creature not much more malevolent than a pixie.*

WHEN WE think of the Roman Empire, we think of cities, trade routes, shipping, coinage, an international economy propped up by slavery, a centralized army. The Christian Byzantine Empire preserved this pattern, but the growth of the West was different. Feudalism, a form of decentralized government administered by the local lords of large areas of farmland and forest, was characteristic of the Middle Ages. Taxes, legal problems, religious appointments, charitable dispositions, and all the minutiae of daily life were governed by these lords under what anthropologists call an artificial kinship structure. At its center was the lord, the leader of the tribe, "father" to all who swore faithfulness to him. The great noble families lived in huge fortified castles in the middle of their vast acreage and stocked them with armies of armed knights on horseback—their vassals. These in turn were supported by even larger numbers of serfs or villeins who performed agricultural and other manual labor in return for the right to earn a living on the land.

The monasteries employed an almost exact clerical counterpart to the secular feudal system: The abbot played the part of the lord, friars being the vassals and lay brothers the serfs. Just as the abbot owed a greater fealty to the pope, the lord might owe formal homage to a king.

Thus it is not surprising that the heavenly hierarchy was often portrayed in the feudal manner with its own Lord, its young prince with his retinue of apostles, its lady of the manor in the Virgin Mary, its senior household in the saints, and its first knight in the archangel Michael, who typically wears armor, wields a sword, and often appears with his angelic troops ranked behind him. When Lucifer fell, he took with him his own knights. Dante's rebel angels lounging about the battlements of the City of Dis, really a walled medieval citadel, are perfect examples of bullyboy knights or gunsels.

Lucifer's sin, the betrayal of faith or fealty to the Lord by a highly

---

*The Renaissance similarly "demonized" classical fauns and satyrs. Look at feet. Early pictures of demons usually have bird claws, unless they are Byzantine and have human feet. The Renaissance preferred Pan's cloven hoofs.

Michael in armor as warrior angel

placed vassal, meant a great deal to the Middle Ages. Betrayal was *the* great sin of feudalism. Keeping faith not only to the lord but to the tenets of religion was imperative to an extremely conservative system rigorously preserved by the collusion of the international Church and the local state. The lowest circle in Dante's Inferno is reserved for the faithless, and, apart from Satan himself, the lowest of the faithless low is Judas, who betrayed his honor and his own Lord with a terrible parody of the kiss of fealty.

The popular term for Muslims or Saracens was "infidels," the unfaithful. They were considered to be far worse than Jews or simple heathens who knew no better, for they too were "people of the book," the Bible, who had fallen away from the true faith centered on the New Testament. In the *Song of Roland*, a very popular French chivalric epic, they are treated as barely human. Christians considered them "servants of Satan," and they returned the compliment.*

In Faustian bargain stories, which began long before Christopher Marlowe, it is fealty that the devil demands. Pledge yourself to me, he says, and I will give you honor, powers, fortune, wealth, all the things that the

---

*According to the Koran, Hell, which is mentioned often and in dire terms, is reserved for unbelievers—non-Muslims, i.e., Christians and Jews, as well as the irreligious.

primitive Christian asks from God or the saints. The kiss of homage was thought to be administered to the buttocks of the Dark Lord.

HOW DID ordinary people react to the constant threat of Hell held over them by the medieval Church? Since the clergy held a near-monopoly on writing, we have to deduce secular attitudes from very few clues. Many, even most, people throughout the Middle Ages may have felt the way François Villon portrayed his mother as feeling in the prayer to the Virgin he wrote for her in the fifteenth century:

> *I am a woman, old and poor,*
> *Who knows nothing, not a single letter.*
> *In the parish church where I worship*
> *Paradise is painted, with harps and lutes,*
> *And a Hell where the damned are boiled:*
> *One fills me with fear, the other joy and delight.*
> *Give me that joy, great goddess . . .*

On the other hand, did Villon believe in Hell? If he did, it certainly didn't stop him from sinning—though there was always the possibility of deathbed absolution. Villon was a professional thief (of Church property among many other things), a womanizer, and a killer, if only in brawls. Possibly he was indifferent to religion. Raymond de l'Aire, one of the peasants quoted in *Montaillou*, Emmanuel LeRoy Ladurie's remarkable reconstruction of a French heretic village at the turn of the fifteenth century, was not only hostile to the clergy, as were his neighbors, he emphatically denied the existence of an afterlife, together with anything miraculous having to do with Jesus. He was unusual, but he could not have been unique. He probably believed that devils caused misfortunes, but that would have been only logical, and he seems to have been a resolutely logical man. His neighbors were conventionally but not excessively shocked by his attitude. They held an interesting variety of views on the afterlife themselves.

The fifteenth century is late, of course. But Gregory of Tours mentions at least one man who did not believe in an afterlife, and then we have the twelfth-century French romance *Aucassin et Nicolette* whose young hero is threatened with the torments of Hell if he makes love to his sweetheart. This is his reply:

In Paradise, what would I do? I don't want to go there but to have Nicolette, my so sweet friend whom I love so much. In Paradise are only people like this: old priests, old cripples, old maimed, who hunch in front of altars and old crypts day and night, and those in ragged old cloaks and old rags, who are naked and shoeless and dying of hunger and thirst, cold and misery. They go to Paradise, and I want nothing to do with them. I want to go to Hell, for to Hell go the handsome clerks and knights who die in jousts and fine wars, and the good officers and noblemen: I want to go with them. And there go the beautiful and gracious ladies who have two or three friends besides their husbands, and there go the gold and silver and furs, and there go the harpers and tumblers and kings. With them I will go, so long as I have Nicolette, my so sweet friend, with me.

The sentiment is perfectly familiar, but here it comes from the twelfth century, at the very height of Church dominance.

From these few clues and from the ceaseless admonitions against incorrigible sinning rests the case that even in the Middle Ages a fair number of individuals remained skeptical or indifferent or defiant toward the orthodox view of rewards and punishments in the afterlife. Most of the written evidence points the other way. The clergy, after all, provided it.

Hell was their great weapon, for only they were authorized to administer the rites of baptism and absolution that could save a soul. Higher Church authorities could threaten excommunication and anathema: they could send a soul to Hell. From the pulpit they thundered reminders of darkness and fire and stench and demons and serpents and "syghynge and sorownge, wepynge and weylynge, hideous cryynge, grugeynnge and murnynge, hunger and thyrst irremediable, wyth gnagyng off tethe wyth-owte ende."

From the confession box they ordained penances: one Irish penitential handbook gives the formula for saving a sinful soul, 365 paternosters, 365 genuflections, 365 blows "with a scourge on every day to the end of a year." More commonly, penances for each sin are listed. Favorite homilies like *The Pricke of Conscience* and *The Agenbite of Inwit* (which mean the same thing) listed "the 14 peynes" and deafening "dyn" of hell.

Exempla were collections of moralizing anecdotes meant to enliven sermons. One French one told of an orphaned girl in danger of enjoying her inheritance too much who was shown first her mother in Hell—burned

112

500 times a day by flames, then doused in icy water while reptiles gnawed on her—then her father in bliss; henceforth she led a good life.

In the *Elucidarium*, a widely used pulpit manual written at the beginning of the twelfth century, Honorius of Autun drew the picture of two Hells, the upper one continuing such sufferings as people already go through on earth and the lower giving a succinct summary of the nine kinds of torture for evil souls: unquenchable fire, unbearable cold, worms and snakes, disgusting stench, demons with whips, horror-filled darkness, agonizing shame, hideous sights and sounds, fiery fetters. They will also be turned upside-down, back to back, and stretched out forever, "they" being the proud, the envious, the cunning, the faithless, gluttons, drunkards, sensualists, murderers, the cruel, thieves, robbers, highwaymen, the impure, the greedy, fornicators, lechers, liars, perjurers, blasphemers, scoundrels, the abusive, the quarrelsome. Members of their own families, looking down from Heaven, will find their agonized suffering "a pleasant sight, like that of a fish jumping in a reservoir."

The greatest preacher of the fourteenth century was said to have been Berthold of Regensburg who predicted that only one in 100,000 would be saved. As for the 99,999, Berthold asked them to imagine themselves "writhing white-hot within a white-hot universe" till Judgment Day, at which time things would get much worse. They could imagine their pains continuing for as many years as "all the hairs grown on all the beasts that have lived since the beginning of the world."

In the allegorical late Middle Ages, sermons frequently invoked the figure of the Castle of Sin: its head knight was Anger, its treasurer Greed, its chef Gluttony, its chamberlain Sloth, its master and mistress Pride and Lust. G. R. Owst, author of *Literature and Pulpit in Medieval England*, discovered in a fourteenth-century manuscript the original sermon from which John Bunyan's *Pilgrim's Progress* was taken. In it the Slough of Despond is actually the Slough of Hell, into which the pilgrim, with his sack of sin, may fall. Owst also suggests that orators who emphasized the Dives and Lazarus story, dwelling upon the fate of the rich at Judgment Day, may have contributed to the widespread peasant unrest at the end of the medieval period. Judgment Day may have seemed too distant a reckoning for some. In any event, sermons provided plenty of drama, and open-air preaching by friars led to the next step, which was drama itself.

113

Mystery Plays

THE EARLY CHURCH DENOUNCED AND killed off Rome's lively theatrical tradition and then reinvented primitive sacred drama in the sung responses of the Latin liturgy. True drama, with actors, dialogue, and a story line, was part of local churches' efforts, during the period when heresies were beginning to look attractive, to reach out and teach illiterate congregations something about the Bible. Sculpture, painting, stained glass, and all the other pictorial decorations of the churches served the same purpose.

The word *mystery*, used for plays developed for the festivals of the Christian year, derives from the Latin *ministerium* or "service"; very early on instructive playlets were performed in church as part of the service. They soon took on a life of their own; the religiously inspired dramatic tradition grew in inventiveness and scope from about the tenth to the sixteenth centuries, vying at holiday times with musicians, dancers, jugglers, and other performers to capture public attention.

Several plays survive from as early as the twelfth century, but many more are lost. They were performed all over Europe, from Czechoslovakia to Britain, and in many places they were elaborated into cycles that presented the "history of the world" from Creation to Last Judgment. England has four of these cycles preserved fairly completely, from York, Chester, Wakefield, and one known as either the Hegge cycle (from an owner of the manuscripts) or the N-Town or the Ludus Coventriae. Italy has lost its medieval plays, but many survive in France, Spain, Germany, Austria, the Netherlands, Switzerland, and other places.

The Oberammergau festival has produced a Passion cycle once in every decade since 1634. This remarkable series persisted through the Reformation, which stopped religious plays everywhere else in Europe, and was only temporarily halted by the Nazis. There are 124 speaking parts, and hundreds more costumed figures in the crowd scenes—in effect, the entire town takes part—and the sequence takes about eight hours to perform. Strictly speaking, Oberammergau is not a medieval cycle, as the text has been substantially revised many times through the centuries, but the presentation gives a good idea of what a big medieval cycle might have been like.

Mystery plays were not always so elaborate nor so secular. We are told of a simple and probably quite moving liturgical performance of the Harrowing of Hell in an English convent where the nuns, representing the souls of the patriarchs, were confined behind the doors of a chapel. After the priest uttered exhortations and flung the door wide, the nuns, carrying palm branches, filed out singing Latin hymns of praise.

By the later Middle Ages, clerics had ceased acting in plays. In the big urban dramas, a union of tradesmen's guilds shared responsibility for increasingly elaborate productions. Each guild produced a separate playlet in its own venue. The Harrowing of Hell was often assigned to the cooks and bakers for the practical reason that guild members were used to working with fire and could supply huge cauldrons and other devices to be used for "tortures," plus pots and pans to bang together for sound effects.

Boisterous Hell scenes inevitably became comic relief to the more solemn goings-on. As time passed, the comedy got lower, with much attention to breaking wind. Critics have often assigned the knockabout capers of the demons in Christopher Marlowe's *Doctor Faustus* to some less worthy playwright, but centuries of tradition supported vulgar stage devilry, and Marlowe was probably playing to his audience.

Hell was everyone's favorite part of the mystery presentations. A scaffolding achieved by something as simple as a ladder might stand in for Heaven in an early production, but even the very earliest plays we know about give careful stage directions for infernal scenes—the twelfth-century *Mystère d'Adam* specifies chains, clouds of smoke, and the clatter of

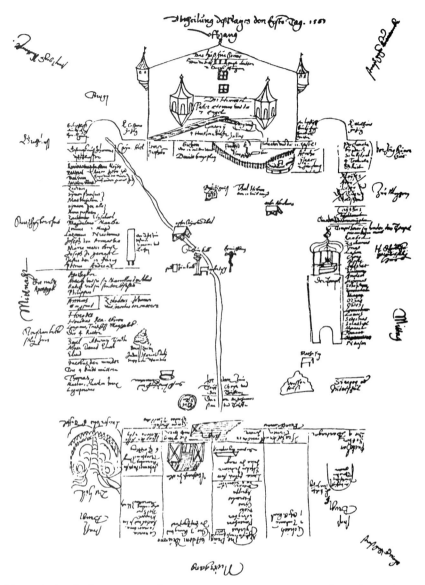

Director's sketch of a mystery cycle set in a German town square. Hellmouth is at lower left, and Heaven, with a ladder, at top.

caldrons and kettledrums, while the Anglo-Norman *Seinte Resureccion* of the same period calls for a jail to be built on one side of the stage to represent Limbo, from which Jesus would rescue the patriarchs. Later productions added fireworks, gunpowder, flaming sulfur, cannons, mechanical serpents, and toads.

116

A Harrowing from the kind of jail that might be built on stage. From the cathedral at Elme, Germany.

The most expensive prop in the entire production was the Hellmouth. Artists had already taken to portraying "the jaws of Hell" quite literally, and theatrical designers took this a step further. Carpenters would make a beast's head out of wood, papier-mâché, fabric, glitter, and whatever else they needed, and set it over a trapdoor. The wide jaws were often hinged and operated with winches and cables so that they could open and close. Smoke, flames, bad smells, and plenty of noise would emerge from within, to the delight of the audience. In one instance, the actual jawbone of a beached whale was employed in the framework.

There would often be fixed locations for the various sets of a dramatic cycle around a cathedral or town square, and in that case the Hellmouth might be so large that actual scenes could be played inside it; one directive specifies that it be nine and a half feet wide. In less lavish productions, the action took place beside the trapdoor Hellmouth, or on a lower scaffolding, curtained off until needed. Sometimes the entire series of playlets was movable. Here is a description of a pageant wagon made for a parade in fifteenth-century Bourges. It was preceded by a group of capering devils darting in and out of the crowd.

> After this *diablerie* came a Hell, 14 feet long and eight wide, in the form of a rock on which was constructed a tower, continually blazing and shooting out flames in which Lucifer appeared, head and body only.

117

"Feeyndes" in a Hellmouth. The pillarlike device was probably used to raise and lower the jaws. From a fifteenth-century German manuscript.

He wore a bearskin with a sequin hanging from each hair and a pelt with two masks adorned with various colored materials; he ceaselessly vomited flames and held in his hands various serpents or vipers which moved and spat fire. At the four corners of the rock were four small towers in which could be seen souls undergoing torments. And from the front of the rock there came a great serpent whistling and spitting fire from throat, nostrils and eyes. And on every part of the rock there clambered and climbed all kinds of serpents and great toads. It was moved and guided by a certain number of people inside it, who worked the torments in place as they had been instructed.

Most were not so magnificent as this, but old bills and documents make it clear that towns competed fiercely on the elaboration of the Hell front. A late German example included "many ghastly and brightly colored devils. And it cost a great deal of money and work."

118

Though it was important to the action mainly at the beginning and the end of the history of the world, the Hellmouth, too large to be easily moved, might be present throughout. It was used almost immediately. The Creation was understandably hard to stage and generally took the form of a speech from the eminence of Heaven, after which God went offstage to rest on the seventh day. The Fall of Lucifer thus began the dramatic action.

Lucifer, glitteringly clad, dares to sit on God's throne and brag, a gesture greeted with gasps of horror or of glee from the other angels, according to their political stance. But then comes the fall. From York:

> *Owe! dewes! All goes down!*
> *My might and my main is all marrande*
> *Help! felawes, in faythe I am fallande.*

Another Hellmouth clearly based on stage design.

And down he goes into the Hellmouth, followed by the "felawes." The Ludus Coventriae indicates the staging:

Now to Helle the way I take
in endeles peyn there to by pyht
For fear of fire a fart I crake.

The role of Lucifer was risky, as the actor might be required to breathe fire and hold a firecracker in each hand as well as the one indicated in his backside. Devil's masks and costumes were backed with mud for protection.

If unscathed, Lucifer would emerge from the Hellmouth in short order (sometimes after a parliament of "feeyndes," just as in Milton) to attend to the Temptation in Eden. He needed a variation in costume here and would either carry or half-wear an imaginatively snaky form with a mask. The successful rout of Adam and Eve might be cause for more gleeful devilry, with the devils now in proper attire with grotesque masks and shaggy suits of hair or feathers instead of their angel costumes. They might appear in scenes from time to time—Cain and Abel, Job, and so forth—while the cycle of plays worked its way through the Old Testament and the beginnings of the New. Satan, now in his third costume of suitably demonic appearance, would be needed for the Temptation of Christ.

Satan was played as a comic failure in the Temptation; in the Ludus Coventriae he flounces toward Hellmouth with a "crakke," and in the Chester play he wills a "testament" to the audience:

To all that in this place be lent,
I bequeath thee shitte.

The Hellmouth's finest hour came after the Crucifixion, when Jesus descended to rescue the prophets. *Nicodemus* offered a perfect dramatic scenario. After the solemnities of the Passion, it engaged the audience with clamor, battling, and more low comedy. In one version, Satan pulled on his "gere" or armor for one-on-one combat with Jesus. The scene ended in triumph for the forces of good, with the devils locked away in their own prison or even in a lower trapdoor Hell.

Sometimes the Harrowing had a little addendum, the story of the ale-wife, sent to Hell for watering the beer, who stays behind to marry one

The alewife and her lover

of the devils. Here she is again, that remarkable barmaid who turns up in every millennium—from *Gilgamesh* to *The Frogs* to a medieval Harrowing!

The Antichrist story was difficult to fit into the dramatic sequence of the life of Jesus. So, though it was a popular dramatic subject—more battling between angels and demons, plus stage trickery and sleight of hand as the Antichrist performs his false miracles—it was usually performed independently, or as the provocative beginning of an independent Last Judgment play. One of the oldest surviving mystery plays is a twelfth-century *Antichrist* from the Tergernsee Abbey in Germany.

At the Last Judgment, the newly resurrected dead appear "naked" in body stockings to be judged by Jesus, while the Virgin Mary acts as intercessor. The saved are greeted by angels and ascend to Heaven, while the damned, bewailing their lot, head for the Hellmouth. Since the damned always featured great folk like kings, queens, bishops, and rich merchants, this was a crowd-pleaser. The Towneley play adds a digression: the devils rejoice at the great number of souls heading their way, so many that the porter at Hell Gate gets no rest. It is this scene that Shakespeare's porter in *Macbeth* imitates in Act II, Scene 3, just after Duncan's murder.

The devils were allowed their moment of jubilation over their captives, but the plays closed on a more decorous note, with music, pageantry, and a joyous ascension to Heaven.

Biblical parables like the stories of Dives and Lazarus or the wise and foolish virgins were not commonly staged, partly because they were not "history," and partly because of an intrinsic dramatic pitfall illustrated by the story of Frederick the Undaunted, margrave of Thuringia. In 1321, he attended a performance of a wise and foolish virgins play put on by a boys' school in Eisnadi and was so distressed by the verdict handed out to the fresh-faced lads who played the foolish virgins that he turned his back on the stage. "What is the Christian faith if the sinner is not to receive mercy upon the intercession of the Virgin and the saints?" he exclaimed in revulsion.

Frederick's story is instructive on several counts. It illustrates the power of dramatic presentation in an illiterate society.* It also demonstrates why other Hell scenes inevitably regressed toward farce. To show a group of pretty "girls" damned for carelessness was discomfiting. Even given an audience's resentment of the rich, Dives's pleas to Abraham for rescue or for warning his living brothers might have had the same effect. To watch a gang of comical imps pretend to torture a hapless dummy fit in far better with the festival mood. It was not the conventional staging of the later mystery cycles, coarse as they had become by the sixteenth century, but the far more controversial "serious" poetry of *Doctor Faustus* that finally ousted religious drama from the British stage.

The later medieval theater offered two other kinds of plays, miracles and moralities. Miracles dramatized the stories that had been told for centuries about the lives and deaths of saints and martyrs. Though these were meant to be inspirational, their popularity, too, was directly related to the action they offered. Jean Bodel's St. Nicholas play (c. 1200) presented battles in the Crusades and scenes in both brothels and taverns, but other

---

*The society need not be illiterate. I have seen an audience become visibly disturbed at a high-school performance of *Godspell*, a modern musical that borrows many techniques from the mystery plays, at the moment when the actor playing Jesus separates the sheep from the goats.

11–12. RIGHT: The Hell detail of the twelfth-century mosaic at Torcello on page 72. Note that a Byzantine Satan is as human as the Antichrist on his lap. Another Byzantine characteristic is the division of the damned into tidy compartments; Western Hells are more chaotic. The angels prod those whose headdresses betray their wealth and pride, while the Hellmouth is part of Satan's throne. Worms that never sleep are at bottom left. BELOW: The unveiling of the grand mosaic on the cupola of the baptistry in Florence in 1300 must have been quite an event. Dante borrowed some of its imagery for his own *Inferno.* Note the jaws on the ears and throne.

13. After his banishment in 1302, Dante very likely visited Giotto in Padua, where he was working on his famous frescoes. Giotto's hideous Satan, who is actually excreting a sinner, moves close to Dante's concept, and the different punishments for the sinners look forward to his inventions. Here the four rivers of fire stream from Christ's throne.

Daily Notes

3

Sunday
July 2011

JULY						
S	M	T	W	T	F	S
31					1	2
3	4	5	6	7	8	9
10	11	12	13	14	15	16
17	18	19	20	21	22	23
24	25	26	27	28	29	30

AUGUST						
S	M	T	W	T	F	S
	1	2	3	4	5	6
7	8	9	10	11	12	13
14	15	16	17	18	19	20
21	22	23	24	25	26	27
28	29	30	31			

Today's schedule	What I need to do

14. Another bestial Satan, by Francesco Traini, at the Camposanto in Pisa achieves a kind of grotesque beauty.

15. An exuberant anonymous fourteenth-century Last Judgment in the Pinacoteca in Bologna includes Dante's *bolge* and bridges.

16–17. Orcagna, or Nardo di Cione, followed Dante exactly in Santa Maria Novella in Florence. The fresco is too faded to reproduce well, but you can see Charon, the philosopher's castle in Limbo, the lustful swirling in air, Minos in the top detail, and the misers and spendthrifts rolling stones, burning coffins, and some harpies in the lower one.

18. Luca Signorelli (1441–1523) painted detailed and somewhat pornographic Hells. This is a good example of Jesuit overcrowding.

19. Detail from Michelangelo's *Last Judgment.*

20. Baciccia's Baroque ceiling of the Gesù, the Jesuit church in Rome. In three places, the frame of the painting is broken by the damned as they fall to destruction.

plays relied on stage wizardry to produce miracles, dragons, wild beasts, and realistic martyrdoms.

The Hellmouth got plenty of use here too. In the *Miracle de Théophile*, a precursor of Faust is saved from the jaws of Hell by the Virgin. St. Michael saves the false "Pope Joan" in a German play. In a Dutch play, the pope is the savior. Demons were needed to tempt the saints and to drag off their persecutors to Hell.

Moralities, or dramatized allegories, came along toward the end of the Middle Ages. On the literary level, allegorizing could become convoluted, as modern students of medieval literature can glumly attest. But on the level of the popular theater, allegory simply added the figure of Death to that of Satan and personified the Seven Deadly Sins who dwelt in Hell-mouth. A Spanish play gives costume directions: Pride wears a scepter and crown; Envy is well dressed with spectacles; Gluttony, well dressed with things to eat; Anger is in armor; Lust, a woman with a mirror; Avarice has a scholar's robe and carries a purse; and Sloth wears droopy breeches and carries a pillow.

Moralities dealt with the end of man, not the end of the world. The journey toward Death and the fate of the soul was their theme; Mercy argued with Justice, and the Vices and Virtues fought for ascendancy. Where they got into trouble is when they forgot to play to the audience. In the longest and oldest of the English moralities, *The Castle of Perseverance*, five settings held the World, the Flesh, the Devil, Covetousness, and God's Throne. The play is tedious beyond modern endurance. A short morality called *Mankind*, written down about 1475, shows far more stage savvy: at a critical point an actor steps forward to say that the chief devil, Titivullus, will appear only after the hat has been passed and filled. *Every-man*, the best known English morality (c. 1500), brought back the popular Titivullus.

By the fifteenth century, the figure of Death personified as an animate corpse or skeleton was ubiquitous in European art. The first precursor of what seems to have been a kind of grisly fad appears toward the beginning of the fourteenth century with the *Legend of the Three Living and Three Dead*, which was illustrated so often that it was frequently abbreviated as simply the *Legend*. In it, three foppishly dressed youths, or sometimes kings, encounter three desiccated corpses. "As you are, so once were we," they intone. "As we are, so you will be."

123

Another more purely visual theme was that of the Dance of Death, which many people remember best from Holbein's sixteenth-century interpretation, based on earlier, more properly medieval models. The *Dance* is a much more sophisticated and ironic concept than the *Legend* and required a number of illustrations rather than the *Legend*'s one, for it indicated that each death is personal, with its own psychopomp. The Dance tended toward sardonic humor, which was certainly the case in Holbein's woodcuts. By his time, Death was more usually a skeleton than a dry corpse, and the word *sardonic* was actually coined to describe its bony grin.

This move toward the personification of Death in the fourteenth and fifteenth centuries is echoed in hundreds of pictures and carvings of morbidly graphic Crucifixions, Pietas, saints' martyrdoms, deathbed images, and even little printed handbooks of cartoons called *Ars Moriendi*, or "Art

---

Death with an arrow, rising from a tomb, by Jean Colombe, from France, late 1470s

An elaborate Italian rendering of the Three Living and Three Dead

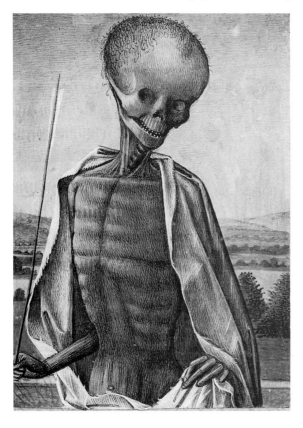

Dance of Death, from a fifteenth-century woodblock

of Dying"; it turns up in poetry as well as in the moralities. Whether or not fascination with the macabre was a response to the plague and other calamities, or whether the times naturally inclined toward pessimism, is moot. What is significant is that the art and poetry indicate that soon after the point at which the Church adopted the doctrine of Purgatory, Hell began to lose its grip on the imagination.

This is not to say that people did not believe in Hell. Most of them undoubtedly did, and the Church never ceased its efforts in that direction. But Purgatory lightened the load, and, from the evidence, fear of death seems to have displaced fear of Hell. By the Baroque period, tombs adorned with horribly realistic sculptures of naked corpses crawling with worms were not at all uncommon.

An unusual mid–fifteenth-century Flemish painting by Jan van Eyck makes the perfect graphic bridge between the two concepts, showing the old Hell topped by the new skeletal and grinning Death. See Plate 17.

Purgatory

THE ETERNITY OF HELL CONTINUED to plague theologians. Hells in older religions, though frightful, were neither static nor eternal; Hindu, Buddhist, and Zoroastrian hells depend on cycles of incarnation that can lead to an improvement of circumstance. Origen's argument that all being in time returns to God was emphatically rejected by Augustine and the orthodox Church, but it never quite disappeared.

One biblical passage seemed to indicate that prayers and offerings for the dead could actually redeem them. In Second Maccabees 12.43–46, Judas Maccabeus orders an offering of 200,000 drachmas for the souls of Jewish soldiers slain in battle:

> For if he had not hoped that they that were slain should have risen again, it had been superfluous and vain to pray for the dead. And also in that he perceived that there was great favor laid up for those who died godly, it was an holy and good thought. Whereupon he made a reconciliation for the dead, that they might be delivered from sin.

Then there was the bosom of Abraham, thought to have rocked Elijah and Enoch (at least) as well as the beggar Lazarus. It was sometimes identified with *refrigerium*, the place of refreshment. The Limbos of the patriarchs and the unbaptized babies were cited. Furthermore, Paul had seemed to indicate (1 Cor. 3.15) some kind of salvation by fire, though the passage is not very clear. And visions, time and again for centuries, had offered glimpses of purgatorial punishments separate from those of Hell.

The history of the Church's adoption of a third major after-death venue has been written by the French historian Jacques LeGoff in *The Birth of Purgatory*, a fine example of scholarly detective work. The chief criticism made of it, by another major medievalist, the Russian Aron Gurevich, is that LeGoff did not give enough credit to visions, which suggest that the idea of Purgatory was well established long before the Church was ready to embrace it officially.* In any event, the "new" doctrine dates back to a papal letter of 1253, though it was not finally confirmed till the Council of Trent.

The Catechism of the Council of Trent, which was drawn up later, says "there is a purgatorial fire in which the souls of the pious are purified by a temporary punishment so that an entrance may be opened for them into the eternal country in which nothing stained can enter." Souls detained there are "helped by the suffrages of the faithful, but especially by the acceptable sacrifice of the altar." While bishops are instructed to teach the doctrine, they are specifically enjoined from imparting "the more difficult and subtle questions relating to the subject which do not tend to edification," particularly those "tending to superstition, savoring of filthy lucre or likely to create scandals and offences." One can hear the horns of Protestantism faintly blowing in that last statement.

In part, Purgatory was adopted as a reaction to heresy, which was not quite early Protestantism, though later Protestants like John Foxe in his *Book of Martyrs* (1563) sometimes claimed that it was. The lively eleventh and twelfth centuries nurtured more free thinking than the orthodox Church could tolerate. Heretical Bogomils (named after a Bulgarian priest) from the East moved westward, and Waldensians (followers of Peter Waldo of Lyons) and Cathars or Albigensians (after the town of Albi) moved north and east from Catalonia and the Pyrenees until they more or less met around Verona. The movement of large groups of people on pilgrimages, and especially on the Crusades, helped to spread heresy.

No more than a superficial look at the long and bloody history of

---

*In the 1984 American edition, LeGoff acknowledges the criticism and adds a new appendix on visions, but does not retreat from his thesis, that there was no real concept of Purgatory until the twelfth century.

medieval heresies and the Inquisition is possible here. Suffice it to say that most of the heretics condemned by the Church did not consider themselves heretics at all, but good Christians, far more devout on the whole than those ministered to by what was, in the heretics' opinion, the increasingly greedy and corrupt Church bureaucracy. The mendicant order of Saint Francis (1182–1226) was founded on just such feelings, but the Church managed to co-opt and embrace the Franciscan movement before it finally drew the line at other departures.

Aside from anticlericalism, the strongest motivation for most heresies, what they had in common, and what the Church seized upon, was dualism, which it called Manichaeism, though it is questionable whether the heretic leaders had ever heard of Mani. What is far more likely is that almost all ordinary nonintellectual medieval people, including minor clerics and the nobility, inclined toward casual dualism. The Church undertook to rout it out by use of the carrot and the stick. The stick was the so-called Albigensian Crusade against heresy and the ferocious Inquisition that followed. The carrot was Purgatory.

Purgatory was a powerful propaganda tool because it offered a new chance to the masses excluded from Heaven by Berthold of Regensburg and other hellfire preachers. Theologically, it handily subsumed the question of Abraham's bosom and the two Limbos—though Dante put his pagan Limbo in the First Circle of Hell. Even the dead babies, after perhaps a very little purgatorial refinement, could now find happiness.

Purgatory also explained how ghosts, which most people believed in, could walk. It solved the complication of what happened between Particular Judgment at death and the eventual Last Judgment. Almost everyone, it was soon widely assumed, would go to Purgatory, the exceptions being saints, martyrs, and the incorrigibly wicked. And the prayers of the living, the Church said explicitly, could help the dead and shorten their time in Purgatory.

But to whom should these prayers be addressed? It seems unlikely that the Church foresaw the extraordinary role the Virgin Mary would take on as Queen of Purgatory. In the *Apocalypse of Mary*, back as far as the fourth or fifth century, she had obtained temporary respite (*refrigerium*) for the sinners in Hell. But so had Paul, and his story was better known in monasteries, though evidently not in storytelling. A miracle story of 1070 features a woman sent to Hell for youthful lesbianism (!) until the Mother of

God intervenes on her behalf and apparently restores her to life. In another story from about the same time, she delivers a noble sinner who had redeeming qualities—generosity to the poor and the Church—from a horde of demons, though she orders that his chains be retained for another sinner, still living. Since no one could leave Hell, they must have been rescued from Purgatory, though it had not yet been defined as such. In about 1220, not long before it *was* so defined, Caesarius of Heisterbach wrote of a young monk named Christian who had a vision of the Virgin saving him from demons; upon awakening he led a life of such reverent humility that when he died he went straight to paradise despite having in his youth fathered two bastards (both of whom became monks). The most famous of Mary's rescues was Theophilus, whose story will be related when we arrive at the Faust legend.

"Pray for us sinners, now and at the hour of our death." Jesus is the Judge, but Mary is the Intercessor, and that is how they are portrayed in hundreds of judgment scenes. Purgatory, together with Mary's increasing power to intervene there, led directly to the medieval cult of the Virgin, Mariolatry, as later Protestants would disdainfully call it. Perhaps following the will of the people, the Church granted Mary more and more supernatural attributes. She was the stainless product of an Immaculate Conception, without sin (sex) on the part of her parents. Unlike her son, she never died but only fell asleep (the Dormition) and was translated to Heaven in her own glorified body (the Assumption, which did not become an article of faith until 1950). In this body, she can appear anywhere on earth, and apparently continues to do so frequently. Her images smile, weep real tears, and grant prayers. (Relics were all but abandoned in the late Middle Ages in favor of images of the Virgin.) She is "the woman clothed with the sun" of Revelation. In Nativity scenes she is the mother of new life, but as the *Mater Dolorosa* she is the pitying death goddess. "Lady of Heaven, earthly queen,/ Empress of the swamps of Hell," is how François Villon had his mother address her in the prayer-poem he wrote for her.

All the saints, alive or dead (most were dead), performed miracles, but Mary's supernatural living status and purview in Purgatory made her foremost in prayers for the dead. John the Baptist had earlier shared her duties as intercessor, but by the end of the thirteenth century—soon after the birth of Purgatory—she was more frequently portrayed alone, sheltering sinners from the wrath of her Son. No wonder she was more popular than

A rather salacious Purgatory from a fifteenth-century French Book of Hours

he during the late Middle Ages when plague, war, and famine wracked Europe, and death seemed everywhere imminent. The Council of Trent tried to limit her powers but was not markedly successful judging from her status even today among Catholics.

Purgatory, which seemed so just and humane in theory, also led to other difficulties. Protestant reformers, who rejected the concept completely, together with "idolatrous" worship of Mary (or other intercessors, such as the saints), publicized these so incessantly that it is necessary only to mention them without comment. In sum, the Church went into the business of selling pardons or "indulgences" for the remission of punishment after death. While this might seem harmless enough when it is simply a matter of lighting a candle in prayer while contributing to the poor box, it could be, and often was, carried to outrageous extents, as when rich men, with far more on their consciences than Dives would appear to have had,

Bosch's fifteenth-century Purgatory, very unusual for its time, looks uncannily like modern descriptions of "near-death experiences."

hired the poor to fast, to pray, to make pilgrimages for them, to fight in the Crusades, even to wear hair shirts and flagellate themselves. All these, Church officials accepted complacently as surrogate penances for sin, together with adequate offerings of money or treasure.

Purgatory gave the Church, so powerful in every aspect of medieval life, new powers that extended beyond the grave. At the same time, it opened a serious chink in the armor of the all-powerful Roman Catholic Church.

Purgatory was thought to be a temporary Hell, as on Dante's mountain, where sins are punished in the same kind but not with the same severity as in the Inferno. More often, Purgatory was associated with fire that would burn away the evil of original and accumulated sin, "refiner's fire." Artists usually portrayed it that way, with angels swooping down to carry naked purged souls to paradise. By the nineteenth century, nearly every Catholic altarpiece featured a depiction of souls in Purgatory.

Dante's Inferno

The volumes of commentary written about Dante Alighieri (1265–1321) would fill his own Inferno, and the part of those volumes that has to do with that Inferno's engineering and geography would form a substantial subdivision. The architectural ingenuity Dante put into his landscape of Hell has always fascinated readers: modern editions of the *Divine Comedy* carry maps and diagrams, while illustrators have presented not only the characters and monsters of the story but also the wonderful underground embankments, moats, castles, paved trenches, and the City of Dis with walls of red-hot iron. Galileo himself did a technical report on the structure of the Inferno in 1587 as a playful student thesis. Virgil's Hades is a spectacular stage set without much depth, but Dante's Inferno is limned in three dimensions, right down to the cracks, fissures, and ruins created in the infrastructure at the time of the great earthquake that followed the Harrowing of the First Circle.

Writing his great poem in exile, Dante was concerned with history, with Florentine politics, with the corruption of the clergy, with the moral position of his contemporaries, and most of all with the state of his own psyche. At a distance of seven centuries, we can no longer easily appreciate any of these things except the last—Dante is generous with his emotions. But anyone reading the *Inferno* "just for the story" can still marvel at not only the stories the Pilgrim is told but also at the sights and sounds—and smells!

133

Dante took every theme traced in this book—philosophic, mythic, Orphic, demonic, repulsive, fantastic, allegorical, grotesque, comic, psychological—and put them together with meticulous care for all time. His religious views were orthodox, but his imagination was not. Even if his artistic contribution had been limited to the radical step of marrying the classical attributes of Hades to those of the Christian Hell of the vision tours, it would be a milestone. But his influence went far beyond that.

On earth, Dante led a complicated life. Orphaned early, he was brought up by well-to-do relatives in the city-state of Florence, where he received an excellent education in both the classics and the poetry of his time. He was interested in vocabulary and at one point wanted to construct an "all-Italian" language merging the many dialects of the peninsula; this project was completely undermined by his decision to write the *Comedy* in his own Florentine dialect, which, together with the later contributions of Petrarch and Boccaccio, made Tuscan once and for all time Italy's literary language. At various times he worked as a businessman, a soldier, a politician, and a professor of philosophy. Because he ran afoul of the tangled politics of the period, he was forced to spend the last twenty years of his life in unhappy, though not uncomfortable, exile.

The most famous event of Dante's childhood was his encounter with Beatrice Portinari when he was nine and she a year younger. Theirs was a model of courtly romance, for they seldom met, each married someone else, and he continued to write poetry to her all his life. She died in 1290, a date remembered because Dante set the *Comedy* in 1300, just ten years later. In the poem, she appears as Divine Love or Grace, which inspires and guides the Pilgrim after Human Reason, represented by the poet Virgil, can go no farther. Dante had other reasons for choosing 1300: he was thirty-five at the time, "midway along life's journey"; it was a centennial year, and numbers are essential to the scheme of the poem. It was also the year his political troubles began.

To picture Dante's physical and ethical universe, think of the round ball of the earth pierced in the northern hemisphere to its center by a hole in the shape of an irregular cone or funnel. The center of that hole is Jerusalem, and its diameter, the width of the circle around Jerusalem, is equal in size to the radius of the earth, about 3,950 miles, though Galileo's calculations showed it a few hundred miles less. This hole was formed by the weight and force of Lucifer and his angels striking the earth as they fell from Heaven. The matter displaced by the impact, forced upward and backward along the tunnel Virgil and Dante use to escape, formed the mountain of Purgatory that rises in an inverted cone on an isolated island in the southern hemisphere. On top of Purgatory is the Earthly Paradise. The opening to Hell is covered by a vault of earth that Galileo calculated to be $405^{15}/_{22}$ miles in depth, though obviously there are irregular shallower fissures such as the one by which the poets enter.* In the Dark Wood of the *Inferno*'s first canto, where the Pilgrim flees from the leopard, the lion, and the she-wolf, is a hill that must be climbed to reach the entrance to the lower depths where the famous words are inscribed: *Abandon hope, all you who enter here.*

To complete the picture, remember that for Dante, though notoriously not for Galileo, the earth was at the center of a Ptolemaic universe around which circled nine crystalline heavenly spheres—the moon, Mercury, Venus, the sun, Mars, Jupiter, Saturn, the fixed stars, and the primum mobile or "first mover," which keeps the universe in order. (The three outer planets had not yet, of course, been discovered.) Beyond the spheres was the vast Empyrean, home of God, the angels, and saints, but Dante's heavens are lodged in the spheres. The nine circles of Hell are a direct inversion of the scheme; the vestibule makes a tenth area, as does the Empyrean, as does the earthly paradise atop the nine levels of Purgatory.

Dante's love of precise structure and symbolic numerology extends to the poetry itself. It is written in *terza rima*, in which the first and third lines of each three-line stanza rhyme while the second rhymes with the first and third line of the next stanza. Each of the three sections, the *Inferno*, *Purgatorio*, and *Paradiso*, is further divided in thirds, of thirty-three cantos each, with an introductory canto to make one hundred in all. To have carried off this structure so readably is amazing.

When the two poets enter the Gate of Hell in Canto III, they find themselves in the vestibule, an area where Dante places the "indecisive," those who have never committed to anything, including life—thus though they have not earned Hell they get no real death either. This vestibule slopes down to the river Acheron, the first of three circular rivers, each of which debouches into the next, finally to flow into Cocytus, the frozen lake at

---

*According to *The Weekly World News* of August 28, 1990, Hell is nine miles beneath the surface of a point in western Siberia where Soviet engineers drilling for oil broke through. They capped their hole after smelling the smoke and hearing the cries of the damned.

Dante's Inferno

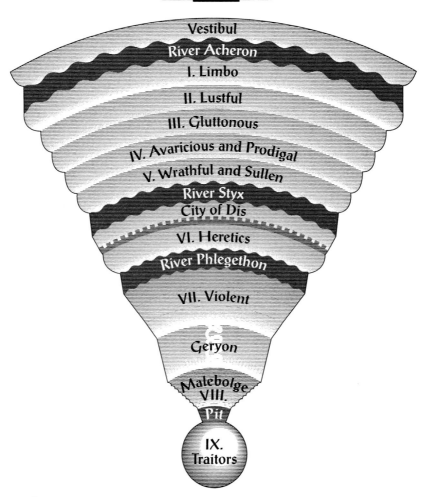

Vestibul
River Acheron
I. Limbo
II. Lustful
III. Gluttonous
IV. Avaricious and Prodigal
V. Wrathful and Sullen
River Styx
City of Dis
VI. Heretics
River Phlegethon
VII. Violent
Geryon
Malebolge VIII.
Pit
IX. Traitors

Map of Dante's Inferno

the center of the earth. The fourth traditional river of Hell, Lethe, Dante locates in Purgatory for dramatic reasons. All of these waters, Virgil tells the Pilgrim in an image worthy of Hesiod, flow from the tears of a great metal statue at the core of Mount Ida in Crete (the statue comes from Nebuchadnezzar's dream in Daniel 2.31–34, but the tears are Dante's).

The entire underground cone is terraced in descending ledges or circles of narrowing size down to the nethermost well or pit at the center of the earth, which holds Cocytus. Between the Acheron, across which Charon

136

the boatman ferries the poets, and the Styx are Hell's first four circles, the highest of which is technically Limbo, the residence of virtuous unbaptized souls, mostly pagan. No one is punished in the First Circle, which resembles the Elysian Fields of asphodel in the *Aeneid* and has its own Castle of Philosophy and its own fresh little stream, which seems to have nothing to do with bitter tears. Virgil himself inhabits this circle together with Homer (Dante is thought to have known Homer's work only by reputation) and other famous pagans. The Hebrews had, of course, been rescued in the Harrowing. Dante avoids the question of unbaptized babies.

The next four circles punish the Incontinent, those who, in life, gave in to their passions. Dante followed Aristotle's ethical system in his classification of sins rather than the more common Seven Deadly Sins listing. Thus the Second Circle, guarded by Minos, holds the lustful, whirled forever in winds of desire. The Third, guarded by Cerberus, traps gluttons in a cold, smelly garbage heap. The Fourth, guarded by Plutus ("Father Rich Man" in yet another guise), pits misers and spendthrifts, many of them priests, against one another. The Styx itself, a filthy marsh, forms the Fifth Circle and also a moat for the City of Dis, as well as the boundary between Upper and Lower Hell. In the swamp, the angry tear at one another, while under the mud the slothful and sullen gurgle incoherently.

The poets are ferried by Phlegyas across the Styx from the great tower on the upper bank to the City of Dis (or Satan), the capital of Hell and home to the fallen rebel angels—who will not permit the poets to enter until an angelic messenger forces the gate. All of Lower Hell lies within the walls of this city—really a citadel—guarded by the Furies and Medusa. Immediately beyond the gate is the Sixth Circle of heretics, who burn in fiery graves; in Dante's Inferno, despite its name, the traditional punishment of fire is used only inside the walls of the citadel.

Down a steep slope guarded by the Minotaur, the poets scramble toward the Seventh Circle and the Phlegethon, the river of boiling blood guarded by the Centaurs, one of whom, Nessus, takes them across it. The Seventh Circle, which punishes the sins of Violence, is divided into three rounds, the first being the Phlegethon itself. Immersed in its horrid flow are the murderous: warmongers, tyrants, predators, gang members, psychopaths. The next round, guarded by Harpies, is the Wood of Suicides (perhaps Dante's eeriest conception), while at the wood's edge are the wastrels. Then comes the Burning Plain of usurers, blasphemers, and homosexuals, which the poets can cross only by following the bank of the paved conduit along which the end branch of the Phlegethon flows to a great waterfall at the edge of a cliff.

The monster Geryon flies them down the cliff's edge to the most elaborate circle of them all, and the beginning of a new and final set of sins, those of Fraudulence and Malice. Malebolge is shaped like a great stone amphitheater with a spokelike series of stone bridges leading down to a central well over ten concentric ditches or *bolge*. Each *bolgia* holds a group of sinners: in the first, horned demons chivy pimps in one direction and seducers in another. In the second, flatterers wallow in excrement; in the third, corrupt ecclesiastics, including at least one pope, are plunged upside down into something resembling a baptismal font while their feet are "baptized" with flames. False prophets and soothsayers trudge through the fourth with their heads twisted entirely around so that their tears flow down to their buttocks; Tiresias, sadly demoted from his position in the *Odyssey,* is here.

The Wood of the Suicides, by Gustave Doré

William Blake put fossils of human bones into the stone of the bridges over the bolge.

At the fifth *bolgia,* Dante introduces us to the Malebranche ("Evil-Claws"), a band of antic devils like those of the mystery plays who athletically and almost playfully toss "barrators"—grafters and public swindlers—into boiling pitch. The mood turns to grotesque comedy, and Canto XXI ends with a traditional fart.

Dante chose to inject comic relief at this particular point because this is his own *bolgia:* back on earth, he had been exiled from Florence on the grounds of barratry, or political corruption, as well as on vaguer charges of intrigue and hostility to the pope. Grim burlesque is his response to the charges, and it is no accident that the next *bolgia* holds the hypocrites with whom he must actually consort.

The poets find that the bridge over the sixth *bolgia* has been broken by the earthquake that followed the Harrowing. In order to escape the angry Malebranche, they must slide down the rubble into the realm of the hypocrites, who shuffle in single file, weeping from the weary weight of their

139

The poets escape from demons down a broken bridge, by Gustave Doré.

lead-lined cloaks. Arduously, the two climb up the ruins on the other bank to regain the bridge, from which they look down to see the amazing shape-shifting in the seventh *bolgia,* where thieves and reptiles merge and remerge.

Deceivers burn in flames in the eighth *bolgia:* among them is Ulysses —Dante was firmly on Virgil's Trojan (and Italian) side when it came to the great war, and Ulysses was known for his trickery. In the ninth *bolgia* are the sowers of discord, horribly mutilated by a demon with a sword. Among them is Mohamet the "infidel," a heretic from Dante's point of view. This *bolgia* is twenty-two miles around; the cone is narrowing severely. The tenth and last *bolgia,* where the falsifiers (impersonators, perjurers, counterfeiters, alchemists) lie stricken with horrible diseases, is only eleven miles around and half a mile wide.

In the well at the bottom of the Malebolge construction stand the Giants, each about fifty feet high, Dante's Titans of Tartarus. Here they guard the Pit, their heads and torsos protruding above it. Antaeus lowers the poets in his huge palm to a point about midway down the Ninth Circle.

Three rings around the center of Cocytus, the icebound lake that is the realm of Treason, hold traitors. Caina (named for Cain) holds those who betrayed their families; Antenora, traitors to their countries (Antenor, who supposedly betrayed Troy, was a hero to Homer, but Dante sided with Virgil and the Trojans). Ptolomea is for traitors to guests: Ptolomy was a captain of Jericho who arranged a banquet for his father-in-law, Simon the high priest, and his two sons, then murdered them. In the absolute center—of the Inferno and of the earth—is Judecca (from Judas, of course), for traitors to their lords, and in its center is the greatest traitor to the greatest Lord: Dis (Satan) himself, frozen fast and mindlessly weeping as he devours the shades of Judas Iscariot, Brutus, and Cassius. It is up his hairy thigh that the poets must climb to find their exit to clean air and starlight.

Dante's portrait of Dis or Satan is both conventional and original. Vision literature tended to avoid Satan or offer only a quick thrilling glimpse, and even if Dante had read *Tundal,* a centipede-like creature would never have suited him. The figure is grotesque enough. It has three faces, red (Judas) in the middle, black on the left (Brutus), yellow on the right (Cassius), and below each is a pair of wings, which fan the freezing wind of Cocytus.

The three heads were inspired by artists' conceptions. Dante, like most of Florence, must have gone to see the spectacular new Last Judgment mosaic on the cupola of the baptistry of the cathedral of San Giovanni, which was completed in 1300, two years before he was banished. Vasari tells us in *Lives of the Artists* (1550) that Dante was a "dear friend" of Giotto, who was also a Florentine. After banishment, he evidently visited the Scrovegni Chapel in Padua, where Giotto completed his famous frescoes around 1307. This chapel was built for Enrico Scrovegni as a penance for the depredations of his father Reginaldo, a blatantly avaricious moneylender who was said to have died screaming for the keys to his strongbox "so that no one can get my money!" Thus, in Heaven (where Giotto also placed himself), the painter shows Enrico respectfully presenting a model of the chapel to the saints. Dante, teasing his friend, retaliated by putting *Papa* Reginaldo in the Seventh Circle of Hell with the usurers; he is the last

Enrico Scrovegni offers his model to the saints. Giotto himself is fifth from the left in the bottom row. Note the dead rising at bottom.

person to whom the poets speak before mounting Geryon to fly to Lower Hell.

Both of these Last Judgments feature bestial Satans with a pair of sinner-swallowing snakes emerging from where their ears should be. In description, the snakes may have seemed more peculiar than poetic, and Dante rearranged the image to parallel the Trinity. Byzantine Last Judgments with their humanoid devils had soul-eating serpents emerging from Satan's throne, a clever way of bringing the Hellmouth into the composition. Both the Florentine cupola and Giotto used that device too; the subsequent excretion of chewed sinners is implied by the seated position. Satan's hairy body developed from the devil suits in mystery plays, which were covered with hair or feathers, which is easy to see in Botticelli's drawings of Dante's Dis. Illustrators quickly gave up on the complicated sets of wings, which go back to biblical descriptions of seraphs, and most show only one pair.

What was new in Dante's literary portrait, though theologically correct and implied by Giotto's beast figure and, arguably, by some vision literature, was Satan as utterly defeated, a blob of mindlessly chewing, weeping, semi-frozen protoplasm, oblivious to the escape of the poets along his own body. Dante's view of Satan is brief, which was traditional in visions, but also artistically wise. When it comes to monsters, the distance from the impressive to the ridiculous is perilously short.

142

The *Inferno* was a sensation as soon as it was circulated and made available to copyists. This was about 1314, while Dante was still working on the later sections of the *Comedy*. Illustrated copies began to appear almost immediately, and the *Inferno*'s enormous influence also extended to public art. The fourteenth century was a great time for cathedral building in Italy, and Last Judgments commissioned for them quickly began to reflect Dante's invention. His purgatorial mountain solved the problem of how to portray Purgatory, but it was his Hell that fascinated artists.

With Dante, the history of Hell entered a new stage. He killed off vision literature altogether, and in a sense he helped to kill off Hell itself by making it possible to think about it in fictional or allegorical terms. He abandoned the old pretense of "truth" in vision literature and invited readers to join him and Virgil in a *story*, an artistic creation by an individual writer looking back with an appreciative and critical eye at the work of other writers. Even a simple soul looking at Nardo di Cione's mural in Florence would understand that it illustrated not a literal Hell but Dante's Hell. Though this was certainly not his intention, Dante made it easier for intellectuals of the Renaissance and the Enlightenment to reject its reality.

Of the three misers watching as the poets prepare to mount Geryon, Reginaldo Scrovegni, usually identified by the pregnant sow on his coat of arms, is in the middle.

From this time forward, the journey portrayed by the *Comedy* also served as a durable interior metaphor. In our post-Freudian age of industrious myth mapping, it is all too easy to see that literary journey to the Land of the Dead, or Hell, or its surrogates are allegories of the individual experiencing "the dark night of the soul" before a spiritual reemergence into starlight. In psychoanalysis, "the modern religion," a patient must explore with his "guide" the deep sources of his unhappiness and inability to follow the true path. Then he must endure the painful Purgatory of examining and challenging his behavior before achieving the relative paradise of mental health. A twelve-step program confronting drug abuse or alcoholism would interpret the downward spiral as the slide into addiction and destructive behavior until an individual has "bottomed out," and can turn on Satan's hairy leg to struggle toward the light; Purgatory is, then, the behavior modification necessary to reach the precarious paradise of sobriety. In the "hero journey" which Joseph Campbell, leaning on Jung, found basic to religious myth and quest adventure, the hero must venture into "the belly of the beast" before undergoing "the road of trials" toward apotheosis.

But this entirely comfortable and pervasive method of modern metaphorical thinking might not exist if Dante had never written the *Comedy*. It gave us a new vocabulary and a wonderfully useful way of looking directly at our spiritual lives.

The High Middle Ages

"R EAL" VISIONS OF HELL STOPPED short with Dante, and fiction, which needed this outlet—for it would be many centuries before realistic fiction was wanted or written—faced with the horrific and eternal Hell outlined and "owned" by the Church, had to turn elsewhere. Dante showed a way to use classical Hades for the purpose, and, accordingly, Virgil's *Aeneid*, which was just at this time being translated into every European language, was eagerly mined by poets in any number of ways.

In Italian epic and chivalric poetry from the fourteenth century into the seventeenth, it became almost de rigueur to feature a trip to Hell in the course of action. Most of these poems, unlike Dante's, were purely secular, and the Hell they explored owed more to Virgil and Ovid than to Christian tradition. There were literally dozens of them. The most successful were Lodovico Ariosto's *Orlando Furioso* (1532) which turned the story of Roland in Charlemagne's war against the Saracens into sheer fantasy and featured the tale of Lydia in Hell, and Torquato Tasso's *Jerusalem Delivered* (1575), about the First Crusade, which deals again with a militaristic war in Heaven, with Satan here called Pluto.

Underworld adventure was not confined to Italy. In France, old legends sent Charles Martel, Charlemagne's grandfather, to Hell, and these were embroidered into romances. In the *History of Charles Martel and His*

145

Successors, which may date back to the twelfth century, Charles sends a scapegrace bastard son along with a magician guide to demand tribute from Lucifer—which is granted! Charles himself then visits Hell to receive homage. The later French *Huon of Auvergne*, the earliest known imitation of Dante, blends his material with Celtic-romance themes. This time Charles sends Huon to Hell so that he can try to seduce Huon's wife. Huon, in the company of Aeneas and William of Orange, engages in an energetic tour of sights and punishments, in the course of which he discovers the truth about Charles Martel's motives. Lucifer agrees to become Charles Martel's vassal and sends tribute: a thousand golden birds, a crown, a ring, a sumptuous litter. The magic litter, of course, carries Charles Martel straight to Hell.

Fairyland was clearly beginning to take over Hell's traditional role. In an English poem called *Sir Orfeo*, written at the end of the thirteenth century but based on the earlier lost *Lai d'Orphee* by Marie de France, Hell simply became "the lond of Faerie," with no explanation offered. It is in this curious hybrid place that the chivalric harper-prince Sir Orfeo (son of King Pluto and "King Iuno") must seek his Dame Heurodis (Eurydice), who has been stolen away by the fairies.

These are courtly medieval fairies who spend their time hunting with hounds, hawking with falcons, and "dauncing in queynt atire." But the poet has not quite forgotten his (or her, with a bow to Marie) sources in Ovid and Virgil, for when Sir Orfeo, posing as a wandering minstrel, gains entrance to the castle courtyard, he sees a fearful collection of "sleepers."

> *Sum strode withouten head,*
> *And sum no arms had,*
> *And sum through the bodi hadde wounde,*
> *And sum lay mad, ybounde,*
> *And sum armed on horse set,*
> *And sum strangled as they ate,*
> *And sum were in water adreynt,*
> *And sum with fire all forschreynt [shriveled],*
> *Wives ther lay on childbedde,*
> *Sum dead and sum awedde [mad];*
> *And wonder many lay there besides,*
> *Right as they slept at their noontides.*

146

And there among them is Heurodis, lying under a tree. Sir Orfeo plays his harp to the fairy king, wins his lady, and leads her back to his own castle for a happy ending.

Clearly, Sir Orfeo could not have gone to the Christian Hell, a frightful place. Fairyland was a necessary alternative.* Signs that Hell and Fairyland were beginning to merge also appear in the prettified pictures in Books of Hours commissioned by the aristocracy and in the *imrams*. In the romance of *Thomas of Erceldoune*, the knight travels with a mysterious lady three days in darkness and then is shown four roads leading to Heaven, Purgatory, Hell—and Fairyland. In the first French "translation" of the *Aeneid* (as the *Roman d'Eneas*) toward the end of the twelfth century, the Sibyl appears as a witch; Aeneas as a feudal knight; and Cerberus as a demon with clawed feet, long arms, and three doglike heads.

The Faerie Queene was the ne plus ultra of high medieval allegorical "tragical-comical-historical-pastoral" romance-epics. Like Dante, Edmund Spenser (c. 1552–1599) looked back to a kind of literature that had already had its day and both summed up and killed off the genre. Dante was avant-garde in using the vernacular, but Spenser's diction was deliberately archaic. He meant to write an English epic in the Italian style, a further mythology of Britain to add to the Arthurian tales. His intended "XII bookes fashioning XII morall vertues" were also to be romantic entertainment for an upper-class audience, which included his fellow poet-knights in the court of Queen Elizabeth, Sir Philip Sidney, and Sir Walter Raleigh. From the point of view of the history of Hell, the most innovative thought in his untidy poem is a new definition of the war between good and evil: Spenser was a Puritan, loyally (and fashionably) anti-Catholic.

Spenser's long allegory takes place in Fairyland, an alternate England ruled by Gloriana, an alternate Queen Elizabeth I, from Cleopolis, an alternate London. Spenser's knights are not quite feudal; they have moved on with the times to become Renaissance courtiers. The Red Cross Knight is a "type" of Christ, thus all the monsters he kills are consciously "types" of Satan. Spenser is almost deliriously lavish with hellish types, which in the England of the time very much included the pope and "papishness." In Canto I, for example, in the Cave of Error is a wonderful monster, half

---

*A fifteenth-century English poem, Henryson's *Tale of Orpheus*, does use "hiddouss hellis house" which Orpheus locates by way of its "stynk rycht odiuss." No escape is possible.

Lithograph for Virgil. Note how cleverly the artist has incorporated Christian imagery: the entire lower right is a huge Hellmouth holding the Eumenides; the Hydra is the Red Dragon; the Sibyl (top left) wears a witch's hat.

woman and half dragon, who when dying "spewd out of her filthy maw" a flood of poison full of old books and papers (Catholic teachings), then her own horrible offspring who lap their mother's poisoned blood until they burst and die. Not exactly subtle allegory.

148

Next Archmiago, who looks like a pious hermit, turns out to be an evil sorcerer, a type of Antichrist complete with attendant demons.

> He bad awake blacke Pluto's griesly Dame,
> And cursed Heaven and spake reprochfull shame
> Of highest God, the Lord of life and light,
> A bold, bad man, that dared to call by name
> Great Gorgon, Prince of darknesse and dead night,
> At which Cocytus quakes, and Styx is put to flight.

The Bower of Bliss is ruled by the enchantress Acrasia (read: Circe); Spenser the poet—as opposed to the moralist—likes this hotbed of wicked lasciviousness and keeps bringing it back. In the House of Pride, Queen Lucifera rides by in a golden chariot drawn by six beasts on which are mounted her Deadly Sin attendants. The witch Duessa, accompanied by Night, descends through the "yawning gulfe of deepe Avernus hole" to Hades, complete with "smoake and sulphure," dreadful Furies, the "bitter waves of Acheron," the fiery flood of Phlegethon, the "house of endlesse paine" with Cerberus on the doorstep. Ixion turns on his wheel, Sisyphus rolls his stone, Tantalus hangs from his tree, Tityus feeds his vulture, the Danaides draw their water, and Aesculapius, the god of medicine (sent to Hell by Boccaccio, not by a classical writer), lies in chains.

The Cave of Despair encourages suicide and leads to another fight with another fiery dragon symbolizing Satan, and most memorably to the Cave of Mammon ("Rich Man") with the underground House of Riches near the gate of Hell attended by allegorical Sins and leading to the Garden of Proserpina where the river Cocytus flows beside a silver chair and a tree laden with golden apples. We know what would happen to anyone who sits in that chair or crunches those apples, and so it seems does the knight Guyon, for he declines hospitality. He peers over the riverbank to see "many damned wights / In those sad waves, which direfully deadly stanke," also Tantalus (again), and Pontius Pilate, endlessly washing his hands.

THE LOW MIDDLE AGES

High-minded allegorical plays and romances are characteristic of the late Middle Ages. So is the lowest kind of folk humor. Most of this was not written down, of course, but it is evident in the Hell scenes of the miracle plays, in the paintings of Pieter Brueghel the Elder, and some of his Flemish followers, and most emphatically in the writings of Rabelais.

Historians estimate that, added together, various festivals took up as much as three months of the late medieval year. Some of them were *festa fatuorum* or "feasts of fools," which were celebrated by both scholastics and lower clerics on certain holidays: St. Stephen's Day (December 26) through New Year's Day, as well as before Lent, at Halloween, and on certain saints' days that varied from town to town. The entire point of these holidays with their noisy charivari parades was loss of dignity, drunkenness, crude abuse of the sacred, a grotesque reversal of the class orders, which were far more stratified in medieval times than in ours. Thus it was permitted, even obligatory, to mock all that was ordinarily feared or revered—Hell and its denizens are still indispensable to this kind of celebration, even if we recognize them only subconsciously.

By the beginning of the seventeenth century, festival Hell parades had become so obstreperous and profane that they frequently led to violence, and religious plays were forbidden everywhere in Europe—except in Catholic countries when presented by the Jesuits, an order founded in 1540, or by other monks. But the role that this kind of festive excitement played in relieving social stress was too essential to abandon. Instead of disappearing, Merry Hell went secular. First came the Dance of Death, a curious manifestation of morbidity meeting allegory and revelry at the end of the Middle Ages: Death and his costumed followers pulled members of the audience into their antic parade. Then came the harlequins.

Herlequin was first a pagan Germanic demon. In France, he became the leader of an army of demons that supposedly rode through the night on the "wild hunt"—England knew him as Herne the Hunter and Germany as the Erlkönig ("the Elf-King"). He appeared on stage at least as early as the thirteenth century as Herlekin Croquesot in *Le Jeu de la Feuillée* ("The Leaf Game") by Adam de la Halle, the oldest French secular drama. As Arlecchino in Italy, he became part of the group of *zanni* or zany improvisational street performers with comical names and rude manners who took over when "religious" devils were banned. Another was Pulcinella (Polichinelle, Petroushka, Punch). After a career in the eighteenth-century puppet theater, Harlequin joined the commedia dell'arte, acquired effete manners and a distinctive costume, and eventually spun off into the street mime who makes a pest of himself today in malls and public parks.

There were written parodies featuring a comic Hell, too. *Saint Pierre et le Jongleur* comes from thirteenth-century France. A jongleur was the kind of street entertainer who would have played a comic devil. After death, this one goes to Hell. While Lucifer and the demons are out gathering souls, he gets into a gambling match with Saint Peter, who wins all the souls in Hell. Lucifer is furious when he returns, throws the juggler out of Hell, and swears never to admit another one. A *Salut d'Enfer* ("Salute to Hell") from about the same period describes all the dishes served at the hall of the demon Tervegan—more roast heretic.

Like Harlequin and Punch, Gargantua and Pantagruel were originally stage demons, and *Gargantua and Pantagruel*, the book that chronicles their adventures is written entirely in the spirit of foolery, a celebration of obscenity, scatology, drunkenness, and the more enjoyable of the Seven Deadly Sins. Because their humor, like most comedy, is highly topical, they are heavy going today. They are just as excessive as *The Faerie Queene*, but one is all courtly artifice, the other all deliberate vulgarity. The fact that François Rabelais (c. 1495–1553), first a Franciscan monk, then a Benedictine, then a medical doctor, got away with them is a sign that times were changing. He is said to have had friends in high places, which is probably why he escaped punishment stronger than censure.

Considering the comic possibilities, Rabelais's Hell is disappointing, even dull. His Roman model was not Virgil or Ovid but Lucian, which turned his Hell into a one-joke academic satire. In the *Menippus*, Lucian showed the philosophers exalted in the afterlife, while kings like Xerxes and Alexander were debased. Rabelais extended the image to a long list of public figures, starting with Alexander (cobbling shoes) and Xerxes (selling mustard) and running through classical history and mythology, the Arthur tales and other romances, the succession of popes, and so forth. The only new torment Rabelais devised for them was syphilis. And there is a great deal of pissing in his Hell.

PEOPLE BEGAN to collect sayings and folklore at the end of the Middle Ages. Brueghel's paintings of proverbs and children's games reflect this interest, as do his illustrations of the Seven Deadly Sins and of Hell. Given the huge amount of infernal material lying about, it should come as no surprise that someone tried to categorize it. The first infernologist's name was Reginald le Queux, and his book, *Baratre Infernel,* dates from 1480.

In it, he attempted to do just what is being done here, to bring pagan and Christian sources together with liberal quotes from each, to describe the inmates of Hell and the sights to be seen there, and to draw conclusions from this material. First he names sixty-two ancient sources, "moral, satyric, elegaic, genealogic, theologic, historic, philosophic and mythologic." The names of fifty Christian writers and ten biblical or apocryphal books follow. His exempla include *Tundal* and the visions of Charles the Fat among many others, and his table of contents is enormous.

FLEMISH PAINTERS AND AN ITALIAN

Jan van Eyck (c. 1390–c. 1441) was the first master of the Flemish school of art which flourished in the fifteenth and sixteenth centuries, and it is his *Last Judgment* that so brilliantly illustrates the point at which conventional images of Hell began to yield to those of Death—or to new and unconventional images. Roger van der Weyden, Dieric Bouts, and Hans Memling painted memorable, even beautiful scenes of Hell for altarpieces. But it is Bosch who moved far beyond convention.

Hieronymus Bosch (c. 1460–1516) is one of the handful of truly original creators of Hell. A Last Judgment altarpiece painted on three wooden panels, as was the custom in the late fifteenth century, would have a Hell on its right-hand panel to balance Heaven or Eden on the left, but in Bosch's triptychs, Hell tended insidiously to take over the entire composition.

Bosch lived in the provincial Flemish town of 's-Hertogenbosch, from which he took his name (the family name was van Aken). It is in the present Netherlands near the Belgian border and the Rhine and was one of the thriving middle-class towns that had begun to make the Middle Ages obsolete. At this point, it was still very much under the control of the medieval Church, and Bosch and most of his family were members of the Brotherhood of Our Lady, one of many religious groups devoted to the Virgin. His grandfather, his father, and at least three of his four uncles were painters, and so was his brother Goosen, though their paintings have been lost except for a town fresco perhaps by his grandfather. He married a woman with money of her own sometime between 1479 and 1481. That is all that is known about his life aside from the dates of some of his commissions.

The paintings, which have so intrigued and puzzled art historians, may seem more comprehensible to those who have persevered through the history of Hell. Whether or not Bosch could read, he was a man of his times, and in those times Hell included a rich tradition of visions, allegorical fantasies, chivalric parodies, myth and folklore, anticlericalism, grotesquerie, scatology, and tomfoolery. This mix is what Bosch painted, trying variants over and over again. Hell clearly interested him more than any other subject: even in his Edens, rebel angels fall from the skies while tiny murders—a mouse, a frog, a deer—occur. In one center panel, his hay-wain lurches toward Hell with a demon atop it; in his Vienna *Last Judgment* the center panel seems to be of Purgatory; the *Garden of Earthly Delights* resembles Venusberg or the mythical Land of Cockaigne more than a conventional terrestrial paradise.

But again and again we see familiar landmarks. Demons roast their victims on spits and fry them in pans on the shores of the river Slith while victims skate along it. Tundal's cow crosses the bridge of the *Hay-wain* Hell, and Tundal's bird devours and excretes sinners in the *Garden* Hell. Pots and pans and kitchenware remind us of the connection with cooks and bakers; together with musical instruments they suggest its "dyn." We can make out the Seven Deadly Sins with their punishments. The architecture is familiar: round ovens, furnaces, doors suggestive of Hellmouth. The demons and tortures are more varied and imaginative than anything we have seen yet, but they are not radically different. Like Dante, Bosch took old material and made it his own. (There is no indication that he knew Dante's work; his sources are all Northern.)

Like Dante's, Bosch's innovations were successful. The printing press had been invented but the photograph had not, and those who knew his work were only those who happened to come across it; luckily for posterity, these included some powerful patrons. Queen Isabella of Spain owned three of his paintings at her death in 1504; at that time the Netherlands was ruled by Spain. Cardinal Grimani of Venice owned Bosch paintings, probably the *Paradise* and *Hell* now in the Doges Palace. Bosch's most avid collector, however, was Philip II of Spain (1527–1598), who set about acquiring works already owned by other people. Philip was an unpleasant man, a fanatic Catholic, infamous not only as the husband of "Bloody Mary" of England

The Harrowing of Hell, *by Pieter Brueghel the Elder*

but for having presided over the most abhorrent excesses of the Inquisition. His enthusiasm for Bosch's work is responsible for the generous collections at Lisbon, the Escorial, and the Prado.

This attention did not go unnoticed in Flanders. So the gentry wanted devilry? Then that's what they would get, agreed the painters who centered around Antwerp and Brussels. And so they went to work, among them Jan Mandyn, Pieter Huys, Pieter Brueghel (c. 1525–1569) and his sons Jan and Pieter. (The latter was nicknamed "Hell" for the sheer profusion of Hellscapes he turned out.)

The best of them was Brueghel the Elder, who brought humor to the Seven Deadly Sins and bustling energy to the *Fall of the Rebel Angels* (1562). His most eerie painting is not of Hell but of Doomsday in *The Triumph of Death*, with ranks of marching skeletons representing the forces of Gog and Magog, while Death on a pale horse pulls a wagonload of skulls. But *Dulle Griet* (c. 1534) is even more original. Brueghel's best-known works often depict folk sayings and proverbs, and this painting illustrates a humorously misogynistic aphorism about a wife so fierce that she could plunder the mouth of Hell and return unmarked. Dulle Griet ("Furious

21. This unusual *Last Judgment*, painted c.1440 by Jan van Eyck, marks a period when many painters were beginning to replace Satan with Death, represented by a skeleton. The bestial demons look forward to Bosch.

22–23. AT LEFT: Hans Memling (c.1430–1494) and (opposite page) Dieric Bouts (c.1410–1475) both painted memorable altar panels of Hell. Note that there are demons but no Satans in Flemish painting.

24–27. Hieronymus Bosch's Hells began relatively "normally" but progressed into strangeness. In the *Hay-Wain* Hell (opposite, left), note Tundal's cow and the icy river. In the *Garden of Earthly Delights* Hell (opposite, right), the knives mark the river as the Slith. Tundal's bird takes Satan's place.

28–29. Two examples of Pieter Brueghel the Elder's vigorous approach to diablerie. ABOVE: The rebel angels change to beasts and goblins in midair. Even here there is no Satan, unless he is attached to the tentacles on Michael's right. BELOW: Dulle Griet frightens even the demons at the gates of Hell.

30–31. ABOVE: Herri met de Bles, or Il Civetta, was a sixteenth-century follower of Bosch, and perhaps the round shape echoes his *Purgatory*. BELOW: Jan Brueghel (1568–1625), son of Pieter the Elder, painted this all-purpose *Orpheus,* which combines elements of Hells past.

32. Even Peter Paul Rubens (1577–1640), foremost of the later Flemish painters, essayed *The Damned* in a very different treatment.

Gretel") wears armor, brandishes a giant cooking spoon, carries a market basket and a bag of loot, and seems utterly unmoved by the demonic activity around her.

The Brueghel sons were less original and more opportunistic. Jan Brueghel's *Orpheus* throws elements from every school of painting together: Renaissance nudity, Boschian grotesquerie, his father's humor. It is an all-purpose Hellscape.

Unlike Bosch who spent his life at it, or the Brueghels who looked to the market, Michelangelo Buonarroti (1475–1564) painted Hell only once. His *Last Judgment*, on the wall of the Sistine Chapel in the Vatican, is one of the most famous paintings in the world, however, and his Hell, though far from the dominant element, is unforgettable.

Michelangelo was the brightest jewel of the most glittering era of the Italian Renaissance. During his long life he always considered himself a sculptor rather than a painter, but not only did he excel at both, he also designed the dome of St. Peter's in Rome. Though the many triumphs of his long life must go unrecorded here, it may be useful to know that although Michelangelo was certainly a Christian and is thought to have become more interested in spiritual things as he grew older, he was also devoted to the ideas of Plato, which he had studied as a youth in the gardens of Lorenzo de' Medici. Certainly the spirit of classical Greece informs all of his work, including the Sistine *Last Judgment*.

The Last Judgment, *by Pieter Brueghel the Elder*

Michelangelo had completed the ceiling and vault of the Sistine Chapel during the years from 1508 to 1512, a grueling marathon that compelled him to lie on a scaffold, face upwards, for long, uncomfortable sessions of work. He was not pleased when, in 1534, Pope Clement VII summoned him back. The great end wall above the Sistine altar was at that time covered with frescoes by Perugino, but the pope wanted a Last Judgment, and he insisted that Michelangelo paint it. There was no way to refuse, although he was nearly sixty. Clement soon died, but his successor Paul III was equally adamant. The great fresco took seven years to complete. Instead of placing his own portrait among the saved, as Giotto had done in the Scrovegni Chapel, Michelangelo, with mordant irony, painted himself, ex-

The detail from Michelangelo's Last Judgment *that shows a sinner realizing for the first time that he really is, finally and irrevocably, going to Hell is one of the most famous images in Western art.*

hausted and limp, in the flayed skin of St. Bartholomew who holds it, according to medieval custom, as an attribute of his martyrdom.

Even when the painting was finished, his trials were not over, for the pope listened to the carping of one of his assistants, Biagio da Cesena, and ordered Michelangelo to cover the genitals of his great male nudes. He refused to do it. Instead, he angrily painted Biagio's not very attractive face on Minos in Hell. When Biagio protested, Paul III replied, "Had the painter sent you to Purgatory, I would use my best efforts to get you released; but I exercise no influence in Hell; there you are beyond redemption." Later, his successor, Pope Paul IV, had the necessary work done by another painter, Daniele da Volterra. Even in the massive cleaning effort of the 1990s these superimposed G-strings and diapers were not removed: the Vatican claimed that after so much time it was impossible.

Michelangelo dispensed with the usual supernatural accoutrements of halos and wings—the only wing in the painting seems rather mysteriously attached to Charon's boat, or perhaps to a creature under it. Demons and angels are humanoid and fully sexed (they were, one should say), though the demons have asses' ears or small horns, and Minos has a serpentine tail. One conventional beast-demon attacks perhaps the most famous figure in the painting—other than that of the virile and implacable Jesus—that of the man who has realized for the first time that he is really going to Hell.

Swirling through the picture are the four rivers of paradise, here rivers of air which, on the left (our right), flow seamlessly into the Styx, with the burning Phlegethon beyond. Hell proper is not in the picture; this is the borderland. The ovenlike structure in which sinners burn at the middle bottom represents Purgatory, from which some few are beginning to be rescued.

The Reformation

DISCONTENT WITH THE CHURCH SWELLED after the twelfth century, despite repression. The perceived corruption, ignorance, hypocrisy, and complacency of much of the clergy distressed people with genuine religious convictions; the blatant sale of indulgences rankled. The great wealth of the monasteries, their huge holdings of untaxed land (between a third and a half of Europe), and their insistence on tribute, their right to interfere politically and to have their own courts of canon law exasperated the secular princes. The growth of middle-class mercantile towns made the feudal system with its autocratic hierarchical structure increasingly obsolete. In the fourteenth century, there were two popes, sometimes three simultaneously, which encouraged contempt for the office. The savagery of the Inquisition outraged people of sensibility even in an age when a public burning was entertainment for the masses, and heretics, Jews, lepers, and—soon—witches were considered fair game.

The invention of the printing press in the middle of the fifteenth century aided protest immeasurably. The Church had long held it heretical for a layman to read the Bible even in Latin, let alone in translation. Copies of translations had, however, been quietly circulating since the thirteenth century, and, though the Church tried to burn them (and the translators, too, when it could catch them), presses made the task hopeless. Moreover, new books with fresh ideas soon began to circulate to a larger reading public.

158

The first best-selling author of the new age was Desiderius Erasmus of Rotterdam (c. 1466–1536), whose books sold by the hundreds of thousands. A graceful writer and a profound humanist, he foresaw the breakup of the medieval Church—which he satirized in *The Praise of Folly* (1511)—but not the bloodbath that would accompany it. Erasmus argued for Plato and against Aristotelian Scholastic metaphysics and theological formulas— "They calculate time to be spent in Purgatory down to the year, month, day and hour as if it were a jar that could be measured accurately with a mathematical formula . . . they draw exact pictures of every part of Hell as if they had spent years in the place!"—and against such commercial ventures of the Church as paid indulgences, pilgrimages, masses for the dead, and other financial means to salvation. He advocated close attention to the Bible itself and peaceful moral reform based on reason and intellectual liberation. It seems entirely fitting that just before he died he was preparing a new edition of Origen, whose work, suppressed for centuries, was beginning to be read again. His critics, looking back at the appalling sixteenth-century slaughter in the name of religion, assailed him for his moderation, which they took to be lack of conviction. If only Erasmus had taken the lead, they believed, the wicked old Church might have been reformed harmoniously and kept its unity, and a century of pogrom, persecution, and massacre might have been avoided.

Instead, the leader of the age turned out to be the monk Martin Luther (1483–1546), a man of passionate intensity. The colorful, eloquent tin-miner's son, who gambled his life against his principles when he nailed his ninety-five theses against indulgences to the door of the Wittenberg church in 1517, was a very different kind of champion. His goals were not dissimilar to those of Erasmus: down with Scholasticism, back to the Bible, away with indulgences and other corruptions. But he did not consider accommodation possible. He was a man of enormous energy and will who believed himself to have been called to the monastery and then to his reformist mission directly by God. To appeal directly to the people and the German princes against the Church, as he did, was extremely dangerous. But he had faith in his destiny.

In the monastery, Luther studied Augustine and became convinced that the scholars of the Middle Ages, particularly the Scholastics in their admiration for Aristotle, had strayed from the path. The idea that struck him most forcefully from his reading was that of predestination. Only God

159

could elect men to salvation or damnation, Luther understood Augustine to say. Therefore the entire structure of Church interference in the afterlife was false and had been concocted by bad men for no other end than greed. He quickly came to "regard the see of Rome as possessed by Satan and as the throne of Antichrist."

Luther threw out Purgatory and all that went with it, including the Virgin as intercessor and deity. His Hell was Augustine's, dire and eternal, constructed by an omnipotent God to punish the wicked. No one would be saved but by God's grace, and there was no way to influence the outcome—good works were only an indication of grace and had no effect in themselves; prayers for the dead were useless. The Devil was God's servant, created by him and destined by him to fall. Like one of the old desert fathers, Luther believed himself to be plagued by demons and, like a proper medieval man, he associated them with his bowels—he evidently had severe problems with both flatulence and constipation. Luther also believed in witches and their pact with the Devil, which explains why the Protestant record on the sorry subject of witch-hunts is worse, if possible, than the Catholic.

John Calvin (1509–1564), the second leader of the Reformation, was born in France but is associated with Geneva, his main base. He came into contact with Luther's ideas when he was still a student and became a convert in his early twenties. He agreed with Luther's principles but went much further with regard to predestination. From the beginning of time, Calvin thought, God's preordained plan has been in effect. "Some men and angels," as the Cambridge Calvinists would write in the mid-seventeenth century, "are predestinated unto everlasting life, and others foreordained to everlasting death." Thus, Christ did not die for all men but only for the elect. Satan acts at God's command to punish the wicked. Prayers, good works, deathbed repentances, and absolutions cannot change inexorable fate. Even Calvin admitted that "double predestination" was harsh. Nevertheless, it was a logically consistent position, given God's all-knowing omnipotence.

Luther and Calvin together with the Swiss Huldreich Zwingli (1484–1531), the third leader of the Reformation, rejected Purgatory, but conceded to a Limbo for unbaptized babies and an interim state between death and the Final Judgment. During this time the elect would go to Abraham's bosom, Calvin thought, and

The lot of the reprobate is doubtless the same as that which Jude assigns to the devils: to be held in chains until they are dragged to the punishment appointed for them.

About resurrection, the Devil, and eternal Hell, they had no doubts. A reform group called the Anabaptists who had been thinking along the lines of Origen about universal pardon were condemned by both Luther and the Catholics, and doubly persecuted. On the other hand, Jacobus Arminius (1560–1609) proposed "conditional predestination," by which those who freely chose to believe in Jesus were thought to have been predestined to salvation. Arminianism was doctrinally suspect, but it crept into and eventually dominated Protestant thinking; nearly all Protestantism today is more or less Arminian.

By the middle of the seventeenth century, the religious wars were finally over. Hardly a European country had been untouched, including Switzerland, which put the matter of religion to the vote of the citizens. Italy, perhaps because its cultural renaissance happened early, because it was closely connected with the classical antiquity which had revived such interest, or because the old papal hierarchy had close family links to the Italian aristocracy, remained Catholic, though there were reformist rumblings in Venice and Florence and some emigration to Protestant Switzerland. The Inquisition kept Spain in line, and Portugal and Ireland remained Catholic, as did Austria, Eastern Europe, and, uneasily, France.

All the Scandinavian countries adopted Lutheranism as a state religion, and by the mid-sixteenth century it was legalized in Germany, which remains about half Protestant, divided between Lutherans and Calvinists. Switzerland followed Calvin, as did Scotland, led by John Knox (1505–1572) who adopted the French Huguenot "presbyterianism." Philip II's attempt to impose the Inquisition on the Netherlands led to a bitter struggle that split them apart, leaving Holland Protestant and Belgium Catholic.

In England, Henry VIII (1491–1547) initiated the break with Rome for reasons of politics, not faith, and his Church of England was intended to be "the papacy without the pope." He burned heretics who subscribed to newfangled Protestant ideas and beheaded bishops who indicated uneasiness about the unity of church and state. He dissolved the monasteries and seized their land and goods. He encouraged an authorized English Bible and a vernacular Book of Common Prayer purged of Catholic "idolatry," but sturdily upholding the old values. His son, Edward VI, continued Henry's policies, and though "Bloody Mary" made notorious efforts to return the country to Catholicism, she was too late.

England's great fortune was Elizabeth I's long reign (1558–1603). The queen seemed to understand the twin arts of negotiation and compromise with an inherent skill alien to most of her fellow rulers. The Church of England continued as the state religion with Elizabeth herself as "Supreme Governor" in spiritual matters. (The term was chosen to avoid offense to those who could not countenance a woman as "Head.") Catholics were fined but not persecuted, nor were John Knox's Scottish Presbyterians, who rejected the mass and papal authority in 1560, a year after the English parliament had done so. In ordinary parlance, the Elizabethan Age is synonymous with the English Renaissance, and fortune seems to have doubly smiled upon England in giving it so reasonable a ruler at so critical a time.

The glory of the Elizabethan period is its dramatic literature, especially the plays of William Shakespeare (1564–1616). It may seem mildly surprising that Shakespeare never attempted the subject of Heaven and Hell, but in fact he was forbidden to do so. The old miracle drama had fallen victim to its own rowdiness and was forbidden nearly everywhere by mid-century. The last miracle play performed in England was at Coventry in 1584, and apparently the very last straw for the English parliament was the presentation of Marlowe's *Tragicall Historie of Doctor Faustus* about 1589. There is evidence for twenty-three performances of the play between 1594 and 1597, but by decree there were to be no more plays of this sort. Religious plays, until only a few years earlier the sole form of popular theater, were banned in Britain at exactly the moment Shakespeare started his career (1589), and it remained up to him and his fellow Elizabethans to construct a new form of popular secular entertainment. Secular drama up to this time had been pedantic and artificial and played to an exclusive upper-class audience.

Doctor Faustus could thus be called a pivot of the age. It was a controversial play, and its author, Christopher Marlowe (1564–1593), was a controversial young man. His enemies accused him of atheism, blasphemy, espionage, and immorality (homosexuality), and very likely all the counts were true. He was the son of a shoemaker, a trade-guild member who could afford to send his son, with scholarship aid, to Cambridge. Though misdemeanors nearly cost him his degree, the Crown itself intervened in

162

his defense—Master Marlowe, it seemed, had neglected his studies "in matters touching the benefit of his country"—and the degree was granted in 1584. He went on to get an M.A. three years later. It is thought that he had been sent to Rheims for a few months to spy on the Jesuits, and university authorities may have feared his conversion to Catholicism; English Catholics of this period could attend universities but could not take degrees.

As a playwright, Marlowe was immediately successful. With *Tamburlaine* (c. 1587), produced when he was twenty-three, he created a strong hero and the sonorous rolling language of "Marlovian" blank verse. But his most famous play is *Doctor Faustus*.

It is based on a 1587 German book, the *Historia von Dr. Johan Fausten*, translated into English by "P.F., Gent." in 1592, but Marlowe's play is thought to date back to 1589. P. F.'s title, *The Historie of the Damnable Life and Deserved death of Doctor John Faustus, Newly imprinted and in convenient places amended . . .* , implies that there was an earlier edition, now lost. It is usually referred to as the Faustbook.

The story of the philosopher who sells his soul to the Devil is an old one, and in Christian legend goes back to Simon Magus of Samaria, the first-century Gnostic sorcerer who was baptized by the apostle Philip (Acts 8.5) and is often pictured magically flying in the Roman Forum before Peter caused him to fall, break his head, and die, according to the second-century apocryphal *Acts of Peter*. Helen was the name of the ex-prostitute who traveled with him, and Simon claimed that she was Helen of Troy reincarnated (as well as Sophia, Eve, Mrs. Noah, and Mary Magdalene); this is how Helen first got into the story, where she has nearly always remained. Simony, the sale or barter of sacred things, was named for Simon Magus, and since to Protestants the Roman Catholic sale of indulgences and benefices was sheer simony, his name was much invoked during the religious wars. Simon was the epitome of the "false prophet" and considered to be the father of all Christian heresy. Dante placed him far down in the Eighth Circle, and he was regarded as a "type" of the Antichrist—at this time the common Protestant epithet for the pope.

A story beloved in the Middle Ages and frequently illustrated was the history of Theophilis, supposedly the church deacon of a Turkish town called Ardana. After a new bishop dismissed him, Theophilis went to a Jewish sorcerer to contact the Devil, with whom he signed a pact in his

Theophilis, from a thirteenth-century French manuscript. The demon is obviously an actor in a devil suit and mask.

own blood: his soul in exchange for success and wealth. These he achieved, but his conscience plagued him. He tried and failed to rebargain with the Devil. While praying to the Virgin, he fell asleep and dreamed that she appeared carrying the deed of his pact. She told him that she had descended to Hell and seized it herself from the Devil, and that Theophilis was pardoned. He woke to find the deed beside him, made a confession, and died in peace. This was the most famous of dozens of rescue tales pitting the Virgin against the Devil.

A real Doctor Faustus received a B.A. from Heidelberg in 1509. One story about him is supposedly historically confirmed: when in prison he

164

offered to show the chaplain how to remove hair from his face and tonsure without a razor in return for free wine. The wine arrived, and Faustus gave the chaplain a salve of arsenic, which removed not only his hair but his skin. Apparently, this sadistic humorist set up shop as an astrologer, alchemist, magician, and "philosopher," a job description that fits all the figures we now think of as early Renaissance scientists: Nicolaus Copernicus (1473–1543), John Dee (1527–1608), Tycho Brahe (1546–1601), Giordano Bruno (c. 1548–1600), Francis Bacon (1561–1626), Galileo Galilei (1564–1642), Johannes Kepler (1571–1630). Well into the seventeenth century, Newton studied alchemy, and, a century later, so did Goethe.

Secular inquiry was a bugbear to the Catholics as Scholastic learning was to the Protestants. It was easy to believe that all learned men were somehow in partnership with the Devil in pursuit of "forbidden" knowledge—we in the nuclear age should not be quick to scoff, and we should keep in mind, too, that the first great wave of witch-hunts swept across Europe from about 1590 to 1620. The notion of pacts with the Devil, or with demonic figures, as in *Macbeth*, was very much in the air when Marlowe was writing *Doctor Faustus*.

Edward Alleyn as Doctor Faustus

The Faust book gathered the many legends that had accrued to the infamous German doctor into a jumble; the reason Marlowe's play is so untidy in the middle is that he followed it closely. He started a tradition here too; all the major works in the long Faust tradition are untidy. (Even smaller ones like *The Picture of Dorian Gray* have muddled middles—one prime attribute of Hell, after all, is chaos.)

Mephostophilis is Marlowe's spelling for the Faust book's new character, "a servant to great Lucifer," exactly as Satan was the worldly agent to the Yahweh of the Old Testament. It's a made-up word that may mean "Not-light-lover," from the Greek; the more common Mephisto leans toward the Latin *mephitus*, "stinking." Marlowe's Devil is grave, ironic, even melancholy, though at times he is attended by traditional capering imps. He may owe something to Rabelais's Panurge ("Make-all," a play on the Gnostic Demiurge), an elegant, sophisticated magician. He is neither a tempter nor a liar but instead is starkly blunt about both his own fate and that of Faustus, who, in his skeptical "scientific" way, believes in neither the soul nor Hell. If there is an afterlife, Faustus cheerfully opts for the classical one:

> *This word "damnation" terrifies not me,*
> *For I confound Hell in Elysium.*
> *My ghost be with the old philosophers.*

Nevertheless, he is curious. He catechizes Mephostophilis:

FAUSTUS: And what are you that live with Lucifer?

MEPHOSTOPHILIS: Unhappy spirits that fell with Lucifer,
Conspired against our God with Lucifer,
And are forever damned with Lucifer.

FAUSTUS: Where are you damned?

MEPHOSTOPHILIS: In Hell.

FAUSTUS: How comes it then that thou art out of Hell?

MEPHOSTOPHILIS: Why, this is Hell, nor am I out of it.
Think'st thou that I that saw the face of God
And tasted the eternal joys of Heaven,

Am not tormented with ten thousand Hells
In being deprived of everlasting bliss?

And again:

FAUSTUS: Tell me, where is the place that men call Hell?

MEPHOSTOPHILIS: Under the heavens.

FAUSTUS: Ay, so are all things; but whereabouts?

MEPHOSTOPHILIS: Within the bowels of these elements,
Where we are tortured and remain forever.
Hell hath no limits, nor is circumscrib'd
In one self place, but where we are is Hell.
And where Hell is there must we ever be.
And to be short, when all the world dissolves,
And every creature shall be purified,
All places shall be Hell that is not Heaven. . . .

And:

FAUSTUS: Think'st thou that Faustus is so fond to imagine
That after this life there is any pain?
No, these are trifles and mere old wives' tales.

MEPHOSTOPHILIS: But Faustus, I am an instance to prove the contrary,
For I tell thee I am damned, and now in Hell.

FAUSTUS: How? Now in Hell?
Nay, and this be Hell, I'll willingly be damned here.
What! Sleeping, eating, walking and disputing?

Mephostophilis is not trying to make the Gnostic point that this earth is Hell, though that is how Faustus chooses to take it. Instead, he employs the old differentiation between *poena sensus* and *poena damni*, cleverly twisting it to explain how a devil condemned to Hell can continue to operate on earth: he suffers the searing pain of deprivation rather than physical torment. Marlowe, who had a better education than the author of the Faustbook, knew that as a Protestant he was permitted the distinction; Catholics, having gained Purgatory, were not. In the end, of course, Faustus is doomed to an actual physical Hell to suffer a melodramatic *poena sensus*. The audience expected no less.

Lucifer, Beelzebub, and Mephostophilis arrive in thunder to watch Faustus's last struggle. The good and bad angels that commonly quarrel for the soul in medieval deathbed miniature paintings arrive, but the good angel relinquishes its claim. A curtain is whisked away to uncover the dreadful Hellmouth.

Faustus's last desperate soliloquy, the one that begins "O Faustus/ Now hast thou one bare hour to live," is famous as a challenge to actors, and Edward Alleyn, for whom it was written, probably tore up the stage with it. But, aside from its powerful verse, it contains some subtle thinking. Faust's story is different from that of Theophilis—for him there can be no rescue, not because of the degree of his sin but because Protestantism does not permit intercession. Because his damnation is preordained (though seemingly freely chosen), there is no escape from "the heavy wrath of God." He calls to Christ with some of the most beautiful lines ever written:

> O, I'll leap up to my God! Who pulls me down?
> See, see where Christ's blood streams in the firmament!
> One drop of blood will save me, O my Christ—
> Rend not my heart for naming of my Christ!
> Yet will I call on him—O spare me, Lucifer—

But Lucifer has already warned Faustus that a deathbed repentance is useless in a Protestant system where mercy cannot temper justice:

> Christ cannot save thy soul, for he is just,
> There's none but I have interest in the same.

Neither his heartbroken pleading nor the Pythagorean philosophy he invokes can mitigate eternity or save Faustus from being torn limb from limb by shrieking devils inside the Hellmouth. The drop of blood refers elegantly to the drop of water for which Dives begged Abraham.*

---

*This long speech, though right on target theologically, was directly responsible, I am convinced, for the final banning of religious drama in Britain. It was simply too incendiary for the times. Not until 1616 did a devil (not counting—possibly—Hamlet's father) appear again upon the English stage, and then only in a light comedy of Ben Jonson's (*The Devil Is an Ass*) with nothing religious about it.

Marlowe was stabbed to death in a brawl before he was thirty. Mercutio, the eloquent jester of *Romeo and Juliet* to whom Shakespeare gave his extravagant Queen Mab speech, is said to be a portrait of him; if that is not true, it ought to be.

Shakespeare, partly thanks to his rival, was forced to step aside from literary tradition, which certainly did him no harm. His plays provide fascinating glimpses of current superstitions and beliefs, all the more reliable for his care in avoiding religious themes. *Hamlet* (c. 1602) is a marvelous mess of eschatological contradictions and—unlike the theologically sound *Doctor Faustus*—a mirror of casual popular belief.

To begin with, there is a ghost. Most people believed in ghosts, and Catholics associated them with Purgatory, as does Shakespeare here— though not in *Macbeth*. Shakespeare was not a Catholic, however, and Article XXII of the Book of Common Prayer had specifically rejected Purgatory as a "fond thing" and "repugnant to the Word of God." Either Purgatory lingered in ordinary Elizabethan belief, or the ghost's mention of a false doctrine offers proof that it is indeed a devil in a pleasing shape:

> *I am thy father's spirit,*
> *Doom'd for a certain time to walk the night,*
> *And for the day confin'd to fast in fires,*
> *Till the foul crimes done in my days of nature*
> *Are burnt and purg'd away. But that I am forbid*
> *To tell the secrets of my prison house,*
> *I could a tale unfold whose lightest word*
> *Would harrow up thy soul, freeze thy young blood,*
> *Make thy two eyes, like stars, start from their spheres,*
> *Thy knotted and combined locks to part,*
> *And each particular hair to stand on end*
> *Like quills upon the fretful porpentine.*

Hamlet, though convinced of his uncle's guilt by his "mousetrap" ruse, will not kill Claudius at prayer for fear that his soul would then go straight to Heaven; he will wait for a moment when the king is engaged in the pleasures of the flesh:

> *Then trip him that his heels may kick at Heaven,*
> *And that his soul may be as damn'd and black*
> *As Hell, whereto it goes.*

That is conventional thinking—the only conventional religious thinking in the play unless Horatio's "Flights of angels sing thee to thy rest" counts—but it may also be merely an excuse, due to Hamlet's lingering hesitation about the ghost's reliability. Elsewhere the afterlife is uncertain:

> *Who would fardels bear,*
> *To grunt and sweat under a weary life,*
> *But that the dread of something after death—*
> *The undiscover'd country from whose bourne*
> *No traveler returns—puzzles the will,*
> *And makes us rather bear those ills we have*
> *Than fly to others that we know not of?*

The prince's musing does not follow church-bred thinking of the time, Protestant or Catholic, but something altogether more modern.

At the graveyard, Hamlet toys with skulls, jokes that Alexander's and Caesar's dust might serve as stoppers for beer barrels, and refers to the Dance of Death ("Now get you to my lady's chamber and tell her, let her paint an inch thick, to this favor she must come"). This is a fifteenth-century *memento mori*, with the emphasis on death, not the afterlife. So, too, is the "dusty death" of *Macbeth* (1606), a play that leans heavily on the magical and the demonic but almost too carefully avoids the afterlife: the Macbeths, three decades earlier, would have been headed straight for Hellmouth.

In *Measure for Measure* (1604), Claudio echoes Hamlet's great speech: even the old imagery of Hell—fire, ice, souls in the wind, like those of Paolo and Francesca, or howling under torture—does not make it seem entirely medieval:

> *Ay, but to die, and go we know not where,*
> *To lie in cold obstruction and to rot;*
> *This sensible warm motion to become*
> *A kneaded clod; and the delighted spirit*
> *To bathe in fiery floods, or to reside*
> *In thrilling region of thick-ribbed ice,*
> *To be imprison'd in the viewless winds*
> *And blown with restless violence round about*

The pendent world; or to be worse than worst
Of those that lawless and incertain thought
Imagines howling! 'Tis too horrible!
The weariest and most loathed worldly life
That age, ache, penury and imprisonment
Can lay on nature is a paradise
To what we fear of death.

That is as far as Shakespeare cared to go on the subject. Even uncensored, playwrights were probably weary of medieval clichés. Shakespeare's great villains are thoroughly human, though both Iago and Macbeth compare themselves (with satisfaction) to devils. Queen Anne roundly accuses Richard III of being one, as, in *Lear,* her husband does Goneril. New images of fear became increasingly bloody and exploitative, especially in the "revenge" plays of John Webster and Cyril Tourneur, though also in Shakespeare's *Titus Andronicus.* But no passage in all of Shakespeare's plays is so evocative of the macabre as this one from Webster's *The Duchess of Malfi* (c. 1613):

I am puzzled in a question about Hell;
He says, in Hell there's one material, fire,
And yet it shall not burn all men alike.
Lay him by. How tedious is a guilty conscience!
When I look into the fishponds in my garden,
Methinks I see a thing arm'd with a rake,
That seems to strike at me.

No French decadent ever topped that imagery or world-weariness.

Baroque Hell

THE DOMINICANS AND FRANCISCANS HAD become an embarrassment to the Church before the Reformation, and though the religious wars granted them a reprieve, they had lost ground. The Benedictines were simply too rich to be left alone by impoverished princes. So it fell to the new and energetic Society of Jesus, founded in 1540 by Ignatius Loyola (1491–1556), the youngest son of an old Basque noble family, to lead the way to the Counter-Reformation. A war wound forced Ignatius out of active life, and reading courtly romances, like those of King Arthur, and the lives of the saints during his prolonged convalescence had set him to thinking about the feudal ideal of holy chivalry. When healed, he decided to get an education—as a young knight, his had been rudimentary—and entered the university at Barcelona at the age of thirty-three. Harassment by the Inquisition drove him to Paris, where he finally achieved his M.A. at forty-five and gathered the friends who helped him to found his new order, which quickly developed an effective leadership network of Catholic reform and resistance to Protestant encroachment.

The Jesuit ideal is not only to save one's own soul but one's neighbor's as well; it is thus a teaching and missionary order. Jesuits carried the faith to Asia, the Indies, and the Americas. They brought sincerity, vitality, and fresh ideas to the old Catholic establishment and also to the new Baroque arts. Within prescribed limits, they were up to date in the sciences, too.

By the early seventeenth century, Jesuit missionaries to China were correctly predicting eclipses; they later sidestepped the Galileo debacle by declaring that the soul revolved around the immobile God as the earth moves around the sun. (Not until 1992 did the Vatican formally admit to possibly having made a mistake with Galileo.)

In the early modern age of printed books and changing educational standards, the teaching Jesuits were shrewdly positioned to influence and change society since most of their pupils were children of the rich and powerful. Jacob Burkhardt writes in *The Civilization of the Renaissance in Italy* that "the feeling of the upper and middle classes in Italy with regard to the Church at the time when the Renaissance culminated was compounded of deep and contemptuous aversion, of acquiescence in the outward ecclesiastical customs which entered into daily life, and of a sense of dependence on sacraments and ceremonies." The Jesuits set about to change that feeling.

One effective approach was to change Hell. Horrid as the old Hell was, it had variety, activity, scenery, and a certain entertainment value—too much, in fact, for the Jesuits. It might serve to frighten the uneducated into good behavior, but it was not taken seriously by people who counted. So the Jesuits dispensed with the frills. They eliminated all tortures except fire, and all monsters except possibly "the worm that never sleepeth," though there remained some doubt as to how these two could co-exist (perhaps the worm was a metaphor for a bad conscience). What they added was unnervingly apt for the times—they added urban squalor.

The Jesuit Hell was unbearably, suffocatingly, repulsively crowded (possibly because of its millions of new Protestant immigrants). In a dank, claustrophobic amalgam of dungeon and cesspool, dainty aristocrats and prosperous merchants jostled, cheek to jowl, buttock to belly, mouth to mouth, with coarse, foul-smelling, verminous peasants, lepers, and slum-dwellers. Just as the bodies of the saved were to be glorified at the Resurrection, those of the damned would be deformed, bloated, flabby, diseased, repugnant, "pressed together like grapes in a wine-press" (a favorite image). There were no latrines. The infernal stench was human stench, and it was disgusting and everlasting and composed of filth and feces and pestilence and running sores and bad breath and everything else creative Jesuits came up with to make their wealthy clients resolve to mend their ways. Whether such a scenario would have frightened the urban riffraff who already lived in unspeakable poverty toiling at foul-smelling jobs is unknown, but it had its effect on the upper and middle classes.

Those who regretted the passing of the old tortures were reassured by the properties of the fire of this alchemical age, for according to Romolo Marchelli in 1682, the fire would "distill and encapsulate" the pangs of starvation, of death by stabbing, strangulation, incineration, and dismemberment by wild animals as well as being eaten alive by worms or serpents, slashed by razors or arrows, having one's breasts sliced, bones shattered, joints disjointed, limbs dismembered, and so forth. Every spark of infernal fire carries all of that pain within it. The fearful sermon that so disturbs Stephen Dedalus in James Joyce's *Portrait of the Artist as a Young Man* presents the Jesuit Hell in grim detail, perfectly preserved for three hundred years.

The Jesuits ousted demons too, or nearly so. They weren't needed in a Hell of "other people" who turned on one another in their pain and terror. At any rate, demons now had a new task, which was tempting and corrupting people here on earth, especially destitute old women. What the Dominicans were to heretics, the Jesuits were to witches during the witch crazes, which began with the Renaissance and lasted intermittently until almost the nineteenth century—and not only, it should be emphasized, in Catholic countries. Satan, or a demonic lieutenant, was supposed to be the master of the witches, but his association with them, which included night flights and diabolical orgies and evil spells and the rest of the rancid nonsense to which thousands of people confessed after torture, was very much of this world, not the next. Serious discussions of Hell after the Reformation, whether Protestant or Catholic, almost never include Satan.

Demons always had time for heretics, atheists, and philosophers like Faustus, according to the Jesuits, and so Bruno was burned at the stake, Galileo escaped only by lying, and John Dee faced dangerous accusations of sorcery. As late as the mid-seventeenth century, Descartes found it advisable to move to Protestant Holland, and later even than that, Voltaire and Rousseau sought sanctuary in Switzerland.

The Jesuits themselves could summon demons when needed. Now that religious plays performed by laymen were forbidden, the Jesuits took over the religious theater. In 1597, the church of St. Michael was consecrated in Munich with an astounding festival pageant involving hundreds of players, brass bands, dragons, sinners, heretics: the final curtain featured a

A sixteenth-century mannerist Pan ogles a nymph. Images of Pan and the Devil drew close in the Renaissance.

tumultuous spectacle in which three hundred masked devils were hurled into what must have been the largest Hellmouth ever designed.

Painters, who were by this time looking for new subjects in religious art, preferably those displaying the rosy flesh of their beloved *putti*, were understandably not attracted to the Jesuit Hell. Nevertheless, the splendid ceiling of the Gesu, the first Jesuit church in Rome, manages to convey with great skill and ingenuity the idea without the ugliness, echoing the spirit of the Munich festival. It was painted by Il Baciccio (1639–1709), a follower of Bernini, between 1670 and 1683, with every one of the latest Baroque tricks and techniques of perspective. The vault of Heaven itself seems to open and the blessed to ascend as cherubs and angels gaze upward in ecstasy into the Empyrean. At the edges and corners of the ceiling, breaking it into sculptured shapes, great writhing clumps of the damned and doomed tumble downward into Hell—or, depending on your point of view, into the congregation. See Plate 12.

The Baroque period is always associated with opera, and the Jesuit orders were deeply involved in opera and ballet, connected as they were with the noble courts of Catholic Europe. The first *three* Florentine operas produced between 1600 and 1607 were based on the Orpheus and Eurydice story, which offered the opportunity for underworld extravaganzas complete with special effects, and allegorical ballets without troubling religious undertones. The third, *Orfeo* by Claudio Monteverdi (1607), was the first big operatic hit.

The pagan Orpheus story has been rivaled in operatic frequency only by Protestant Faust and Don Juan, the Catholic libertine, who, like Faust, is usually (not always) dragged off to Hell for his sins. By the late eighteenth century, after Mozart had finished *Don Giovanni* and Goethe had added the story of Faust's seduction of Gretchen to his first published fragment of *Faust*, Faust and Don Juan converged. Though in 1829 they appeared together as rivals in love in a German play by Christian Dietrich Grabbe, it is Goethe's amalgam of the two in the first part of *Faust* that inspired operas by Berlioz, Boito, and Gounod.*

*A chronological survey compiled by E. M. Butler in *The Fortunes of Faust* (1952) lists more than 30 Don Juan dramas, some musical, some not, and more than 40 featuring Faust (composers became interested only after Goethe added the Gretchen story). These do not include innumerable semi-improvised anonymous puppet plays of the eighteenth and nineteenth centuries. Butler says, without listing them, that there are more than fifty post-Goethe German *Faust*s.

Paradise Lost

JOHN MILTON (1608–1674) WAS VERY different
from Marlowe, who had attended Cambridge a generation earlier. He
was the younger son of a Protestant convert who was a stenographer and
sometime moneylender. At Cambridge, Milton was nicknamed "the Lady,"
more for a certain high-minded prudishness than for his unquestioned good
looks. His family considered him suited for the ministry, but he thought
otherwise. Poems written during his seven years at the university (for a
B.A. and M.A.), which include "On the Morning of Christ's Nativity,"
as well as "L'Allegro" and "Il Penseroso," had brought him local fame and
the confidence to envision a literary career.

It was his father's generosity that permitted him to travel to Italy—
where he visited Galileo—to continue his studies and spend twenty years
writing tracts in favor of religious liberty: the Stuart kings had brought
religious dissension and civil war back to England. In addition, he worked
as a translator, editor, and sometime politician in Oliver Cromwell's government. He married three times, had three daughters by his first wife,
and lost his eyesight gradually, becoming completely blind by 1652, before
a word of the great epic he had always hoped to write was set down. It is
possible that his blindness saved him from hanging when Charles II was
restored to the throne: Andrew Marvell is said to have pleaded for him.

Milton is sometimes called "the Puritan poet," but, at least in his greatest work, nothing could be farther from the truth. He was raised an Anglican at a time when Calvinism permeated the Church of England, but the entire concern of *Paradise Lost* is to confute predestination and demonstrate the freedom of will. Satan chooses to rebel in Heaven and chooses further wickedness; we share every twist of his thinking. Eve, beguiled and foolish, might be excused from choice, but Adam certainly understands the issues, if not the consequences, when his love for Eve overwhelms his love for God. Actually, Milton seems to have become quite independent in his religious views by the time he began to dictate *Paradise Lost* (published in 1667). In this he was in step with other intellectuals of the day, though most were wise enough to conceal their opinions. Milton obfuscated his in poetry, and generations following him have co-opted *Paradise Lost* for their own, often opposed, religious (or irreligious) sides.

The poem's source material was vast. The great Spanish Renaissance playwrights, Miguel de Cervantes (1547–1616), Lope de Vega (1562–1635) and Calderón de la Barca (1600–1681) had all taken the fate of the Devil as a theme. In Holland, Hugo Grotius (1583–1645) had written a Latin play, *Adamus Exul,* which Milton knew, while Joost van den Vondel's (1587–1679) *Lucifer* was famous. A Huguenot poem about the creation and fall by Guillaume du Bartas (1544–1590), translated in 1605 by Josuah Sylvester as *The Divine Weeks and Works,* was widely read in England and certainly known to Milton: he borrowed from it the line "Immutable, Immortal, Infinite" for the angels' hymn in Book III.

The character of Milton's magnificently outsized Satan has been discussed, often passionately, for centuries, but we will avoid the debate in order to concentrate on cosmography. We learn that, following a more hard pressed than usual war in Heaven, during which the Son had to be sent in to back up Michael and the angelic troops, Satan and his host are:

> *Hurl'd headlong flaming from th' Ethereal Sky*
> *With hideous ruin and combustion down*
> *To bottomless perdition, there to dwell*
> *In Adamantine chains and penal Fire.*

For nine days they fall through Chaos till:

> *Hell at last*
> *Yawning receiv'd them whole, and on them clos'd,*
> *Hell their fit habitation fraught with fire*
> *Unquenchable, the house of woe and pain.*

They splash down into a burning lake, and, looking around, find themselves much changed from their bright angelic forms, while their surroundings are:

> *A Dungeon horrible, on all sides round*
> *As one great Furnace flam'd, yet from those flames*
> *No light, but rather darkness visible*
> *Serv'd only to discover sights of woe,*
> *Regions of sorrow, doleful shades, where peace*
> *And rest can never dwell, hope never comes*
> *That comes to all; but torture without end*
> *Still urges, and a fiery Deluge, fed*
> *With ever-burning Sulphur unconsum'd:*
> *Such place Eternal Justice had prepar'd*
> *For those rebellious, here their Prison ordain'd*
> *In utter darkness and their portion set*
> *As far remov'd from God and light of Heav'n*
> *As from the center thrice to th' utmost Pole.*

Note that the prison is "ordain'd," but not necessarily its inhabitants. Hell is ready, but they were not foredoomed to occupy it. How they escape from the adamantine chains is never explained (none of Milton's predecessors managed to explain this either), but they make their way to land:

> *yon dreary Plain, forlorn and wild,*
> *The seat of desolation, void of light,*
> *Save what the glimmering of these livid flames*
> *Casts pale and dreadful.*

Nevertheless, Satan is determined to make the best of circumstance; in a curious reversal of Mephostophilis's lament, he proclaims his defiance:

179

Farewell happy Fields
Where Joy for ever dwells: Hail horrors, hail
Infernal world, and thou profoundest Hell
Receive thy new Possessor; One who brings
A mind not to be chang'd by Place or Time.
The mind is its own place, and in itself
Can make a Heav'n of Hell, a Hell of Heav'n.
What matter where, if I be still the same,
And what I should be, all but less than he
Whom Thunder hath made greater? Here at last
We shall be free; th' Almighty hath not built
Here for his envy, will not drive us hence:
Here we may reign secure, and in my choice
To reign is worth ambition though in Hell:
Better to reign in Hell, than serve in Heav'n!

With truly Puritan zeal, the demons set to work on the side of a volcano to build a splendiferous palace, supposed to conjure up in the mind of the reader the worst excesses of Baroque Rome and Byzantine Constantinople, not to mention sinful Babylon. The architect is Mulciber, another name for Hephaestus or Vulcan, the craftsman of pagan Olympus, and the builder is Mammon, our old plutocratic friend, "the least erected Spirit that fell/ From Heav'n, for ev'n in Heav'n his looks and thoughts/ Were always downward bent, admiring more/ the riches of Heav'n's pavement, trodd'n Gold,/ Than aught divine or holy." Their combined effort results in something astonishing. Pandemonium ("All-Demons") is the most palatial structure in Hell's history, grander than anything in Spenser, more majestic than Dante's City of Dis, more glittering than Hesiod's House of Styx. In the opulent meeting hall, Satan calls a council. The infernal council is traditional in literature and drama but Milton's treatment is something else entirely. The new monarch sits in sumptuousness rivaled only by Shakespeare's Cleopatra on her gilded barge:

High on a Throne of Royal State, which far
Outshone the wealth of Ormus and of Ind,
Or where the gorgeous East with richest hand
Show'rs on her Kings Barbaric Pearl and Gold,

Satan exalted sat, by merit rais'd
To that bad eminence.

The demons swarm to the council in the thousands "as bees in spring-time." Each senior devil gives a speech. Moloch counsels war—he is Anger. Belial, who is sensibly, but ignobly, against any warlike activity, is Sloth. Mammon, who is willing to put up with fiery inconveniences for Hell's "Gems and Gold," is Avarice. Beelzebub, second in rank, is Envy; he tells of "another World, the happy seat/ Of some new Race call'd Man," and suggests that they subvert it "and drive as we were driven,/ The puny habitants; or, if not drive,/ Seduce them to our Party." His plan delights the council and they vote to adopt it. But who shall make his way through the "dark unbottom'd infinite Abyss" to visit this world? Who but Satan himself in his Pride.

The Stygian council dissolved, the demons disperse, some to engage in heroic games, others to play the harp, to philosophize, and, most importantly, to explore their new world.

Another part adventure to discover wide
That dismal World, if any Clime perhaps
Might yield them easier habitation, bend
Four ways their flying March, along the banks
Of four infernal Rivers that disgorge
Into the burning Lake their baleful streams;
Abhorred Styx *the flood of deadly hate,*
Sad Acheron *of sorrow, black and deep;*
Cocytus, *nam'd of lamentation loud*
Heard on the ruful stream; fierce Phlegethon
Whose waves of torrent fire inflame with rage.
Far off from these, a slow, a silent stream,
Lethe *the River of Oblivion roules*
Her wat'ry Labyrinth, whereof who drinks,
Forthwith his former state and being forgets,
Forgets both joy and grief, pleasure and pain.
Beyond this flood a frozen Continent
Lies dark and wild, beat with perpetual storms
Of Whirlwind and dire Hail, which on firm land

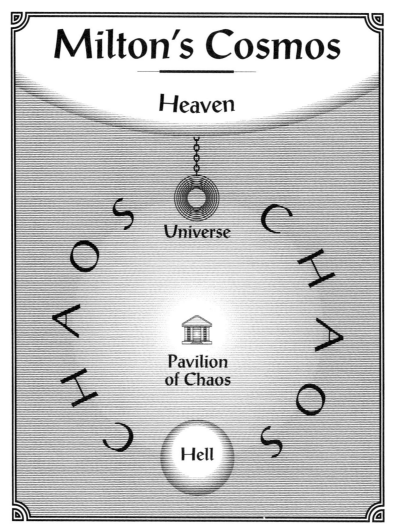

Map of Milton's cosmos

Thaws not, but gathers heap, and ruin seems
Of ancient pile; all else deep snow and ice.

The terrain and fauna are not hospitable:

Thus roving on
In confus'd march forlorn, th' adventurous Band,
With shudd'ring horror pale, and eyes aghast
View'd first their lamentable lot, and found

182

No rest: through many a dark and dreary Vale
They pass'd, and many a Region dolorous,
O'er many a Frozen, many a Fiery Alp,
Rocks, Caves, Lakes, Fens, Bogs, Dens, and shades of death,
A Universe of death, which God by curse
Created evil, for evil only good,
Where all life dies, death lives, and nature breeds,
Perverse, all monstrous, all prodigious things,
Abominable, inutterable, and worse,
Than fables yet have feign'd, or fear conceiv'd,
Gorgons *and* Hydras *and* Chimeras *dire.*

Meanwhile Satan "puts on swift wings" and soars toward the "thrice threefold" gates of Hell, three of brass, three of iron, three of adamantine rock, guarded by two formidable shapes who turn out to be Sin and Death personified. Sin

seem'd Woman to the waist, and fair,
But ended foul in many a scaly fold
Voluminous and vast, a Serpent arm'd
With mortal sting: about her middle round
A cry of Hell Hounds never ceasing bark'd
With wide Cerberean *mouths full loud, and rung*
A hideous peal: yet, when they list, would creep,
If aught disturb'd their noise, into her womb,
And kennel there, yet still there bark'd and howl'd
Within unseen.

Illustrators, whose favorite Miltonic subject was "Satan, Sin, and Death" always had trouble with Sin, understandably. With Death, they usually paid no attention to Milton's own description of a crowned shapeless shadow shaking a spear, but simply used the traditional fifteenth-century skeleton or desiccated corpse.

Once it is established that Sin is Satan's daughter, sprung full-grown from his forehead like Athena from the head of Zeus, and Death his incestuous son by her, Sin unlocks the gates, and for a moment they all contemplate Chaos.

183

At this point, one might well begin to wonder just where Milton's Hell is. It certainly is not in the center of our own earth, the traditional site. Earth had not yet been created when Milton's rebel angels fell. It is not a claustrophobic Jesuit prison but a vast world, unpopulated (yet) except for the rebels, Sin, Death, and a few prodigious monsters. It seems to be located on, or rather inside another planet altogether. When Sin unlocks the gates, it is as though Satan were about to step out into space, though here it is Chaos. And Chaos is outside the universe, as the universe was generally understood.

In Chaos the elements noisily battle one another while Satan is buffeted back and forth until he reaches his first stop, the pavilion of Chaos personified and his consort Night. Here we learn that Hell is "beneath," this situation and that the new "World" hangs "over" Chaos, "link'd in a golden Chain/ To that side Heav'n from whence your Legions fell." Actually, this dangling object is not a world at all but the old Ptolemaic universe with its nine spheres circling the earth. Despite his acquaintance with Galileo, Milton found it too poetically useful to abandon.

Satan looks back to see Sin and Death forging a bridge behind him, then ahead to the opal towers and sapphire battlements of Heaven, together with, hanging from it on a golden chain, the "pendent world," looking as small with regard to Heaven as a star does next to the moon.

Satan alights on the outermost sphere of this "world," which seems to house a Limbo called the Paradise of Fools, reserved for unreconstructed Roman Catholics. He finds a stairway to Heaven, but heads away from it through the sphere of the fixed stars, past Saturn, Jupiter, and Mars to the sphere of the sun, ruled by the archangel Uriel. Disguised as a winsome cherub, he asks directions, and Uriel points him toward Paradise, Adam's abode. And off Satan speeds to Mount Niphates to intone his great soliloquy, which runs in part:

> *Me miserable! Which way shall I fly?*
> *Infinite wrath and infinite despair?*
> *Which way I fly is Hell; myself am Hell;*
> *And, in the lowest deep, a lower deep*
> *Still threat'ning to devour me opens wide,*
> *To which the Hell I suffer seems a Heav'n.*

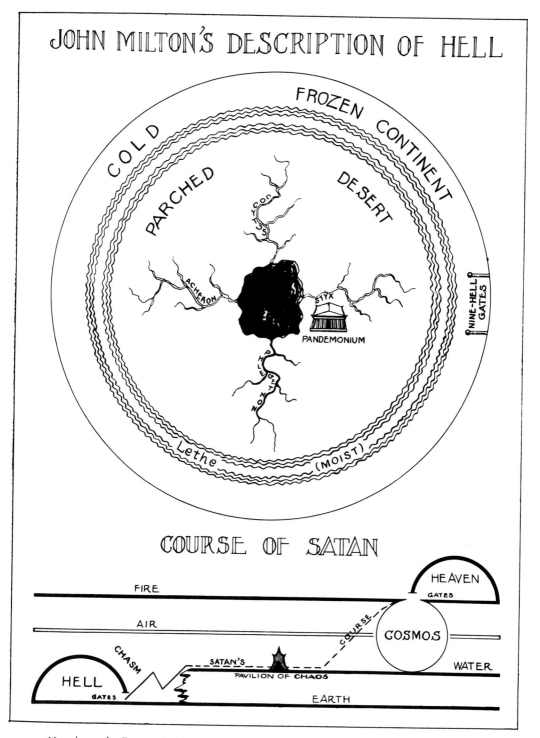

Map drawn by Eugene Cox in 1928

O then at last relent: is there no place
Left for Repentance, none for Pardon left?
None left but by submission; and that word
Disdain *forbids me, and my dread of shame*
Among the Spirits beneath, whom I seduc'd
With other promises and other vaunts
Then to submit, boasting I could subdue
Th' Omnipotent.

This fragment is interesting for at least three reasons. First, there is the echo of Marlowe and the *poena damni* of deprivation; second, it underlines the poem's argument for free will; third, it hints at Origen's theory of universal salvation, which was beginning to be seriously discussed in the seventeenth century. Even Satan could repent, but to do so now would be to betray his troops as well as his pride.

Satan's travelogue is confusing. Milton removed Heaven and Hell from the Ptolemaic universe entirely while, instead of the Empyrean, Chaos rings the Primum Mobile, with Heaven and Hell on opposite sides of it in two separate spheres or universes—or perhaps Heaven is a kind of ceiling or platform. To map Milton's cosmos logically is impossible, which hasn't stopped mapmakers from trying. Milton himself says in the *Christian Doctrine* that "Hell appears to be situated beyond the limits of this universe," and cites Luke 21.8 to justify Chaos. He might have welcomed the vocabulary of the particle physicist or science-fiction writer to speak of a "parallel universe." One early wag complained, quite correctly, that when Milton wrote of Chaos, his writing turned singularly chaotic. And T. S. Eliot acerbically remarked that "Milton's celestial and infernal regions are large but insufficiently furnished apartments filled by heavy conversation."

One of Milton's many illustrators made notably good sense out of Hell, however. This was John Martin (1789–1834). Martin was much admired in his own time, but his reputation has not lasted, partly because his paintings now seem florid and overwrought, but also because he simply could not draw a credible human figure. Apocalypse and epic were his specialties, but architecture and engineering (especially of sewers) on a heroic scale also

---

Illustrations by John Martin for Paradise Lost

33. In the late Middle Ages, Hell could get downright winsome. From the French fifteenth-century *Hours of Catherine of Cleves.*

Comment les vuroughes sont tormentez par les diables qui leurs gettent a grans floles en la gorge ploinb et souffre bouillant puant et ardant.

Pres regarde des luxurieux qui ont demoure en leurs obstinatios et mis leur aieur en amour char

34–35. Hell has often been somewhat prurient. From the French fifteenth-century *Le Trésor de Sapience.*

es pillars et tous ceulx q̃ auoient robe et ransonne leurs freres crestiēs

36. More late-fifteenth-century French *diablerie*.

37–38. Blake illustrated both Dante and Milton. Above, right, "The Simoniac Pope" from the *Inferno;* below, "Satan Rousing the Rebel Angels" from *Paradise Lost.*

39. Blake may have been the last major artist to paint a Last Judgment.

40. *Satan, Sin and Death*, by William Hogarth, c.1735–40.

41. *The Fallen Angels Entering Pandemonium,* by John Martin, c.1840.

42. *The Gates of Hell,* by Auguste Rodin, early twentieth century.

interested him. He had grown up in a mining town, and one of his brothers was a famously insane arsonist. Perhaps this combination of interests and circumstances explains how, in the series of engravings, mezzotints, and paintings he made for *Paradise Lost*, he managed to convey the sense of vast underground gloom lit by dim fires but all somehow enclosed. He was the only illustrator who understood that Milton's Hell, for all its geographical features, was actually a cavernous interior underworld, if not exactly a sewer. He did an admirable job with the Bridge over Chaos too. Pandemonium intrigued him so much that he returned to it several times, and collectors of movie trivia will be pleased to know that the sets of Babylon (254 acres of them) in D. W. Griffith's *Intolerance* owe their grandeur directly to Martin's visions of demonic palaces. See Plate 41.

He was not the first artist to portray these visions as spectacular, however, for we have a wonderful description of a theatrical panorama of "Satan Arraying his Troops on the Banks of the Fiery Lake, with the Palace of Pandemonium: from Milton." This was a kind of magic lantern show, a precursor of the movies, created by Philippe Jacques de Loutherbourg in London in 1782 and called the Eidophusikon:

Here in the foreground of a vista, stretching an immeasureable length between mountains ignited from the bases to their lofty summits with many-colored flame, a chaotic mass arose in dark majesty which gradually assumed form until it stood, the interior of a vast temple of gorgeous architecture, bright as molten brass, seemingly compiled of unquenchable fire. In this tremendous scene, the effect of colored glasses before the lamps was fully displayed, which being hidden from the audience threw their whole influence on the scene as it rapidly changed, now to a sulphurous blue, then to a lurid red, and then again to a pale vivid light and ultimately to a mysterious combination of the glasses, such as a bright furnace exhibits in fusing various metals. The sounds which accompanied the wondrous picture struck the astonished ear of the spectator as no less than preternatural, for to add a more awful character to peals of thunder and the accompaniments of all the hollow machinery that hurled balls and stones with indescribable rumbling and noise, an expert assistant swept his thumb over the surface of the tambourine which produced a variety of groans that struck the imagination as issuing from infernal spirits.

The Eidophusikon was unfortunately destroyed by fire at the beginning of the nineteenth century.

In *Paradise Regained,* Milton took Satan's story through the Temptation of Christ, but not through the Harrowing. By the late seventeenth century, the Harrowing was falling from favor. Breakaway Protestant sects always included "He descended into Hell" in their creeds, but this seems to have been more from tradition than conviction; in the twentieth century, later divisions, especially Methodist councils, quietly dropped the phrase, probably because the difference between Hell and Limbo is no longer commonly understood. Also, the Harrowing very prominently features Satan, and, after Milton, Satan and other devils became increasingly dissociated from Hell.

The Mechanical Universe

FOR CATHOLICS, THE EXISTENCE OF Hell and eternal punishment were emphatically affirmed by the Catechism of 1564 ordered by the Council of Trent, and the Inquisition's treatment of Bruno and Galileo made them wary of challenging church dogma. But it was hard to dam the progress of secular knowledge. In the early, heady days of the Copernican revolution, new discoveries in science and mechanics came from every part of Europe,* Protestant and Catholic, but by the seventeenth century Protestant countries had a distinct scientific advantage. René Descartes (1596–1650), who was, with Newton, the most influential thinker of the century, had studied with the Jesuits but found it prudent to move from France to Protestant Holland after his own studies confirmed Galileo's astronomical findings. Virtually all the intellectuals of the eighteenth-century French Enlightenment found sanctuary at one point or another in Holland, England, or Switzerland.

Meanwhile, fascination with mathematics and astronomy, coupled with great advances in optics and in the manufacture of clocks and watches— the pendulum clock was introduced in mid-century, as was the balance spring for watches—led to a widespread view of a "mechanical" or "clock-

---

*Copernicus was Polish; Tycho, Danish; Bruno and Galileo, Italian; Kepler, German; Dee and Bacon, English.

work" or "watchmaker's" universe, in which all phenomena were the result of matter set in motion according to natural laws set down by God. It is sometimes difficult to remember that for centuries *supernatural* history and law, as well as religion, had prevailed. Calvinist predestination seemed to encourage inexorable natural law, at least at first.

The idea of the mechanical universe dated back to the fourteenth century, but it was underlined by Galileo's discoveries and articulated philosophically by Thomas Hobbes (1588–1679), remembered for his Gnostic characterization of human life as "nasty, brutish and short." His own life was long, intellectually rich, and quite comfortable despite the virulent antagonism stirred up by his books: the common and serious charge against him was that he was an atheist. In later life, he was protected by Charles II of England, once Hobbes's pupil in mathematics and always fond of him.

Geometry was Hobbes's first love, followed by mechanics and physics; he sought out Galileo in Italy to discuss astronomy and the nature of the universe. He was not an atheist in the modern sense, but he was an original thinker, more concerned with the logical purity of his mathematical approach than with subverting science to scripture. He was a materialist and the first of the "English deists," as the scientifically minded members of the Royal Society came to be called—though the Society shunned him. His sardonic humor and contempt for superstition (see the fourth part of *Leviathan*, "Of the Kingdom of Darkness") would have fit perfectly into the climate of the eighteenth century, but he was precariously ahead of his time. On the subject of Hell, he pointed out that it could not possibly be both a bottomless pit and contained in the globe of the earth, that a reading of Isaiah 14.9 might suppose it to be underwater, and that Matthew's hellfire might be taken simply as a metaphor for dying—a radical interpretation.

Hobbes eventually advocated annihilation theory, the idea that only the saved will be resurrected and the damned are doomed to everlasting death. This is one of the two principal modern Christian theories opposed to Augustinian damnation, the other being universal salvation more or less along the Origenian line.

Descartes's discussion of reason deliberately moved the traditional soul-body dichotomy to a less touchy one, opposing the mind and the senses. He professed Christianity but insisted that the material universe was completely separate from the spiritual universe, with no further interference from God after the Creation itself. Following Hobbes and Galileo, he presented the universe as a mechanism operating in accordance with God-given laws; if it was not perfect that was because only God can be perfect—this was a tricky step away from blaming the woes of the world on Original Sin. Descartes's position on materialism went beyond Hobbes in denying the possibility of supernatural events, including the miracles of the Bible—an extreme that triggered anguished debate. He backtracked to make the subtle (and politic) argument that revelation from God could hardly be denied, even though it could not be demonstrated, but he threw open the doors to later skepticism.

The boldest of the skeptics was Baruch Spinoza (1632–1677) of Holland. As a Jew, he had a certain distance from squabbles over predestination and free will as well as New Testament miracles, but because he denied that biblical evidence supported an immortal soul or the existence of angels, he was excommunicated from the synagogue before he was twenty-five. Spinoza undertook to correct the three flaws he found in Descartes's mechanical universe: a transcendent God, mind-body duality, and insistence on free will. For God, he substituted the "being of the universe," which contains everything and may be worthy of worship though it is not concerned with worship. Though it may be conscious, it has no "will" as we understand it and is very far from being interested in or capable of anything like a Last Judgment or eternal punishment. Mind and body are two parts of an intrinsic unit, the mind being that part which is aware. But bodily instinct, appetite, and desire override any freedom of will, and joy and grief transform feeling; a person is "free" only insofar as he strives for one rather than the other. What is "good" is what is useful to an individual or a species and means nothing to God. Miracles are mistaken impressions of natural events.

Spinoza did grant that some part of the mind is eternal, which seems to go against the rest of his system. He was, of course, decried as an atheist in the seventeenth century and embraced as an atheist in the eighteenth.

For a more conventional mind, the task of explaining why, in a mechanical universe, so many souls were created only to be damned was difficult. Gottfried Leibnitz (1646–1716) of Germany tried to integrate Cartesian rationalism, which included an individual's free will to choose good or evil, with Calvinist double predestination, and ended up with a somewhat Arminian "optimism," retreating toward the position that if God could have created a better universe he would have; the faults are intrinsic to creation: he is the Dr. Pangloss ("Explain-it-all," or "Polish-it-all," a nice pun) ridiculed by Voltaire in *Candide* for proclaiming this to be "the best of all possible worlds."

But Voltaire belonged to the anti-Christian Enlightenment, while the earlier scientific era struggled to integrate what it had been taught with what it was learning. Seventeenth-century scientists and philosophers (no real difference separated them as yet) operated under constraints other than those of scripture. First, they had no idea of the real age of the universe and of the earth; both were thought to be only a few thousand years old, usually dating back to 4004 B.C., the agreed-upon biblical date* and to have been created in fixed mechanical working order with flora and fauna intact, roughly as described in Genesis. Because they had no concept of evolution, the remarkable balance of nature was seen as proof of God's divine handicraft and creative omnipotence and, for Protestants, of predestination. This is called "argument from design."

Moreover, the watchmaker's universe was small. Despite Roman Catholic opposition, scientifically inclined men all accepted the sun-centered Copernican universe, but they did not yet see beyond the solar system. Only six planets were known, Copernicus having added the earth as the sixth. It was not long before the adventurous began to speculate that stars might be other suns, but telescopes were not nearly advanced enough to discern galactic nebulae. The notion of incalculable millions of other "universes," each containing billions of suns around which trillions of planets might whirl, was far in the future.

Isaac Newton (1642–1727) was the most prominent member of the Royal Society, which gathered together most of the like-minded Englishmen of the day, with the pointed exception of Hobbes. They took their model of the universe from Descartes, built on it with Newton, and labored to reconcile it with scripture. Steadily but cautiously, they began to move away from Calvinistic Anglicanism toward a simpler deism, or "natural religion." Newton, the greatest of them all, was cited admiringly as a man of science who had kept his faith. Not until the twentieth century, when his private papers were published, was it discovered that Newton, sincerely devout but a sincere and dedicated mathematician too, had gradually

---

*Johannes Hevelius (1611–1687), a German astronomer, dated the moment of creation to six P.M., October 24, 3963 B.C.

193

abandoned faith in miracles, including that of the Resurrection, and in so doing he had had to reject the Trinity, a position identical to that of Locke. Miracles and Newtonian mathematics could not co-exist, though he could believe in God and even in a Last Judgment. But he had also begun to doubt the eternity of Hell.

What, after all, was the *point* of Hell after the Last Judgment? Punishment can be deterrent, corrective, curative, or vindictive. Hell was certainly a deterrent: even those who doubted privately felt it was a useful concept for others, particularly the lower classes. The Catholic Purgatory was corrective and curative. But infinite pain at the end of time for those whose sins were, after all, finite? This would be neither curative nor deterrent. How could it be other than vindictive? Add double predestination, and you have the truly fearful concept of a God who creates an overwhelming majority of the damned ("many are called, but few are chosen") and teases them with the doctrine of salvation only to punish them forever for a situation he has himself created, and for no purpose other than to entertain the elect. Seventeenth-century rationalism could not tolerate such a view of God, let alone such detritus clogging the cosmic machine.

Of course, most people did not really believe in double predestination; they probably believed in a muddled form of free will that justifies punishment—for others. But many of those who tried to think things through were quietly beginning to abandon eternal punishment. Hobbes, John Locke, and numerous others came to the conclusion that after a period of torment appropriate to their sins—perhaps a thousand years or so—the wicked would be simply and tidily annihilated.

Some thought that annihilation might happen immediately after death. The Socinians were said to believe this.* Jews were thinking along these lines. A century earlier, Anabaptists had held similar views. All of these groups were considered suspect, but by the eighteenth century David Hume had advanced to rejecting any form of afterlife, serenely embracing his own deathbed annihilation, much to Boswell's pious distress.

Even in the Royal Society, scientific method could mimic medieval literalism. In 1714, Tobias Swinden published *An Enquiry into the Nature and Place of Hell* in which, following all the latest theories, he proved that

---

*There is considerable ambiguity about just what Socinians did believe about the afterlife or lack of it; their names were invoked rather as "Manichaeans" were during the Albigensian Crusade. See D. P. Walker, *The Decline of Hell*, 1964, Chapter V.

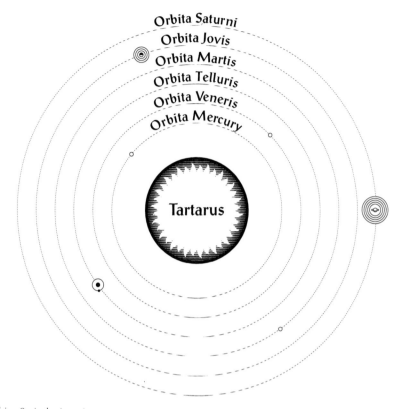

Orbita Saturni
Orbita Jovis
Orbita Martis
Orbita Telluris
Orbita Veneris
Orbita Mercury

Tartarus

Tobias Swinden's universe

the sun was logically and scientifically the site of Hell. By his calculations, the accumulation of souls would have long since overrun any subterranean space, and not enough oxygen could penetrate to keep the fires stoked. Only the sun was big enough, fiery enough, and eternal enough to hold the enormous number of damned souls, past and future. Furthermore, as the center of the Copernican universe, it had the place farthest away from the Empyrean that the earth had mistakenly been thought to have held. Surely the conclusion was obvious.

Apparently not. Three years later, William Whiston, who had succeeded Isaac Newton as professor of mathematics at Cambridge but had been expelled for unorthodox beliefs, published *Astronomical Principles of Religion, Natural and Reveal'd,* dedicated to Newton, whose second law of motion had helped to establish the idea of comets as orbiting bodies with elliptical but traceable orbits within the mechanical universe. In 1705, Edmund Halley had published the calculated orbits of twenty-four periodic

195

comets and, using Newton's revolutionary mathematics, correctly predicted the return in 1758 of the one that bears his name. Whiston studied this book and the evidence for Hell, particularly with regard to extremes of heat and cold, and decided that the path of a comet, which took it so near the sun and so far into "the cold regions near Saturn" was the logical "Surface or Atmosphere" for the place of torment.

Whiston received some incredulity from fellow members of the Royal Society and retreated to his own form of annihilation theory. In 1740, in *The Eternity of Hell Torments Considered*, he placed *all* dead souls in a nonpunitive (but certainly uncomfortable, considering the crowd) Hades inside the earth, where they would have a chance to mend their ways. At the Last Judgment (Whiston was a millenarian) the blessed would rise in spiritual bodies and the incorrigible in the diseased or damaged bodies they had at death. That explained the worms, while the fire would follow at world's end "till they expired in the utmost agonies."

JOHN DONNE (1573–1631), the dean of St. Paul's Cathedral in London, wrote a satire on the Jesuits called *Ignatius, His Conclave* which takes place in Hell, not the Jesuit version but the satirical Hell that Lucian invented to air his political views. Donne pretends to visit this region, passing through its "suburbs," Limbo and Purgatory, to find Lucifer hobnobbing with Ignatius Loyola in order to judge the scientists and thinkers of the new world order: Copernicus; Paracelsus, a medical alchemist whose work interested Donne; and Machiavelli, who so intrigues the Devil that he nearly deserts Ignatius. With the aid of Galileo's telescope, they decide to form a new colony of Hell on the moon over which Ignatius will rule: this is to hold all the heretics condemned by the Vatican.

The essay is slight and intended to amuse but is noteworthy for its interest in contemporary discoveries, not only in the sciences but in travel, for it brings in the reports of voyages to the Americas and the Indies and the Orient that made the age so exciting. Donne had been raised a Roman Catholic and was taught by the Jesuits before attending both Oxford and Cambridge, where, because of his religion, he could not take a degree. He was always interested in science; just as Hobbes and Milton went to visit Galileo, Donne sought out Kepler in a remote town in Austria.

Donne is remembered for his ardent and exalted poetry both religious and sensual, but after his rather late conversion to the Anglican faith, he also became a celebrated preacher. He was not a hellfire preacher—although he had morbid tendencies in later life, this would have been entirely foreign to his temperament—but he did preach one famous sermon that illustrates perfectly the *poena damni* that moderate, educated, middle-class Protestants who kept up with science but held to the faith could believe in:

> That that God who, when he could not get into me by standing and knocking, by his ordinary means of entering, by his word, his mercies, hath applied his judgments and hath shaked the house, this body, with agues and palsies, and set this house on fire with fevers and calentures and frightened the master of the house, my soul, with horrors and heavy apprehensions and so made an entrance into me; that that God should loose and frustrate all his own purposes and practices upon me, and leave me, and cast me away, as though I had cost him nothing, that this God at last should let this soul go away, as a smoke, as a vapor, as a bubble, and then that this soul cannot be a smoke, nor a vapor, nor a bubble, but must live in darkness; . . . what torment is not a marriage bed to this damnation, to be secluded eternally, eternally, eternally from the sight of God?

The use of the first person in this sermon is wonderfully effective. Though Donne was a contemporary of Marlowe and Shakespeare, he lived longer than they did and both his poetry and his prose seem to look forward to the age of science and self-revelation of a sort not practiced since the days of Augustine and Marcus Aurelius.

A parallel confessional passage from the *Religio Medici* of Thomas Browne (1605–1682) probes an Anglican position similar to but a little to the left of Donne. Browne, in tune with other intellectuals, was moving toward the deist position. He reflects that he has never feared Hell and thinks that God must use it only as a last resort "upon provocation."

> I can hardly think there was ever any scared into Heaven; they go the fairest way to Heaven that would serve God without a Hell; other mercenaries that crouch to him in fear of Hell, though they term themselves the servants, are indeed the slaves of the Almighty.

197

On the other hand, hundreds of Puritan preachers were terrorizing their audiences with threats like this one by Christopher Love (1618–1651):

Should you pray till you can speak no more; and should you sigh to the breaking of your loins; should every word be a sigh, and every sigh a tear, and every tear a drop of blood, you would never be able to recover that grace which you lost in Adam; you obliterated the beautiful image of God; you lost that knowledge by the commission of one sin, which you cannot regain by ten thousand sermons, or doing ten thousand Duties.

The antithetically named Love, an extremist, defended his position by saying that "sermons of terror have done more good upon unconverted souls than sermons of comfort have ever done"; for "stout and knotty" souls, "nothing but flashes of hellfire will make their conscience startle." In *The Anatomy of Melancholy* (1621), the moderate clergyman Robert Burton (1577–1640) described sufferers who had been cast into conditions of morbid despair by "those thundering ministers" and undertook to provide a list of scriptural reassurances.

By far the best known of all seventeenth-century preachers, however, was John Bunyan (1628–1688), a Baptist whose allegory of a Christian's journey toward salvation, the massively popular *Pilgrim's Progress, from This World to That Which Is to Come* (1678), had gone through 160 editions by 1792 and remained, after the Bible, the best-selling book in the English language right through the nineteenth century. Hell enters only peripherally, but Bunyan's second most famous book was *A Few Sighs from Hell*, with thirty editions between first publication in 1658 and 1797. Bunyan's outlook and technique in both books is entirely medieval: their huge popularity serves to prove how distant the outlook of the elite can be from that of the masses. *A Few Sighs*, developed from an actual sermon, is no more than a vision journey updated with Puritan terrorist eloquence: bellies crammed with burning pitch or molten lead, red-hot pincers shredding flesh to bits, limbs torn apart, souls abandoned to "fry, scorch and broil, and burn forever." Copies of Bunyan's books were frequently presented to Puritan children.

The Enlightenment

IN THE EIGHTEENTH CENTURY, THE center of in-
tellectual activity veered from England to France and it has become
conventional to call the group at the center of the Enlightenment *philosophes*, whether they were French or not. The word does not quite mean
philosophers, though some of them were. They were primarily thinkers,
writers, polemicists, critics, men of letters who shared a belief in rationality,
science, and freedom from oppression, which very much included freedom
from the heavy hand of organized religion. *"Écrasez l'infâme!"* was Voltaire's cry, and by *l'infâme* he meant quite specifically what Hume called
"Stupidity, Christianity & Ignorance," with an emphasis on the fear of
Hell as a coercive device.

For convenience, let us call Pierre Bayle (1647–1706) the first of the
philosophes. Although he lived only a few years into the century, he had
its ironic tone, and he engaged in one of its characteristic occupations, the
industrious compilation of fact and opinion to prove a point. John Ray
(c. 1627–1705) had just parsed the definition of *species*, a useful way to
classify and group things; and intellectuals of the eighteenth century,
whether philosophes or their opponents, were indefatigable makers of dictionaries, encyclopedias, catalogs, libraries, compendia, collections, and
systems of all kinds.

Other well-known French philosophes included Voltaire; Montesquieu;
Diderot; scientists Jean d'Alembert and the Comte de Buffon, who wrote

a forty-four volume *Natural History;* and Rousseau, who eventually quarreled and broke with the other philosophes. Best known in Britain were the philosopher David Hume, the economist Adam Smith, and the historian Edward Gibbon. In America, Ethan Allen, the frontier hero, and Thomas Paine, the political theorist, may be counted, while Benjamin Franklin and Thomas Jefferson collaborated to make their new nation's Declaration of Independence the most triumphant political document of the Enlightenment.

The difference between the investigators of the seventeenth century and those of the Enlightenment is that the latter were no longer interested in attuning their findings to scripture—except to decry it—which, for the first time, opened the way to a true empiricism. Thus Buffon looked to a past of eons, not merely of thousands of years, and a creation not constrained to six days or even six "epochs." The reports and merchandise and sometimes people coming from the New World and the Far East with increasing frequency made Europe less parochial. The steady accumulation of works in translation added to respect for the past and for other cultures.

A proper Enlightenment demon wearing spectacles

The industrial age was beginning, and philosophy, science, and religion had begun to sort themselves into different categories.

To see how the philosophes used the "scientific" approach to confute orthodoxy on the subject of Hell, it is useful to look into their compilations, beginning with Bayle's encyclopedic *Dictionnaire Historique et Critique*, published in 1697. In his dictionary, which is really a collection of essays, Bayle was fighting not only a general war against doctrine but a specific one against the Calvinist Huguenot leader Pierre Jurieu. Jurieu stated that God permitted sin in order to demonstrate his hatred of it. Bayle retorted that such hatred would be better demonstrated by preventing it. Jurieu argued that Hell was necessary "by reason, custom and all the laws of the world." Bayle disagreed.

The *Dictionnaire* does not have a section on *"enfer"*; that would not have been prudent. Bayle attacked from the sidelines, through camouflage provided by his articles on heresy, paganism, atheism, revelation, and philosophers such as Spinoza. His weapons were wit and great erudition, his points that ethics and virtuous living had little to do with the fear of offending God (or the gods) and that one man's pious mystery is another's murky superstition. Jurieu, attacking Catholicism, pointed out heretical inconsistencies in the early Church. Bayle used his own arguments against him to prove that Calvinism could not logically exclude from salvation any of the new heresies against which orthodoxy inveighed. One of Bayle's best ironic positions was that atheists, lacking the fear of Hell, are naturally virtuous, while the truly vicious are kept in bounds only by their belief in eternal punishment.

Fifty years later, Diderot's enormous *Encyclopédie* began to appear. This time the attack on Hell was direct. In an article on "Damnation," the illogic of the orthodox position is exposed, step by step: the disproportion between mortal sin, however severe, and eternal punishment; the pointlessness of post-judgment punishment; the difficulties of reconciling eternal pain with a merciful God or with the sacrifice of Jesus. Must virtuous pagans, noble savages, and all Protestants and other heretics be damned? Swinden and Whiston are trotted out solemnly, only to be held up as preposterous. There is only one argument for damnation: evidence for it is "clearly revealed in Scripture." Diderot's skepticism regarding scripture slashes through the bland statement.

The final volume of the *Encyclopédie* appeared in 1772, but Voltaire did not wait for it to bring out his own *Dictionnaire Philosophique*, which is no more a dictionary than Bayle's was, though much shorter. His motive in writing it was entirely subversive; the *Encyclopédie* was too large and ponderous to make a revolution, he said, but his cheap portable book, published anonymously in 1764 to immediate official excoriation, might do the trick.

Voltaire did not present arguments but stated facts, usually accurately, then drew logical but devastating conclusions from them. Dozens of barbs in deadpan homilies and "Chinese catechisms" relate to all aspects of death, resurrection, eschatology, apocalypse, miracles, biblical "facts," and philosophical theories. *"Enfer,"* his Hell entry, is not as amusing as some others, but it is accurate. He says that the Persians, Chaldeans (Mesopotamians), Egyptians, and Greeks invented Hell, not the Jews who believed in punishment only "to the fourth generation," and that it takes prodigious ingenuity to find obscure support for the idea in the Old Testament. He acknowledges belief in Hell among the Pharisees and Essenes, who got it from the Romans via the Greeks, and remarks that several church fathers rejected it because "it appeared ridiculous that a poor fellow should burn forever because he had stolen a goat." And lastly he quotes a priest who pooh-poohs the idea of eternal Hell but says that it is "well for your maid, your tailor, and especially your lawyer to believe it."

It is interesting to compare this approach with the *Dictionary* of Samuel Johnson (1709–1784). Johnson was a sincere Anglican and tended to look down his nose at the philosophes, despite the uncanny similarity of his satirical novel *Rasselas* to Voltaire's *Candide*, published in the same year. He gives six definitions of Hell, each backed with appropriate literary and biblical quotes, and a seventh comment:

> **HELL** n.f. [helle, Saxon]   1. The place of the devil and wicked souls.   2. The place of separate souls, whether good or bad.   3. Temporal death.   4. The place at a running play to which those who are caught are carried.   5. The place into which a tailor throws his threads.   6. The infernal powers.   7. It is used in composition by the old writers more than by the modern.

Nothing could be more correct or decorous. There is an odd little story that Boswell tells about Johnson, however, that throws some light on the variances among educated men of eighteenth century, men who, in this case, belonged to the same social set, or "club," as Boswell would put it.

On Saturday, June 12, 1784, the great man was dining with the reverend Dr. Adams, the "learned and pious" Mr. Henderson, and Boswell. At one point Johnson suddenly declared:

> "As I cannot be *sure* that I have fulfilled the conditions on which salvation is granted, I am afraid I may be one of those who shall be damned." (looking dismally) DR. ADAMS. "What do you mean by damned?" JOHNSON (*passionately and loudly*) "Sent to Hell, Sir, and punished everlastingly." DR. ADAMS. "I don't believe that doctrine." . . . [Johnson] was in gloomy agitation, and said, "I'll have no more on't."

To be sure, Johnson was seventy-five at the time. But Dr. Adams, the demurring clergyman, was three years his senior.

Compare this with Boswell's visit to David Hume, the Scottish philosopher, on Sunday, July 7, 1776, seven weeks before Hume's death. Rather untactfully, considering, Boswell introduced the subject of immortality and was astonished to find that Hume did not believe in it, nor in any kind of religion. Was not a future state possible? Boswell asked.

> He answered, It was possible that a piece of coal put on the fire would not burn; and he added that it was a most unreasonable fancy that he should exist forever. I asked him if the thought of Annihilation never gave him any uneasiness. He said not the least, no more than the thought that he had not been.

The thoroughly orthodox Boswell was dismayed, but persisted.

> "But," said I, "would it not be agreeable to have hopes of seeing our friends again," and I named three Men lately deceased, for whom I knew he had a high value. He owned it would be agreeable, but added that none of them entertained such a notion. I believe he said such a foolish, or such an absurd notion, for he was indecently and impolitely positive in incredulity.

Boswell took his leave, "with impressions that disturbed me for some time."

An eighteenth-century Tantalus by Honoré Daumier

THE EIGHTEENTH century left its mark on Hell in other ways as well. The form Lucian had invented, the "dialogue of the dead," was revived in magazines and pamphlets and became a favorite form of satire, religious and political commentary, and sometimes scandal. Equivalent illustrations were the sometimes macabre caricatures of William Hogarth (1697–1764), Francisco José de Goya (1746–1828), and many lesser artists. The participants of the dialogues were often classical or recently deceased celebrities, with Dr. Johnson a particular favorite. Others might be Minos, Pluto, Julius Caesar, Socrates, Montaigne, monarchs, bishops, society ladies, journalists like Addison and Steele. George Bernard Shaw's *Man and Superman*, featuring Don Juan in Hell, takes these as a model. Dialogues of the dead still turned up in early twentieth-century magazines.

Don Juan's career had been flourishing, together with that of his sorcerous equivalent, Faust. The Don, his beautiful paramours, and the Statue that flings him to Hell first came to the stage in *El Burlador de Sevilla*, a play written in about 1630 by a Spanish monk using the name of Tirso de Molina. In one version or another, notably in Mozart's *Don Giovanni* (1787), they have stayed there ever since. Here is an irresistibly silly song-and-dance Hell number written for the banquet scene of *The Libertine* (1676), a Don Juan play by a Restoration playwright named Thomas Shadwell:

FIRST DEVIL: Prepare, prepare, new Guests draw near,
And on the brink of Hell appear.

SECOND DEVIL: Kindle fresh Flames of Sulphur there.
Assemble all ye Fiends,
Wait for the dreadful ends
Of impious men, who far excel
All th' Inhabitants of Hell.

CHORUS OF DEVILS: Let 'em come, Let 'em come,
To an eternal dreadful Doom
Let 'em come, Let 'em come.

THIRD DEVIL: In mischiefs they have all the damn'd outdone;
Here they shall weep, and shall unpiti'd groan,
Here they shall howl, and make eternal moan.

FIRST DEVIL: By Blood and Lust they have deserved so well
That they shall feel the hottest flames of Hell.

SECOND DEVIL: In vain they shall here their past mischiefs bewail,
In exquisite torments that shall never fail.

THIRD DEVIL: Eternal Darkness they shall find,
And them eternal Chains shall bind,
To infinite pain of sense and mind.

CHORUS OF DEVILS: Let 'em come, Let 'em come,
To an eternal dreadful Doom
Let 'em come, Let 'em come.

At almost exactly the same time, William Mountfort produced and acted in *The Life and Death of Doctor Faustus Made Into a Farce*, which brought Harlequin and Scaramouche into the action. In 1724 a fancy-dress pantomime called *Harlequin Doctor Faustus* was produced at Drury Lane. Of a similar production by Colley Cibber, Pope comments in *The Dunciad*:

All sudden, Gorgons hiss and Dragons glare,
And tenhorn'd fiends and Giants rush to war.
Hell rises, Heaven descends, and dance on Earth:
Gods, imps and monsters, music, rage and mirth,
A fire, a jig, a battle and a ball,
Till one wide conflagration swallows all.

All over Europe in public squares and markets, puppet theaters thrived. Puppet plays were portable, cheap to produce with only a few actors (only one, in a real pinch), and could easily evade the state censorship of full-dress plays. Though children crowded into the audiences, the plays were not for their ears, but relied on the broadest possible folk humor. Originality was not the point of these shows, which counted, exactly like a present-day television sitcom, on repetitive stories featuring familiar characters. Punch and Judy is the last puppet tradition to survive, but the earlier exploits of Don Juan and Faust, the first featuring his successive seductions and the second his miracles and pranks, could be spun out as long as an audience's attention held. The Don and the Doctor were not even the real heroes of the plays; the audience cheered on their clownish servants, Hans

Pickelhäring, Hans Wurst, or Herlekin, whose adventures imitated and parodied their masters' until, at the end, when demons dragged the gentry toward Hellmouth, the bumpkins outwitted them and escaped, to laughter and applause. The Faust puppet plays, not Marlowe's drama—though traveling companies of actors playing Marlowe in translation had first inspired the puppeteers—were Goethe's source for *Faust*.

MOST PEOPLE in the eighteenth century were not engaged in the pursuit of reason, nor had they abandoned religion or even Hell itself. In 1732, Alphonso de' Liguori founded the order of Redemptorists specifically to send hellfire preachers to Catholic pulpits. Here is a sample from his parish handbook, *The Eternal Truths:*

> The unhappy wretch will be surrounded by fire like wood in a furnace. He will find an abyss of fire below, an abyss above, and an abyss on every side. If he touches, if he sees, if he breathes, he touches, sees, breathes only fire. He will be in fire like a fish in water. This fire will not only surround the damned, but it will enter into his bowels to torment him. His body will become all fire, so that the bowels within him will burn, his heart will burn in his bosom, his brains in his head, his blood in his veins, even the marrow in his bones; each reprobate will in himself become a furnace of fire.

The Jesuits were great sermonizers and during the time that the Encyclopedists were preparing their subversive messages the famous Abbé Bridaine and others were thundering imprecations on all Paris. But the glory of the Puritans was in their sermons and this was never more true than in America, where Protestant dissenters and extremists often chose to live.

Anglicans settled in the Virginia colonies. The *Mayflower* Puritans of Massachusetts were Congregationalists in revolt against the Anglican hierarchy. The Baptists broke away at about the same time, soon establishing themselves in Rhode Island. Persecuted in England, the Quakers settled Pennsylvania and Scottish Presbyterians joined them there and in New Jersey. John Wesley founded Methodism in the eighteenth century, and it took root in New York state, though the main church splintered into many branches.

Beginning in the 1730s, a wave of evangelical revivalism swept across the colonies. The so-called Great Awakening started in New Jersey with the Presbyterian evangelist Gilbert Tennent (1703–1764), but was quickly taken up in New England by the famous Congregationalist theologian Jonathan Edwards (1703–1758), followed by George Whitefield (1714–1770), a Calvinist Methodist whose sensational pulpit manner, as he said himself, combined "Flame, Clearness and Power." Their avowed purpose was "to drive the nail of terror into slumbering souls." Audiences responded with tears, shouts, convulsions, fainting fits, and mass conversions.

Edwards, the son and grandson of New England clergymen, had studied Newton and Locke at Yale, where he received his M.A. in 1723, and he endeavored, with considerable success, to draw natural science into the fold of Puritanism. He was a strict predestinarian, considering evil and its punishment to be part of the grand design, but something of an ecstatic too and skillful in the "preaching of terror." His first great revival meeting was in Northampton, Massachusetts, in 1734–35, and one of his most celebrated sermons, "Sinners in the Hands of an Angry God," was preached in 1741 when the Great Awakening was in full cry. "Their foot shall slide in due time," was his text and, "There is nothing that keeps wicked men at any one moment out of Hell but the mere pleasure of God," his interpretation, and his lurid imagery that of spiders dangling over flames from frail threads attached to God's fingers.

The polite Sunday behavior of those who shared the "innate, sinful depravity of the heart" evidently annoyed him. He ended another sermon entitled "The Future Punishment of the Wicked: Unavoidable and Intolerable":

> It will not be long before you will be wonderfully changed. You who now hear of Hell and the wrath of the great God, and sit here in these seats so easy and quiet and go away so careless, by and by will shake and tremble and cry out and shriek and gnash your teeth, and will be thoroughly convinced of the vast weight and importance of these great things which you now despise. You will not then need to hear sermons in order to make you sensible; you will be at a sufficient distance from slighting that wrath and power of God, of which you now hear with so much quietness and indifference.

Edwards is said to have thought that Whitefield's intensely emotional open-air evangelism went much too far. Unfortunately, none of it has survived in writing to contrast with his own moderation.

The first Great Awakening (others followed throughout the nineteenth century) had two distinct effects on American history. The emotions unleashed by it surely contributed to the revolutionary fever that soon caught the colonists, and that was seen by many as the start of the millennium.

The second effect was more subtle, and not one that revivalist leaders anticipated. The mass controversy and religious ferment caused by the revivalists were not lost upon the Founding Fathers. Distaste for religious zeal pushed men like Franklin and Jefferson, both of whom lived for a time in the France of the Enlightenment, away from the moderate Christianity to which they might otherwise have subscribed. Franklin became an out-and-out deist, Jefferson a tacit one. Both had the wit to see that America's religious pluralism must be supported in order to preserve her independence from factionalism and fanaticism. And so it happened that America's Declaration of Independence, written by Jefferson with the help of Franklin, refers only to "the Laws of Nature and Nature's God," a formulation Hume himself might have approved. In the Constitution, the name of God is nowhere mentioned, and church is firmly separated from state.

Swedenborg's Vision

ONE LAST TOWERING FIGURE OF the eighteenth century was Emanuel Swedenborg (1688–1772) of Stockholm, though his influence pervaded the nineteenth century rather than his own. Like so many of his contemporaries, Swedenborg, a bishop's son, was intensely interested in the sciences. In fact, he seems to have been something of a scientific genius, with interests ranging from astronomy to algebra to metallurgy to remarkably advanced physics to anatomical studies. Emerson admired him as "a colossal soul," and also, less admiringly, "one of the missouriums and mastodons of literature."

Swedenborg's accomplishments in science and philosophy have been obscured by the fame he achieved from the visionary spiritual revelations he began to record in his fifties. The accounts of these in his most famous book, *Heaven and Hell* (1758), are fascinatingly similar, yet dissimilar, to medieval vision literature. The approach is entirely different, the language cool, clear, and unemotional—the eyewitness records of a geographer—but the form is quite similar, though at immensely greater length. Unlike medieval visionaries, he was far more interested in angels and heavens than in hells. (These are plural in his cosmology, though they are subdivisions of a whole, as in many medieval visions.) Nevertheless, he dutifully records his visits to the lower world, to which he descended in a sort of brass elevator.

The spiritual world, he explained, has its own landscape, with plains, mountains, and streams, just like the natural world. The heavens are in the highest section, the world of spirits under that, and beneath both are the hells. Spirits cannot see the heavens except when their "inner sight" is opened, nor can the damned see above them. There is, however, an equilibrium between Heaven and Hell, for "from Hell there continually exhales and descends the effort of doing evil, and from Heaven there continually exhales and descends the effort of doing good." The echo of Origen is provocative, and so is the echo of *Tundal's* Lucifer, inhaling and exhaling sinners. Swedenborg allowed for no conversion after a choice was made, however, which irritated Emerson, the passionate universalist, as well as William Blake, another visionary who, at first fascinated, later recoiled from every whiff of predestination, and hence from Swedenborg.

Swedenborg's intermediate world of spirits is the one that most intrigued nineteenth-century "spiritists," and twentieth-century chroniclers of the "near-death experience." Its equivalent is the Catholic Purgatory without the punishments, or the place between Heaven and Hell that some Protestants were trying hard to define, and that occultists and mediums believed retained some commerce with our own world. In this gray Limbo-like area, spirits walk slowly, as Swedenborg saw them doing, toward Heaven or Hell, according to their natures.

Every heavenly division has a correspondent infernal one. The worst hells are those in the west, especially the northwest; in them are Roman Catholics "who wished to be worshiped as gods and who consequently burned with hatred and revenge against all who refused to acknowledge their power over the souls of men and over Heaven." In others are atheists, the worldly, the rancorous, the hostile, thieves, robbers, misers, and the greedy and unmerciful. Behind the northwestern hells are "dark forests in which malignant spirits prowl about like wild beasts," and behind the southwestern are deserts, where dwell those who "were most cunning in plotting artifices and deceits." The hells are classified in rigorous order according to the infinite varieties of evil.

> There are hells everywhere, both under the mountains, hills and rocks, and under the plains and valleys. These apertures or gates leading to the hells . . . appear to the sight like the holes and fissures of rocks, some wide-stretching, some confined and narrow, and most of them rugged.

All, when looked into, appear dark and dusky; but the infernal spirits who are within them wind themselves in a sort of light resembling that emitted from ignited charcoal. Their eyes are adapted to receive that light in consequence of their having been, while they lived in the world, in darkness with respect to divine truth. . . . All [the apertures] are covered over except when evil spirits from the world of spirits are cast in. When they are open, an exhalation proceeds from them, either like smoke or like fire or like soot or like a thick mist. I have heard that the infernal spirits do not see or feel these fires, smokes or mists because, when immersed in them, they are as if in their own atmosphere and thus in the delight of their life.

Swedenborg examined the hells and found the upper parts dark because their inhabitants were "immersed in the falsity of evil," while the lower parts were fiery, for there the sinners were immersed in evil itself.

In the milder hells are seen what appear like rude cottages, sometimes arranged contiguously as in a city with lanes and streets; and within these houses are infernal spirits who are engaged in continuous altercations, displays of enmity, beatings and efforts to tear one another to pieces; while in the streets and lanes are committed robberies and depredations. In some hells are brothels disgusting to behold, being full of all sorts of filth and excrement.

Despite the bucolic scenery, they smack of inner-city squalor and depravity. Emerson, who did not believe in them but was willing to salute visionary thinking, called both the heavens and hells ultimately dull: Swedenborg, he thought, lacked poetry. This opinion would have surprised Swedenborg himself; he appeared to believe he was still a scientist recording sober fact.

Emerson predicted that Swedenborg would not be read much longer, and this came to pass. But he cast a long shadow over the nineteenth century. As science continued to march forward, there began to be a revulsion against everything the Age of Reason stood for, a shift toward romanticism, spiritualism, intuition, ambiguity, and new forms of fantasy, much of it dark fantasy that toyed with the old views of Hell and the otherworld.

The Nineteenth Century

O N   J U N E   1 8 ,   1 8 1 5 ,   N A P O L E O N ' S forces fell at Waterloo, ending a quarter century of political upheaval. In October, he was sent to Saint Helena, there to end his life almost inevitably mythologized as a powerful symbol, a Satan in exile, a fallen hero who had appeared like an angel from nowhere—or like the Antichrist—to take charge of demoralized, bankrupt, blood-washed France and then to lead her on a terrifying crusade of world conquest.*

The French Revolution had far more impact on Europe than did the other in faraway America. The tyranny, corruption, and injustice that had rallied the French people offended liberals and reformists in the surrounding countries too. Primed by the Enlightenment, people thrilled in sympathy to the Declaration of the Rights of Man (1789). Poetry at the century's turn was full of hope and excitement, millennial in the most positive sense: France was to lead the way to the promised kingdom of God on earth. Disillusionment, when it came, was profound. It was no longer bliss to be alive.

The Spirit of the Age was much talked about; a series of thoughtful articles by John Stuart Mill that began to be published in the 1830s took

---

*Emerson tells us that Napoleon, who enjoyed debate, argued against the existence of Hell—expedient, since so many were convinced it was his natural home.

213

that title. On one level, the century moved straight ahead, accelerating ever faster. Industry prospered, science, exploration, conquest, trade, and railroads advanced, and great fortunes were made by men whom American historians have straightforwardly called "robber barons."

But underneath its progressive surface, the Spirit was uneasy. The earlier philosophes used wit, reason, and erudition to attack what they considered to be the tottering superstructure of superstition and imperial heritage. But the new age swept tradition aside, bringing uncertainty, a sense that reason had failed. Hence the Spirit was to a marked degree anti-intellectual, with a strong interest in the metaphysical. The historian Peter Gay notes: "Before the eighteenth century was over, the philosophes were under severe pressure from a Germanic ideology, a strange mixture of Roman Catholic, primitive Greek, and folkish Germanic notions—a kind of Teutonic paganism." By the end of the next century, the strange mixture had produced Gothic and Romantic literature and music, a strong interest in fantasy and folklore, and dozens of different occult and mystical sects including "diabolism." There was also the secular approach to soul-searching that would become psychoanalysis, as well as a morbid late-century fascination with death and dying such as had not been seen since the fifteenth century.

The "sublime" was much talked of. It is the word we associate with the drastic Alpine landscapes and fevered emotions of the Romantic period; it reaches beyond the order and harmony of mere beauty to the chaos of the infinite. In a 1756 essay, Edmund Burke said that "infinity has a tendency to fill the mind with that sort of delightful horror which is the most genuine effect and truest test of the sublime." The definition flirts with a revisionary nineteenth-century view of Hell.

The prose novel was developed in the eighteenth century with the reliable traditions of Don Juan and Faust as useful models. Don Juan was disguised as Lovelace in Samuel Richardson's *Clarissa* (1748) and as Valmont in Pierre Choderlos de Laclos's *Les Liaisons Dangereuses* (1782). Virtue is rewarded in both books (in Heaven, for both heroines die), but what drives their plots and keeps the reader turning pages is, emphatically, vice. The machinations of their aristocrat hero-villains bent on sin do not, however, lead them to their just rewards below. Something new was in the air.

Raw vice was the muse of the most notorious demonic aristocrat of the age, the Marquis de Sade (1740–1814). He spent much of his life either in prison or an insane asylum, which gave him plenty of time to fantasize,

LES LIAISONS DANGEREUSES.

BY CHODERLOS DE LACLOS

Proposed title page by Aubrey Beardsley from The Yellow Book

215

and he claimed that his pornographic inventions of bizarre rapes, tortures, and murders in the name of pure sexual pleasure (*Justine*, 1791; *Histoire de Juliette*, 1796) were legitimate extensions of Enlightenment ideas. If there is no God, there is no accountability, no social contract, and everything is permissible, including the wanton destruction of others. If people are objects (sex objects in the most literal sense of an often misused term), their wills count for nothing in a world where morality is subjective.

De Sade's influence was considerable. He stretched sensationalism and prurience beyond all previous limits of taste, and his violent secular scenarios went beyond apocalyptic visions of Hell, gruesome accounts of martyrdoms, or the most lurid revenge melodramas. No moral was attached to de Sade's writing; quite the opposite. The heavens themselves, enraged by the heroine's obstinate attachment to virtue throughout her multifarious degradations, strike her dead in *Justine*. The Marquis himself became, in later imagination, a kind of underground hero, a prototype of "mad, bad Lord Byron," the personification of the romantic doomed aristocrat.

The Gothic novel—so-called because of its "medieval" setting—started at about the same time and kept pace with the development of the "realistic" novel; *Clarissa* is, in fact, very close to a classic Gothic. Horace Walpole put his stamp on the genre in *The Castle of Otranto* (1764), investing the Don Juan theme with gothic paraphernalia: gloomy castles, clanking chains, stormy weather, brooding heroes, persecuted heroines, and the creaking Inquisitorial machinery we associate with this genre and with a great deal of Romantic poetry.

Despite the trappings, there was less about Hell in the Gothic novel than one might think. What very quickly happened—it seems almost inevitable after de Sade—was that Gothic authors began to re-create Hell on earth. They employed horror and terror—carefully differentiated, the first being natural, the second supernatural—for titillation, not for moralizing. Punishment was almost always the lot of the innocent; the guilty did the punishing.

In Matthew Gregory Lewis's *The Monk* (1789), the sadistic Gothic hit its stride. Written before he was twenty-one, the book won him lasting fame as "Monk" Lewis. De Sade thought it a masterpiece, and Byron agreed; more conventional opinion held that it was "poison for youth and a provocative for the debauchée." Lewis connected Roman Catholicism, via the depraved Abbot Ambrosio, with rape, orgies, and hair-raising violence. Lucifer himself steps in at the end to tear the sinful monk to pieces, but there is no actual Hell scene. Claustrophobia, imprisonment, torture, and underground gloom provide a satisfyingly hellish atmosphere, and those of Lewis's human beings who are not victims behave entirely demonically—the temptress Matilda *is* a demon.

The trend toward Hell on earth is even more apparent in Charles Robert Maturin's *Melmoth the Wanderer* (1820), an episodic Faust story set in a murky world of increasing decadence, despair, and corruption but with no final Hell scene either. In all of Poe, there is no literal Hell scene. In Victor Hugo's *Notre Dame de Paris* (1831), a dark underground kingdom of grotesquely deformed beggars stands in as a kind of earthly Hell, but the hunchback Quasimodo becomes a kind of reverse angel. Old supernatural formulas were useless to an age that increasingly embraced the psychologically uncanny. In a grand gesture that sums up the genre, Byron's Manfred categorically and contemptuously rejects them.

Goethe's Faust

WHERE DOES ONE PLACE THE great German poet Johann Wolfgang von Goethe (1749–1832) historically? His life was so long and so productive that his work spans entire creative periods, from eighteenth-century classicism through Germany's Sturm und Drang era, which he virtually created and later rejected, through the French Revolution and the Napoleonic Wars—he met and rather approved of Napoleon—right past Gothic Romanticism into Victorianism and on to the phantasmagoric experimentalism of the modern age. *Faust,* the masterwork that concerns us here, was written and revised over a period of sixty years. Nineteenth-century Romantic opera found its inspiration in the first part of the drama,* while an entire lineage of twentieth-century literature owes an immeasurable debt to the second part, published, by his request, after Goethe's death.

Goethe was born in Frankfurt, the son of a lawyer, and studied law himself, first at Leipzig till he fell ill, then at Strasbourg where he took a degree in 1771. He was interested in art and architecture, in medicine and

---

*Berlioz, Boito, Gounod, Schumann, Liszt, and Mahler all tackled *Faust,* the latter two in symphonies. Wagner, too, was influenced by it though he did not approach it directly. Goethe himself did not care for the Romantic approach and regretted that Mozart could not have set it to music. He greatly admired *Don Giovanni* and actually began a sequel to *The Magic Flute,* which is thought to have influenced the "Helena" section of Part II of *Faust.*

218

science (he anticipated Darwin's work on evolution), in philosophy where he particularly admired Spinoza, in occult mysticism, Swedenborgian and otherwise, and—very much—in women. From his early teens until his death, Goethe was nearly always paying passionate court to one woman after another, though he was married only once—for expedience—to a servant who had some years earlier borne him a son.

Sturm und Drang ("Storm and Stress") was a deliberate reaction against the classical cadences of Corneille and Racine, the French playwrights who dominated the eighteenth-century stage. Its first sensational success was Goethe's novel of unrequited love, *The Sorrows of Young Werther* (1774), which is said to have triggered a continent-wide wave of suicides among rejected lovers. It also put Germany, which had been considered a backward nation culturally, on the literary map and caught the eye of Charles Augustus, the young duke of Saxe-Weimar, who invited the author first to visit him and then to become his minister of state. Goethe lived in the duchy for the rest of his life, occupying himself with agriculture, mining, the sciences, and, for more than twenty years, directing a theater for the duke.

All this time he continued to write, mainly for the theater, though he completed two more popular novels, *Wilhelm Meisters Lehrjahre* (1796) and *Die Wahlverwandtschaften* (1809). But his masterpiece, which occupied him on and off for most of his life, was *Faust*.

In his early twenties, before he went to Weimar, he began to work on the basic plot of Part I in which Faust, encouraged by Mephistopheles, seduces and abandons an innocent virgin, Gretchen. He had not read Marlowe's play, but he was familiar with the marketplace puppet plays of *Dr. Faustus* and *Don Juan*, whose plots he appropriated and combined. In 1790, he published *Faust: A Fragment*, to great admiration. In 1808, Part I was published in the completed form that became the basis of subsequent operas and plays. Twenty years later, he published "Helena," the self-contained fragment of Part II which includes his tribute to Byron. He finished and sealed up Part II shortly before he died.

Strictly speaking, there is no underworld scene in *Faust*. One was planned for Part II: Faust was to descend to Proserpine's court to ask for Helena's hand. Obviously, this would not have worked with the Christian ending he decided on, so instead he let the female demons of Hades loose on earth in "Classical Walpurgis Night," sending the bewildered but captivated Gothic demon Mephistopheles to dance among them in a fine satiric scene that parallels the witches' conclave of Part I.

Goethe's ending was something of a shock to intellectual circles. Gretchen had been a Catholic in early versions of Part I, but it was clear that she was only a simple girl and Faust himself was, if anything, an occultist like Goethe. The Prologue's wager between God and the Devil, echoing Job, indicated that God (or Goethe) planned to save Faust. But after the intellectual ironies and fantasies of Part II, written in a succession of literary styles, including the classical and the Miltonic, the final scene pulls some surprises. At the moment of reckoning, traditional demons tumble from Hellmouth on one side of the stage to fetch him away—but a battalion of *putti* and *amoretti,* heavenly choruses, and the Virgin herself descend from Heaven on the other in a scenario worthy of a Victorian candy box. It seems to be a neo-Baroque parody of a miracle play. Gretchen, the "eternal feminine," intercedes for Faust though he hardly deserves it. Mephisto loses the day only because he is distracted and aroused sexually by bare cherubic bottoms. No wonder Goethe preferred to seal up his manuscript rather than argue, as he surely would have had to do, over an outcome bound to startle everybody but the most willfully un-imaginative Catholic apologists—who probably took it as a sign that the old man had undergone a deathbed conversion.

The Romantics

THE RENAISSANCE REVELLED IN ITS rediscovery of classical myth, Milton extended the Christian myth, the deists made a myth of science, and the Enlightenment tried to explode any kind of mythmaking. Romantic writers, rebelling against the past, made new or syncretic myths which sought to overturn and discredit the old ones. As the century progressed, these new myths became more perverse, more occult or fantastical (though arguably less original), more dependent on induced visions or drugs, more self-consciously decadent. A point of view began to emerge all over Europe that could legitimately be called a "counterculture."

This radical perspective can be seen at the very beginning of the century in the writings and illustrations of William Blake (1757–1827), which in some ways stand as an epitome of what was to come. Blake, the son of a London hosier or stocking maker, was apprenticed to an engraver as a boy. At twenty-one, he set up shop for himself and worked all his life at his trade, assisted by his wife Catherine.* He had no higher education, though he was a great reader. His theology was self-invented, but he can fairly be

---

*It was a happy marriage. A splendid anecdote tells of a neighbor who came calling only to find Mr. and Mrs. Blake sitting in their garden summerhouse reciting passages from *Paradise Lost,* both of them stark naked. "Come in!" cried Blake. "It's only Adam and Eve, you know!"

called a profoundly religious and visionary man. In a series of complex epic poems, he replaced classical, Christian, Miltonic, Swedenborgian, and even Dantean mythological systems with one of his own.

These systemic poems were scarcely known in Blake's lifetime, and even today his reputation depends on his beautiful short lyrics and on his hundreds of stylized paintings and illustrations that seem to take on more depth and meaning with time. Still, Blake is like a litmus paper for his times, sensitive to everything that now seems to define them. He responded to the American and French revolutions with apocalyptic poems, radiant or despairing according to the course of history, to *Paradise Lost*—the essential poem for half a century of poets—with his own *Milton*, and to Swedenborg with *The Marriage of Heaven and Hell*. He echoes the occult or mystical stirrings of the era. It is in his poetry that we first see the negative side of the industrial revolution; in "London" and "Jerusalem" the city slums are represented as a Hell for the neglected poor. Later poets would take up these images to the point of cliché, but Blake has not lost his power. Like an Old Testament prophet, he excoriated the hypocrisy and cruelty of the age. In his epics, too, we first see the Satan figure presented as a heroic rebel against an oppressive tyrant; no other theme is so central to high Romantic poetry.

Blake's allegorical system is difficult to decipher even with a guide because his symbols and identifications shift. It helps to know that "demonic" figures are presented positively because Blake identified them with the genius or *daemon* of poetry, what Nietzsche would call the Dionysian force of the chaotic sublime as opposed to the orderly Apollonian force of classical beauty; this is what Blake meant by saying (of Milton) that "a true poet is of the Devil's party."

No later poet attempted so complex a mythology as Blake's, though *Prometheus Unbound*, by Percy Bysshe Shelley (1792–1822), also presents a tyrannical Jupiter, a Gnostic "all-miscreative" Demiurge who must be overthrown to achieve a millennial new Heaven and new earth. Opposed to him is Prometheus, the suffering Titan chained to his precipice. Shelley's preface to the poem holds up Prometheus directly, and favorably, to Milton's Satan as "susceptible of being described as exempt from the taints of ambition, envy, revenge and a desire for personal aggrandisement." Prometheus's immovable position on the Caucasian peak complicates the descent motif, which Shelley solves by sending Asia, a spiritual avatar of his hero, down to the Deep, the otherworld "underneath the grave," where among "Terrible, strange, sublime and beauteous shapes" she will find the gods and powers of nameless worlds, phantoms, heroes, beasts, and "Demogorgon, a tremendous Gloom."

The Deep is not Hell or even Hades, which Shelley associates with Jupiter and his Furies (read: perverted Christianity, or the established authority of a combined church and state). Demogorgon is a great, dark, formless being whom Shelley identified with the force of the inchoate and inarticulate masses. Overthrown, Jupiter falls to what seems like a Christian Hell (though it could be Platonic), echoing both Greek tragedy and the old mystery plays:

> *Let Hell unlock*
> *Its mounded Oceans of tempestuous fire,*
> *And whelm on them into the bottomless void*
>
> . . . .
>
> *Ai! Ai!*
> *The elements obey me not. I sink*
> *Dizzily down—ever, for ever, down.*
> *And, like a cloud, mine enemy above*
> *Darkens my fall with victory! Ai, Ai!*

Earth, the Moon, and the spirit rejoice in a great celebration of Love, joined by a newly articulate Demogorgon celebrating freedom from "Heaven's Despotism."

John Keats (1795–1821) chose Hyperion, the sun god deposed by Apollo, as his Titan. His first attempt at the myth, *Hyperion*, ran into Shelley's technical problem: in underworld Tartarus, the fallen Titans are paralyzed—almost literally turned to stone—by grief and gloom, making any kind of action difficult. Keats solved the problem of mobility in his second attempt, *The Fall of Hyperion*, by sending himself, in a dream-vision, into the underworld (he had been reading Dante). He finds himself before what appear to be the steps of Purgatory, which he is ordered to climb by the Titaness Moneta. Fearfully, he obeys, shrieking from pain at the icy cold. Moneta tells him that he has now learned what it is to die. He next sees Tartarus itself. His poet-self must suffer, die, and conquer Hell in order to be reborn as Hyperion's successor, Apollo, who is not only the sun god but the god of poetry.

223

The incomplete poem remains a fascinating early look at the descent motif as a metaphor for creative ambition and the artist's struggle with the titanic figures of his predecessors or father-figures. Sometimes, the whole nineteenth century seems to be lying in wait for Freud.

In his own day, George Gordon, Lord Byron (1788–1824) was widely agreed to be the central figure of Romantic poetry, as much for the Romantic hero-villain he himself represented as for what he wrote. Byron had taken dissipation a long way: rumor of incest with his half-sister had blackened his reputation, his marriage had foundered amid reports of domestic sadism, and various sexual scandals had forced him out of England. His sardonic response to exile was to publish *Manfred*, a Faust-drama about an unregenerate "Satanic," or indeed "Byronic" nobleman recognizably steeped in incestuous sin. Manfred refuses allegiance to either God or the Devil (here called Arimanes) and at the end, with ultimate machismo, he refuses to go to Hell, treating the traditional demons sent to drag him off like presumptuous lackeys:

> *Back to thy Hell!*
> *Thou hast no power upon me, that, I feel;*
> *Thou never shall possess me, that I know:*
> *What I have done is done; I bear within*
> *A torture which could nothing gain from thine:*
> *The mind which is immortal makes itself*
> *Requital for its good or evil thoughts—*
> *Is its own origin of ill and end—*
> *And its own place and time. . . .*
>
> Thou *didst not tempt me, and thou couldst not tempt me*
> *I have not been thy dupe, nor am thy prey—*
> *But was my own destroyer, and will be*
> *My own hereafter—Back, ye baffled fiends!*
> *The hand of death is on me—but not yours!*

Byron flung his contempt straight in the faces of the "baffled fiends" of the British bourgeois establishment and could not have been more successful. He represented himself, not without irony, as the solitary Promethean rebel against tyranny, the exiled artist, the doomed Don Juan that women longed for, the disdainful Gothic anti-hero, exploiting his dark reputation to the hilt. The public bought his act—and his books. Goethe celebrated him as Euphorion, the Spirit of Poetry, interrupting *Faust* with an elegy after Byron's "poetic" death at Missolonghi; surely another kind of tribute was also intended in Goethe's giving Mephistopheles a single deformed hoof—a reference to Byron's famous clubbed foot.

Byron went back to the demonic theme in *Cain*, in which, predictably, Lucifer himself is the Byronic hero. The Hell here is interesting because it shows another side of the age and of the poet himself. Byron had been reading the French geologist and paleontologist Baron Georges Cuvier (1769–1832), an intermediate figure between the Comte de Buffon and Darwin. The baron had come to the conclusion, still current, that a catastrophe, or a series of them, had killed off the creatures whose huge bones were being collected increasingly by nineteenth-century fossil hunters. Byron used the biblical account of "giants in the earth in those days" to propose the "poetical fiction" that these included bones of "rational beings much more intelligent than man and proportionately powerful to the mammoth, etc., etc." With the spirits of these lost beings, he populated a sort of science-fictional Hades somewhere in space. Lucifer transports Cain thither in much the same way that Superman carries Lois Lane over Metropolis. Cain, fascinated but fearful, asks:

> *Oh ye interminable gloomy realms*
> *Of swimming shadows and enormous shapes.*
> *Some fully shown, some indistinct, and all*
> *Mighty and melancholy—what are ye?*
> *Live ye, or have ye lived?*

"Somewhat of both," replies Lucifer, piloting him past "beautiful and mighty" shapes that once were:

> *Intelligent, good, great, and glorious things,*
> *As much superior unto all thy sire,*
> *Adam, could e're have been in Eden, as*
> *The sixty-thousandth generation shall be,*
> *In its dull damp degeneracy, to*
> *Thee and thy son;—and how weak they are, judge*
> *By thy own flesh.*

Great beasts lie beyond the "phantasm of an ocean":

> *And yon immense*
> *Serpent, which rears his dripping mane and vasty*
> *Head ten times higher than the haughtiest cedar*
> *Forth from the abyss, looking as he could coil*
> *Himself round the orbs we lately look'd on—*
> *Is he not of the kind which bask'd beneath*
> *The tree in Eden?*

The brontosaurus as the Eden serpent!

The theme of incest (yet again) and the celebration of rational disobedience to mindless orthodoxy (Cain's defiance of Yahweh) branded the poem as blasphemous, which Byron obviously intended it to be. His message was also obvious. Knowledge and love are worth having, Lucifer states categorically, and any God (or government) that prevents them may fairly be called evil.

BYRON AND Shelley may have experimented with drugs in Italy, but other nineteenth-century poets went beyond experimentation into a region that they very naturally equated with Hell. Though there was as yet no medical concept of addiction, when Samuel Taylor Coleridge (1772–1834) and Thomas De Quincey (1785–1859) began taking their "anodynes" of laudanum, or tincture of opium, early in the century, they understood the Faustian bargain: charmed magic casements, yes, but at a price.

Visions have always had their price, which some men and women have always been willing to pay. In the Middle Ages that price included marathon hypnotic prayers, fasting, flagellation, fever, induced sleeplessness, and, some think, the ingestion of such naturally occurring hallucinogens as ergot, a fungus that attacks wheat. For some people, like Blake or Bosch, visions seem to have come naturally. But drugs, more readily available in the industrial age, made visions easy to achieve. A brave new world of discovery lay in the antipodes of the mind, brilliantly colored and poisonously seductive, a dangerously "poetical" allegorical Hell.

Drug-related experiences so frequently take the form of journeys into the otherworld that psychedelic experimenters of the late twentieth century

Gustave Doré's illustration for the Ancient Mariner

---

routinely referred to them as "trips." Coleridge's *The Rime of the Ancient Mariner* is a prototype. The Mariner's vessel bursts into a strange sea where, under an unnatural tropic sun, it is at once becalmed and surrounded by uncannily bright waters filled with "a thousand, thousand slimy things" and hostile spirits. A spectral ship manned by Death and "the Night-mare Life-in-Death" appears, and one after another the sailors drop down dead till the Mariner is left alone, parched for water. For seven days and nights of private penance (for having killed an albatross) he yearns for death with no avail till, by moonlight, he looks down at the "slimy things" he has despised and sees their "rich attire" in the phosphorescent light. When love for the watersnakes gushes from his heart—another example of a Romantic reversal—the spell is broken and rain comes, followed by a wind that blows the ship, now manned by angels inhabiting the dead men's bodies, back to the real world.

It has been argued that the *Ancient Mariner*, even with Coleridge's own (quite beautiful) margin glosses, does not make a great deal of sense. But sense, in the outer reaches, is not the whole point and, in any event, is not completely under control, which is not to say that the sensibility of drug-induced visions is completely random. The *Ancient Mariner* and Coleridge's other brilliant supernatural fragments, *Christabel* and *Kubla Khan* (which he admitted was drug-induced), have never lost their appeal.

Like the English, the French Romantics sparred with Milton's Satan, but Napoleon had lived among them, and their attempts at rebellion were not so successful. Chateaubriand transported Hell to North America (*Les Natchez*, 1826), while Victor Hugo wrote an unfinished trilogy on Satan, whom he intended to redeem. Meanwhile, younger French poets took their own road, washing down hashish and opium with absinthe, an addictive drink based on wormwood, which causes hallucinations and, eventually, brain damage. The syphilis contracted by Charles Baudelaire (1821–1867) brought him close to madness before he was forty. Baudelaire, a disciple of Swedenborg and an admirer of Byron and Poe, called his first collection *Les Fleurs du Mal*, "The Flowers of Evil" (1857). In it, nearly every poem refers in some way to Satan, Hell's inhabitants, corpses, vampires, or at least vice of some ominous sort. The poet does not exactly identify with them, but he feels their attraction, their glamor. He has freely, if somewhat ironically, chosen to wander in Hell, with drugs as his guide and his downfall; at its worst it is a change from the drab world, and, at its best, it defies the Jehovah that he, too, rejected. The interpenetration of good and evil in this poetry, the celebration of "cold and sinister beauty" is complete. The book was taken to court for obscenity, and six of its poems were condemned but it was too much a product of its time not to remain in vogue.

Arthur Rimbaud (1854–1891) was Baudelaire's disciple, a *poète maudit* even to the point of similarly contracting syphilis. His poetic career lasted only from his sixteenth to his nineteenth year, and he is said to have made a virtual religion of drugs. *Une Saison en Enfer* ("A Season in Hell") is less about drugs than about his affair with Paul Verlaine, a third poet dedicated to narcotics, but Rimbaud also wrote perhaps the most famous "trip" poem of all. "Le Bateau Ivre" ("The Drunken Boat") depicts a wild ride down a hallucinatory New World river. The poet has lost control of his vomit-stained body, his boat, to the drug or drink which carries him higher and faster down the river which becomes every river, soaring up and out into the Milky Way. Bosch-like landscapes—"fantastic Floridas"—flash by, mixing strangeness with memory, so that the experience becomes one of exhilarating terror, the infinite sublime, a Hell that he both loathes and loves.

Vision-journeys into the soul need not be drug-induced, of course, but it often helps to sound as though they were. Herman Melville's early sea stories were straightforward, even jolly, in tone but for the long, allegorical vision-voyage of *Moby-Dick* (1851) he found a hallucinatory style that seems intrinsic to the material. One also might recall the turbulent, gleaming twentieth-century vision-voyages of Hart Crane, and the elegant parodies of the entire genre by that least druggy of poets, Wallace Stevens, for instance in "The Comedian as the Letter C."*

Drugs were frequently associated with late Victorian occultism, especially with diabolist groups like the Hermetic Order of the Golden Dawn, whose members included William Butler Yeats, Algernon Swinburne (in whose poetry erotic sadomasochism of the Hell-on-earth kind was extreme), and Oscar Wilde. (Yeats, a lifelong believer in the occult, took as his "spiritual" name Demon Est Deus Inversus, "The Devil Is God Reversed"). Diablerie was chic in the "heavy purple smoke" of the fin de siècle, though it was often infused with irony, as in Aubrey Beardsley's illustrations.

The oddest Victorian drug poem must certainly be Christina Rossetti's *Goblin Market* (1862). Though she was linked to London artistic circles by her brother, the poet and artist Dante Gabriel Rossetti, it seems unlikely that she had much firsthand experience of drugs. But what is one to make of Laura's sojourn among the "cat-faced" and "rat-faced" demonic goblins

---

* The Beatles have stoutly denied that their 1967 song "Lucy in the Sky with Diamonds" was drug related; it is nevertheless a perfect miniature vision-voyage, perhaps the nursery version.

who tempt her with strange fruit? Poor Laura is an instant addict, though the goblins torment her by disappearing from her ken. Virtuous Lizzie, who cannot bear her sister's misery, visits the goblins herself, who show her their true nature:

> *Their tones waxed loud,*
> *Their looks were evil.*
> *Lashing their tails*
> *They trod and hustled her,*
> *Elbowed and jostled her,*
> *Clawed with their nails,*
> *Barking, mewing, hissing, mocking,*
> *Tore her gown and soiled her stocking,*
> *Twitched her hair out by the roots,*
> *Stamped upon her tender feet,*
> *Held her hands and squeezed their fruits*
> *Against their mouth to make her eat.*

It is a scene warped from a medieval mystery play by way of *Sir Orfeo*. But stranger still is to come. Brave Lizzie will not taste, but, drenched with goblin juices, she runs home to Laura and cries:

> *"Did you miss me?*
> *Come and kiss me.*
> *Never mind my bruises,*
> *Hug me, kiss me, suck my juices*
> *Squeezed from goblin fruits for you,*
> *Goblin pulp and goblin dew.*
> *Eat me, drink me, love me;*
> *Laura, make much of me."*

And Laura falls on her. "Shaking with aguish fear and pain,/ She kissed her and kissed her with a hungry mouth." The juice is bitter this time, but Laura cannot stop. Luckily, Lizzie's virtue turns the juice on her body into an antidote, and Laura is delivered from the "poison in the blood"— which, together with its cozy moral about sisterly love and a willful Victorian blindness to nuance, is all that saved this eyebrow-raising poem for family reading.

AS THE Victorians, fascinated with spiritualism or mesmerism or theosophy and following the example of their queen, made a fetish out of mourning and the cult of the dead, especially if the corpse was a young person; they also loved ghost stories, horror stories, and fantasies, few of

Illustration by Laurence Houseman for Goblin Market

which were notably Christian, though some had saccharine morals troweled on at the end.* Like American horror stories, which were more or less invented by Edgar Allan Poe (1809–1849), they avoided Hell in favor of bogeys and apparitions, revenants from the occult and mysterious spirit world "beyond the grave." Soon science fiction would send in replacements from beyond the galaxy.

Out of all the rich available material, three Gothic novels provided the essential popular fantasies for the twentieth century. They have been copied and adapted over and over again with no end in sight. These are, of course, Mary Shelley's *Frankenstein* (1818), where science brings to life and then abandons a monster; Robert Louis Stevenson's *The Strange Case of Dr. Jekyll and Mr. Hyde* (1886), in which the Faustian scientist creates life not from spare parts but from the Id made manifest; and Bram Stoker's *Dracula* (1897), the ultimate Gothic demon-lover serial-killer story.

Hell has no place in any of these novels. Dracula and his minions are demons, but they are not Christian demons, despite the hocus-pocus with crucifixes. They are night creatures from the black forests of folklore, and no one thinks for a moment that when the dust crumbles away the vampire spirits or their victims are destined for Hell. Hyde is a demon, too, but despite some conventional Victorian hand wringing on the narrator's part, he is an important modern metaphor, not a supernaturally damned soul; his counterpart is Dorian Gray (1891), who hides the soul of Hyde behind the face of Jekyll. (Oscar Wilde seemed to feel that the shame of having his true hideousness discovered by the servants would be punishment enough for Dorian—no doubt he was right.) Mary Shelley was a progressive, well ahead of her time, while Stoker and Stevenson were very much of theirs, but none of them found any need for a punitive Hell for their benighted creatures.

Thus, by the end of the nineteenth century, Hell had virtually disappeared from the popular culture. Even if a literal Hell had still been part of the middle-class mind-set, where would it be situated? Certainly not underground, not after 1865, when Lewis Carroll published *Alice's Adventures in Wonderland*. It would have to be somewhere out in space with William Whiston, or with Byron.

---

*It is strange, and not very comfortable, to find Lutheran moralism tipped into the Nordic fables of Hans Christian Andersen; one can hardly blame the twentieth century for censoring him so heavily. I find his Hell fable, "The Girl Who Trod on a Loaf," repellent, though unforgettable.

Universalism

The late nineteenth century was also seeking to dispense with Hell inside the Christian fold, though not without a fierce struggle. Ever since Origen had first speculated about eventual forgiveness for all, the concept of universal salvation had lurked in the background of Christianity, sternly repudiated by both Protestant and Catholic hierarchies but never entirely vanquished. At the time of the Enlightenment, deviant theories were openly discussed for the first time in 1,500 years. The Romantic view of God as Love, familiar to us now but something of a novelty one hundred and fifty years ago, demanded a new look at damnation.

One of the first men to proclaim the doctrine of universal salvation, in about 1750, was the Englishman James Relly (c. 1720–1778), at first a Baptist follower of the notorious George Whitefield, whose fire-breathing revivalism gave pause even to Jonathan Edwards. Relly was apparently still more dismayed by it. He abandoned Whitefield for John Wesley's more moderate Methodism, but soon moved further to the left, eventually repudiating orthodox Calvinism—which would, at this point, include most English denominations except, perhaps, the Quakers—to become an itinerant preacher whose message was, "If Christ died for all, then all will be saved."

One of Relly's converts was the Calvinist John Murray (1741–1815), who arrived in Good Luck, New Jersey, in 1770, and began immediately to preach universal salvation all over the northeast colonies. His Baptist colleague, Elhanan Winchester (1751–1797), founded the Universal Baptist Church in 1781. By 1790, conversion had proceeded to the point where a Universalist Convocation was held in Philadelphia, and by the 1820s the church was securely established in America.

Early Universalists held to the orthodox views of whichever Protestant denomination they professed on all subjects except eternal torment. Like the early English deists, they believed in Hell, but regarded a sojourn there as temporary and corrective. Murray argued that God's goodness forbade anything more punitive, and also—following Origen, whether or not he knew it—that men would retain free will in Hell and could there repent, which they surely would, considering the horrors therein. But the influential leader Hosea Ballou (1771–1852), though no more educated than his predecessors, had a thoughtful and intellectual bent; he had read the deists and believed in reason, and he admired Thomas Jefferson and Ethan Allen. He began to face squarely the theological difficulties of the universalist position: If God's nature guarantees salvation, and man's nature is such that he will eventually choose good, what is the meaning of Christ's sacrifice? Why would one need to believe in his deity or his resurrection? Why is a Trinity needed? What meaning can be given to the Fall of Man or Original Sin? Most of all, if there is no everlasting Hell, what is there to be "saved" from?

Ballou concluded, radically, that none of the orthodox theological baggage was necessary: the Crucifixion guaranteed salvation from a doom that, since its time, no longer existed. He went from disbelief in eternal torment to disbelief in Hell altogether, which caused consternation leading to schism in his own church. Universalists shifted back and forth along this ground, moving toward transitory punishment in the late nineteenth century—it was known as "restoration"—then away from it toward Ballou's extreme position in the twentieth, by which time many Universalists had stopped believing in any afterlife.

Universalism prospered, however, establishing its own schools—the American public school system owes much to Universalist Horace Mann —and universities. It handled the Darwin crisis of the 1860s much better than rival Christian denominations and generally established itself as pro-science. And pro-business, too: P. T. Barnum, the impresario and circus master, was a prominent Universalist, which did not prevent him from proclaiming that a sucker was born every minute. In the twentieth century, deciding that true religion is "universal" in all senses of the word, the Universalists reached out to the other great world religions. In 1960, the Universalist Church of America was consolidated with the American Unitarian Association.

But in the nineteenth century, when tempers ran hot among the orthodox, the doctrine of universal salvation, especially when even a temporary Hell was doubted, was attacked from all sides on precisely the grounds Ballou had identified. To put God in the position of having to save all men, even the worst sinners, seemed immoral and blasphemous, and, as Arminian free-will proponents pointed out, just as deterministic as Calvinism. To deny the reality of Hell, and thus the vital importance of the Crucifixion, was to abandon Christianity altogether. This was mere "humanism," anathema to many people by no means as restricted in their views as America's late-twentieth-century fundamentalists.

Most American theological seminaries were either founded or already operating in the nineteenth century, and a look through the dusty shelves of their old library collections is an education in the fervor of the argument. Some Victorian titles from Emory in Atlanta, founded by Methodists in 1836, include *A History of Opinion on the Scriptural Doctrine of Retribution* (1878), *Everlasting Punishment and Eternal Life* (1879), *Everlasting Punishment* (1880), *What is of Faith as to Everlasting Punishment* (1880), *What is the Truth as to Everlasting Punishment?* (1881), *The Endless Future: The Probable Connection between Human Probation and the Endless Universe that Is to Be* ("The author prefers to publish this book anonymously. Truth, not notoriety, is his aim and inspiration." 1885), *Doom Eternal* (1887), *Future Retribution: Viewed in the Light of Reason and Revelation* (1887), *God's Mercy in Punishment* (1890), *Future Retribution* (1892), and so on, on both sides of the debate. As many of these tracts were written by the British as by Americans, and many of the authors were not clergymen but simply outspoken Victorians with strong convictions.

The right wing was determined, however. Pope Leo XIII issued a bull in 1879 affirming an eternal Hell and the existence of the Devil, and Catholic intellectuals were expected to toe the line. Conventional Victorian parents presented their children with Bunyan's books or with *The Sight of Hell,* a

Illustrations from Hell Opened to Christians to caution them from Entering into it, *Dublin, 1841*

This figure represents the person convinced of sin, and is endeavouring to flee the wrath to come.

From The Spiritual Mirror or Looking-Glass Exhibiting the Human Heart as Either the Temple of God or the Habitation of Devils, *1830*

best-seller by the Reverend Joseph Furniss, in which damned souls shrieked in dungeons:

> The little child is in the red-hot oven. Hear how it screams to come out; see how it turns and twists itself about in the fire. It beats its head against the roof of the oven. It stamps its little feet on the floor. . . . God was very good to this little child. Very likely God saw it would get worse and worse and never repent, and so it would have been punished more severely in Hell. So God in his mercy called it out of the world in early childhood.

Convention won the battle but not the war. Most Christian denominations still affirm belief in an eternal Hell, but only Catholic traditionalists and Protestant fundamentalists put much emphasis on it. Hell has become something of an embarrassment, and a bishop who resorts to threats of damnation is quickly roasted in the popular press. Privately, most people who believe in an afterlife seem to take a loose Universalist position, either the modern one or the older corrective one.

Publicly, no other Christian denomination has yet taken the step of the Unitarian-Universalists who ringingly proclaim, in near-Emersonian prose:

The doctrine of an eternal hell we unqualifiedly reject, as the foulest imputation upon the character of God possible to be conceived, and as something which would render happiness in heaven itself impossible, since no beings whose hearts were not stone, would be happy anywhere knowing that half the human family, including many of their own loved ones, were in torments. Instead of such a dark and God-dishonoring doctrine, we believe that the future existence will be one ruled by Eternal Justice and Love, that he whom in this world we call "our Father" will be no less a Father to all his human children in the world to come, and that the world will be so planned as not only to bring eternal good to all who have done well here, but also to offer eternal hope to such as have done ill here.

The Age of Freud

FOUR FIGURES ARE FREQUENTLY CITED as the prophets of the modern world. The intellectual shock of the mid-nineteenth century was the publication of *The Origin of Species* in 1859, in which Charles Darwin (1809–1882) put forward a theory of biological determinism that profoundly altered the most advanced philosophical ideas. The mechanical universe, already creaking as it expanded outward, fell to pieces at once as the organic struggle was seen to extend down eons of geological time. The harmonic design that had been thought to demonstrate God's power and goodness now appeared to be the result of a series of individual sexual successes. It was a nasty thought, implying atheism and immorality, and many took (or take) great offense at it, as well as at the prospect of being ourselves descended from apes or near-apes instead of created whole in God's image. Others hailed the new gospel as a sure sign of progress, a demonstration that nature and the nation can and do move onward and upward.

Even earlier, in 1848, Karl Marx (1818–1883) had published the *Communist Manifesto*, though the more influential *Das Kapital*, edited by Friedrich Engels, would not appear till the end of the century. Marx simply swept religion aside as a distraction, "the opium of the people" historically used to promote and protect exploitation and tyranny. Progress demanded its elimination, together with that of private property, class differences, and unfair division of labor and wages. Before these ideas were tested in the great national caldrons of the twentieth century, they presented a formidable intellectual and humanitarian argument.

Friedrich Nietzsche (1844–1900) did not believe in progress, especially by enforced egalitarianism. Human beings were far too conformist and mediocre as it was, he thought, and Christianity was used, despicably, to keep them in line with bizarre supernatural threats. The *Übermensch*, or "superman," a word that has become permanently perverted by the Nazis, was, for Nietzsche, the individual who has the will and the power to resist conformity (especially to anything resembling fascism, including organized religion) and to set his own high personal ethical standard. Goethe was Nietzsche's example of a proper "superman." Like the poets of his time, he celebrated sublime or "Dionysian" joyousness as something beyond the order of "Apollonian" beauty.

But for the modern view of Hell, Sigmund Freud (1856–1939) is central. Metaphorical or "poetical" thinking advanced in the nineteenth century, but Freud's ventures into mental topography threw new light into dark areas and permanently and importantly changed the modern vocabulary. Questions of predestination versus free will are peripheral to an age preoccupied with the struggle of the primitive Id with the Ego and Superego.

Demons themselves can't break into the safe. Nineteenth-century ad.

We speak of anxiety, inhibition, repression, and Oedipal guilt now, not Original Sin, though Freud (unlike many of his followers) was as determined as Augustine to link all of these to the sexual act.

Freud was opposed to religion, which he considered to be institutionalized neurosis. His younger colleague Carl Jung (1875–1961), who had a somewhat mystical turn of mind, differed with him here, as elsewhere, and added the notion of a collective unconscious, drawing upon archetypal figures with significance to the race as well as the individual. The Shadow was what he called the despair resulting from repression of the unconscious. Jung's influence on artists and writers may be even greater than Freud's; they certainly understand the Shadow.

Far from disappearing in the twentieth century, Hell became one of its most important and pervasive metaphors. Even John Bunyan had known what he was doing on some level when he changed the Slough of Hell in the old sermon to the Slough of Despond for *The Pilgrim's Progress*. But it was an entirely different level from that used by an intellectual writer like Thomas Mann, deeply influenced by Freud and Nietzsche, who set *Doktor Faustus* (1948) in Hitler's Germany, where his obsessed and despairing musician-hero goes mad. Fyodor Dostoevsky (1821–1881), in a series of powerful novels exploring good and evil, sanity and madness, had already brought demonic imagery to realistic writing; no one has ever made a stronger case for what Nietzsche called the death of God than Ivan in *The Brothers Karamazov*.

Modern writers have used the Hell metaphor with great imagination in a number of ways. Ironic phantasmagoria is pervasive. Goethe's *Faust*: Part II led to the "Night-town," or underworld brothel section of James Joyce's *Ulysses* (1922), and hence to Mann's *Doktor Faustus*, William Gaddis's *The Recognitions* (1955), and Salman Rushdie's *The Satanic Verses* (1988), though the last is more about devils than Hell.

A straightforward journey into dangerous territory, frequently a jungle or a war zone, can also parallel an inner journey; Joseph Conrad's novel *Heart of Darkness* (1902) is a well-known example. But when Francis Ford Coppola updated it to the period and setting of the Vietnam War for his 1979 film, *Apocalypse Now*, he chose a phantasmagoric technique, which seems more natural to the post–World War II era. Joseph Heller used the same technique in *Catch-22*, as did Günter Grass in *The Tin Drum*, Jerzy Kosinski in *The Painted Bird*, and J. M. Coetzee in *The Life and Times* of *Michael K.* Similarly, Picasso's anguished *Guernica* (1937) is a war painting but recognizably a Hell painting too, squarely in the tradition.

There is a kind of intellectual's Hell, too. In *Don Juan in Hell*, George Bernard Shaw had the Comandatore, the traditional figure of virtue in Don Juan plays, descend to Hell because he found Heaven too symmetrical and stiff. In Jean-Paul Sartre's *No Exit*, on the other hand, people bore each other for all eternity.

Another modern view of Hell is that of the wasteland, which first appeared in the "starved ignoble nature" of Robert Browning's "*Childe Roland to the dark tower came.*" Browning claimed not to know where the blighted nightmare imagery of the poem came from or what it meant, but T. S. Eliot was more sanguine when he appropriated it for *The Waste Land* (1922). Eliot is one of the great chthonic poets, borrowing from and adding to the entire tradition. His is a Hell of exhaustion and anomie, an arid void where emptiness of heart and meaning add up to "rat's alley,/ Where dead men lose their bones." He returned to this landscape in other poems, notably "The Hollow Men" (1925), which takes its epigraph from *Heart of Darkness*, and in "Little Gidding" (1942), the last of the *Four Quartets*, where his guide to the underworld is a "familiar compound ghost," mainly of Dante and the recently deceased Yeats.

This existential waste or a neighboring half-acre is also, I suggest, where the protagonists of nearly all the novels and plays of Samuel Beckett crawl or loiter or, like the denizens of one of Dante's *bolge*, are buried up to their necks. It is not so far from Kafka's territory either. Even in J. R. R. Tolkien's fantasy trilogy, *The Lord of the Rings*, the evidence of the Dark Lord's power is a blighted terrain populated with grotesque figures, almost like a post-nuclear holocaust desert.

Hell is effectively allied to madness, either depression or schizophrenia, in other books, not all of them fiction. Hannah Greenberg used luminous Miltonic imagery in *I Never Promised You a Rose Garden*, the famous novel of schizophrenia. Mark Vonnegut described his own bout with drugs and schizophrenia in *The Eden Express*. In about the middle of the century, an English psychoanalyst, R. D. Laing, suggested that a descent or lapse into willful madness, with or without the aid of drugs, could be profitable to the soul; the procedure turns up in several novels by Doris Lessing, notably *Briefing for a Descent into Hell*.

Treatment of Hell in the movies or on television is mostly gothic and

Auguste Rodin (1840–1917) worked on his Gate of Hell for many years. He did not follow any one tradition, but this is a relief of Ugolino, from Dante.

---

trivial, a chance for set designers and special-effects people to strut their stuff. Metaphor can play well on film—as in two wonderful Orpheus movies, Jean Cocteau's *Orphee* (1949) and Marcel Camus's *Black Orpheus* (1959)—but commercial studios usually avoid it. One commercial movie that handled an old theme strikingly was *Aliens* (1986), a science-fiction adventure in which actress Sigourney Weaver, a space-age Inanna, descends to a fearful Hell to rescue a child from a monstrous Ereshkigal. A comic Hell with amusing imps often turns up in cartoons, both still and animated. A dark comic novel, *The Living End* (1979) by Stanley Elkin is set entirely in a Hell of the most traditional medieval dreadfulness—a neat trick.

Hell will probably continue to fade from religious teaching, especially as research into the "near-death experience" continues. But as a flexible metaphor it is far too valuable to lose, though it will surely continue to change, as it has so frequently and remarkably since Mesopotamian days.

Acknowledgments

Though this is not a scholarly work, some distinguished scholars have been kind enough to read parts of it. Many thanks to Harold Bloom of Yale and New York University; Norman Cantor and James P. Carse, both of New York University; Emily Vermeule of Harvard. Any errors in the text are my own responsibility, certainly not theirs. The relatively new Liberal Studies department of New York University's Graduate School of Arts and Sciences provided an ideal cross-disciplinary springboard for the first chapters, and I am particularly grateful to Cynthia Ward for extending library privileges. Thanks to Carol Hill for being my school buddy, to Margaret Atwood for Gothic inspiration; to Ted Klein for some good suggestions, to Tom Disch for John Martin, to Jeffrey Schaire for publishing a handsome preview in *Art & Antiques*, to Ken Feisel, who did the maps, and to Anne Freedgood, for both her enthusiasm and her hard-line editing. Two special thank-yous: To Eric Ashworth, my agent and friend. And to Anne Stainton Dane, my dear Roo, for endless moral support, useful books, and infinite wisdom.

In a bibliography all books are equal, but in reality some are more equal than others. Though no one knows better than he how different infernology is from diabology, the pioneer scholarly work of Jeffrey Burton Russell in five very readable books on the Devil was a constant touchstone. Other dog-eared books are Robert Hughes's *Heaven and Hell in Western Art*,

244

D. P. Walker's *The Decline of Hell*, Jacques Le Goff's *The Birth of Purgatory*, Paul Johnson's *A History of Christianity*, and Howard Rollin Patch's *The Other World*. A. R. L. Bell's unpublished thesis on the Harrowing of Hell was useful, and I am grateful to Alan Bernstein for sending reprints of several articles; Mr. Bernstein's forthcoming scholarly work on Hell in the Middle Ages is greatly anticipated in infernal circles.

I have been asked a number of times what put the idea for this book in my head. The truth is that it was my belated discovery of Gilgamesh, Enkidu, Inanna, and Ereshkigal. I was so surprised and delighted by Mesopotamian myth that I thought I might explore the rest of the Great Below. It has been a journey that has taken me in directions I never anticipated.

Bibliography

Abrams, M. H. *Natural Supernaturalism: Tradition and Revolution in Romantic Literature*. New York: Norton, 1971.

Apuleius. *The Golden Ass of Apuleius*. Translated by Robert Graves. New York: Pocket Library, 1958.

Arbes, Rudolph. *Tertullian, Father of the Church*. 1959. Reprint. Washington, D.C.: Catholic University Press, 1977.

Ariès, Philippe. *Images of Man and Death*. Translated by Janet Lloyd. Cambridge: Harvard University Press, 1985.

Ariès, Philippe. *The Hour of Our Death*. Translated by Helen Weaver. New York: Knopf, 1981.

Aristophanes. *Five Comedies*. Translated by Benjamin Bickley Rogers. Garden City, NY: Doubleday, Anchor Books, 1955.

Auerbach, Erich. *Mimesis*. Translated by Willard R. Trask. Princeton: Princeton University Press, 1953.

Bakhtin, Mikhail: *Rabelais and His World*. Translated by Helene Iswolsky. Bloomington: Indiana University Press, 1984.

Bate, Walter Jackson. *John Keats*. Cambridge: Harvard University Press, 1979.

Bate, Walter Jackson. *Samuel Johnson*. New York: Harcourt Brace Jovanovich, 1975, 1977.

Bayle, Pierre: *Dictionnaire historique*. Le Havre: P. de Hondt, 1759.

Becker, Ernest J. *A Contribution to the Comparative Study of the Medieval Visions of Heaven and Hell, with Special Reference to the Middle-English Versions*. Baltimore: John Murphy Company, 1899.

Bell, A. R. L. "The Harrowing of Hell: A Study of Its Reception and Artistic Interpretation in Early Medieval European Literature," Ph.D. diss., University of Maryland, 1971.

Berthold, Margot. *The History of World Theater: From the Beginnings to the Baroque*. Translated by Edith Simmons. New York: Continuum, 1972, 1990.

Blake, William. *The Complete Poetry and Prose of William Blake*. Edited by David V. Erdman. Berkeley and Los Angeles: University of California Press, 1981.

Bloch, Marc. *Feudal Society*, vols. 1 and 2. Translated by L. A. Manyon. Chicago: University of Chicago, 1961.

Bloom, Harold: *The Visionary Company: A Reading of English Romantic Poetry*. Ithaca: Cornell, 1971.

Boase, T. S. R. *Death in the Middle Ages: Mortality, Judgment and Remembrance*. New York: McGraw-Hill, 1972.

Bosing, Walter. *Hieronymus Bosch: Between Heaven and Hell*. Cologne: Benedikt Taschen, 1987.

Boyce, Mary, ed. and trans. *Textual Sources for the Study of Zoroastrianism*. Manchester: Manchester University Press, 1984. Reprint. Chicago: University of Chicago Press, 1990.

Brown, Peter. *Augustine of Hippo: A Biography*. Berkeley and Los Angeles: University of California Press, 1967.

Brown, Peter. *The Making of Late Antiquity*. Cambridge: Harvard University Press, 1978.

Brown, Peter. *Society and the Holy in Late Antiquity*. Berkeley and Los Angeles: University of California Press, 1982.

Budge, E. A. Wallis. *The Egyptian Heaven and Hell*. Vol. 3, *The Contents of the Books of the Other World Described and Compared*. New York: AMS Press, 1976.

Burckhardt, Jacob. *The Civilization of the Renaissance in Italy*. Translated by S. G. C. Middlemore. New York: Random House, Modern Library, 1954.

Burkert, Walter. *Greek Religion*. Translated by John Raffan. Cambridge: Harvard University Press, 1985.

Burkert, Walter. *Homo Necans: The Anthropology of Ancient Greek Sacrificial Ritual and Myth.* Translated by Peter Bing. Berkeley and Los Angeles: University of California Press, 1983.

Bush, Douglas, ed. *John Keats: Selected Poems and Letters.* Boston: Houghton Mifflin, 1959.

Butler, Eliza Marion. *The Fortunes of Faust.* London: Cambridge University Press, 1952.

Byron, Lord, George Gordon. *Byron: Selections.* Edited by Jerome J. McGann. New York: Oxford University Press, 1986.

Campbell, Joseph. *The Hero with a Thousand Faces.* 2nd ed. Bollingen Series, vol. XVII. Princeton: Princeton University Press, 1968.

Camporesi, Piero. *The Fear of Hell: Images of Damnation and Salvation in Early Modern Europe.* Translated by Lucinda Byatt. University Park, PA: Pennsylvania State University Press, 1991.

Cantor, Norman. *Medieval History: The Life and Death of a Civilization.* New York: Macmillan, 1963.

Cohn, Norman R. C. *The Pursuit of the Millennium.* 1957. 2nd ed. New York: Oxford University Press, 1972.

Coughlan, Robert, and the editors of Time-Life Books. *The World of Michelangelo:1475–1564.* Alexandria, VA: Time-Life Books, 1966.

Dalley, Stephanie, trans. *Myths from Mesopotamia: Creation, the Flood, Gilgamesh, and Others.* New York: Oxford University Press, 1989.

Dante Alighieri. *Dante: The Divine Comedy. vol. I: Inferno.* Translated by Mark Musa. Bloomington, Indiana University Press, 1971. Reprint, New York: Penguin, 1984.

Dante Alighieri. *The Inferno.* Translated by John Ciardi. 1954. New York: 2nd ed. New American Library, 1982

Dante Alighieri. *The Inferno.* Translated by Dorothy Sayers. Baltimore: Penguin, 1950.

Davidson, Clifford and Thomas H. Seiler, eds. *The Iconography of Hell.* Kalamazoo: Medieval Institute Publications, Western Michigan University, 1992.

Davidson, Gustav. *A Dictionary of Angels, Including the Fallen Angels.* New York: Free Press, 1967.

Davidson, H. R. Ellis. *Gods and Myths of Northern Europe.* Baltimore: Penguin, 1964.

248

Davidson, H. R. Ellis. *Myths and Symbols in Pagan Europe: Early Scandinavian and Celtic Religions.* Syracuse, NY: Syracuse University Press, 1988.

Delumeau, Jean. *Sin and Fear: The Emergence of a Western Guilt Culture 13th–18th Centuries.* Translated by Erich Nicholson. New York: St. Martin's Press, 1990.

Diderot, Denis: *Encyclopèdie ou Dictionnaire raisonne des sciences, des arts et des metiers.* New York: Adler, 1967.

Dodds, E. R. *The Greeks and the Irrational.* Berkeley and Los Angeles: University of California Press, 1951.

Dodds, E. R. *Pagan and Christian in an Age of Anxiety: Some Aspects of Religious Experience from Marcus Aurelius to Constantine.* New York: Norton, 1965.

Dolan, John P., ed. and trans. *The Essential Erasmus.* New York: New American Library, Mentor-Omega, 1964.

Donne, John. *The Complete Poetry and Selected Prose of John Donne.* Edited by Charles M. Coffin. New York: Modern Library, 1952.

Ebor, Donald *et al.*, trans. *The New English Bible with the Apocrypha.* New York: Oxford University Press and Cambridge University Press, 1970.

Eimerl, Sarel. *The World of Giotto.* New York: Time, Inc., 1967.

Eliade, Mircea *et al.*, eds. *The Encyclopedia of Religion.* New York: Macmillan, 1987.

Elsen, Albert E. *The Gates of Hell by Auguste Rodin.* Stanford, CA: Stanford University Press, 1985.

Emerson, Ralph Waldo. *Essays and Lectures.* New York: The Library of America Series, Literary Classics of the U.S., 1983.

Emmerson, Richard Kenneth. *Antichrist in the Middle Ages: A Study of Medieval Apocalypticism, Art, and Literature.* Seattle: University of Washington Press, 1981.

The Encyclopedia Britannica. Chicago: William Benton, 1963.

Euripides. *Four Tragedies.* No. I. Edited by David Grene and Richard Lattimore. Chicago: University of Chicago Press, 1955.

Eusebius of Caesaria. *The History of the Church From Christ to Constantine.* Translated by G. A. Williamson. New York: Penguin, 1965, Reprint 1989.

Faulkner, R. O., trans. *The Ancient Egyptian Book of the Dead.* Edited by Carol Andrews. Austin: University of Texas Press, 1990.

Feaver, William. *The Art of John Martin.* Oxford: Clarendon Press, 1975.

Ferguson, John. *The Religions of the Roman Empire*. Ithaca: Cornell University Press, 1970.

Forsyth, Neil. *The Old Enemy: Satan and the Combat Myth*. Princeton: Princeton University Press, 1987.

Gardiner, Eileen, ed. *Visions of Heaven and Hell Before Dante*. New York: Italica Press, 1989.

Gardner, John and John Maier. *Gilgamesh*. New York: Knopf, 1984.

Gay, Peter. *The Enlightenment: An Interpretation, The Rise of Modern Paganism*. New York: W. W. Norton, 1966.

Gay, Peter. *The Party of Humanity: Essays in the French Enlightenment*. New York: W. W. Norton, 1971.

Gibson, Walter S. *Brueghel*. New York: Oxford University Press, 1977.

Gibson, Walter S. *Hieronymus Bosch*. New York: Oxford University Press, 1973.

Ginzburg, Carlo. *Ecstasies: Deciphering the Witches' Sabbath*. Translated by Raymond Rosenthal. New York: Pantheon, 1991.

Goethe, Johann Wolfgang von. *Faust, Part I*. Translated by Philip Wayne. New York: Penguin, 1949.

Goethe, Johann Wolfgang von. *Faust, Part II*. Translated by Philip Wayne. New York: Penguin, 1959.

Graves, Robert: *The Greek Myths*. New York: George Braziller, 1955.

Green, V. H. H. *Renaissance and Reformation: A Survey of European History between 1450 and 1660*. London: Edward Arnold, 1952.

Gurevich, Aron. *Medieval Popular Culture: Problems of Belief and Perception*. Translated by James M. Bak and Paul A. Hollingworth. New York: Cambridge University Press, 1988, 1990.

Guthrie, W. K. C. *Orpheus and Greek Religion: A Study of the Orphic Movement*. New York: W. W. Norton, 1966.

Hadas, Moses. *A History of Greek Literature*. New York: Columbia University Press, 1950.

Haskell, Ann S., ed. *A Middle English Anthology*. Garden City, NY: Doubleday, Anchor Books, 1969.

Hearn, M. F. *Romanesque Sculpture: The Revival of Monumental Stone Sculpture in the Eleventh and Twelfth Centuries*. Ithaca: Cornell University Press, 1981.

Heidel, Alexander. *The Gilgamesh Epic and Old Testament Parallels.* Chicago: University of Chicago Press, 1949.

Herbermann, Charles George *et al.*, eds. *The Catholic Encyclopedia.* Vol. 17. New York: Appleton, 1907–1912.

Hesiod. *Theogony, Work and Days.* Translated by M. L. West. New York: Oxford University Press, 1988.

Himmelfarb, Martha. *Tours of Hell: An Apocalyptic Form in Jewish and Christian Literature.* Philadelphia: University of Pennsylvania Press, 1983.

Hinnells, John R., ed. *A Handbook of Living Religions.* New York: Penguin, 1984.

Holmes, Richard. *Coleridge: Early Visions.* New York: Viking, 1989.

Homer. *The Odyssey.* Translated by Robert Fitzgerald. 1961. Garden City, NY: Doubleday, Anchor Books, 1963.

Hooke, S. H. *Middle Eastern Mythology.* Baltimore: Viking-Penguin, 1963.

Houghton, Walter E. *The Victorian Frame of Mind.* New Haven: Yale University Press, 1957.

Hughes, Robert. *Heaven and Hell in Western Art.* New York: Stein & Day, 1968.

Huizinga, Johan. *The Waning of the Middle Ages: A Study of the Forms of Life, Thought, and Art in France and the Netherlands in the XIVth and XVth Centuries.* Translated by A. Hopman. Garden City, NY: Doubleday, Anchor Books, 1949, 1954.

Huxley, Aldous. *Heaven and Hell.* New York: Harper, 1956.

James, Montague Rhodes. *The Apocryphal New Testament.* Oxford: Clarendon, 1924, 1953.

Johnson, Paul. *A History of Christianity.* New York: Atheneum, 1976.

Johnson, Samuel. *A Dictionary of the English Language.* London: W. Strahan, 1765.

Jonas, Hans. *The Gnostic Religion: The Message of the Alien God and the Beginnings of Christianity.* 2nd ed. Boston: Beacon Press, 1963.

Keener, Frederick M. *English Dialogues of the Dead: A Critical History, an Anthology, and a Checklist.* New York: Columbia University Press, 1973.

Kirk, G. S. *Myth: Its Meaning and Functions in Ancient and Other Cultures.* Berkeley and Los Angeles: University of California Press, 1970.

Kirk, G. S. *The Nature of Greek Myths.* Hammondsworth: Penguin, 1974.

Koester, Helmut. *History, Culture and Religion of the Hellenistic Age.* Philadelphia: Fortress Press, 1982.

Kovacs, Maureen Gallery, trans. *The Epic of Gilgamesh.* Stanford, CA: Stanford University Press, 1989.

Kramer, Samuel Noah. *Mythologies of the Ancient World.* Garden City, NY: Doubleday, Anchor Books, 1961.

Kramer, Samuel Noah. *Sumerian Mythology: A Study of Spiritual and Literary Achievement in the Third Millennium B.C.* Philadelphia: University of Pennsylvania Press, 1961, 1972.

Kren, Thomas and Roger S. Wieck. *The Visions of Tondal from the Library of Margaret of York.* Malibu, CA: The J. Paul Getty Museum, 1990.

Ladurie, Emmanuel Le Roy. *Montaillou: The Promised Land of Error.* Translated by Barbara Bray. New York: G. Braziller, 1978.

Lambert, Malcolm. *Medieval Heresy: Popular Movements from Bogomil to Hus.* New York: Holmes & Meier, 1977.

Lane Fox, Robin. *Pagans and Christians.* New York: Knopf, 1987.

Le Goff, Jacques. *The Birth of Purgatory.* Translated by Arthur Goldhammer. Chicago: University of Chicago, 1984.

Le Goff, Jacques. *Time, Work and Culture in the Middle Ages.* Translated by Arthur Goldhammer. Chicago: University of Chicago Press, 1980.

Lurker, Manfred. *Dictionary of Gods and Goddesses, Devils and Demons.* New York: Routledge and Kegan Paul, 1987.

Lurker, Manfred. *The Gods and Symbols of Ancient Egypt: An Illustrated Dictionary.* New York: Thames and Hudson, 1980.

McDannell, Colleen and Bernhard Lang. *Heaven: A History.* New Haven: Yale University Press, 1988.

McGinn, Bernard. *Visions of the End: Apocalyptic Traditions in the Middle Ages.* New York: Columbia University Press, 1979.

McManners, John. *Death and the Enlightenment: Changing Attitudes to Death among Christians and Unbelievers in Eighteenth-Century France.* New York: Oxford University Press, 1981.

McNeill, John T. and Helena M. Gamer. *Medieval Handbooks of Penance.* New York: Columbia University Press, 1938.

Marlowe, Christopher. *The Complete Plays.* Edited by J. B. Steane. Hammondsworth: Penguin, 1969.

252

Melton, J. Gordon, ed. *The Encyclopedia of American Religions.* "Religious Creeds." Detroit: Gale Research, 1987.

Meredith, Peter and John E. Tailby. *The Staging of Religious Drama in Europe in the Later Middle Ages: Texts and Documents in English Translation.* Translated by Rafaella Ferrari. Kalamazoo: Medieval Institute Publications, Western Michigan University, 1983.

Meyer, Marvin W., ed. *The Ancient Mysteries: A Sourcebook, Sacred Texts of the Mystery Religions of the Ancient Mediterranean World.* San Francisco: Harper & Row, Perennial Library, 1986.

Migne, J. P. *et al.,* eds. *Encyclopedie Theologique.* Paris: Chez 1 Editeur, 1845–1873.

Milton, John. *The Student's Milton.* Edited by Frank Allen Patterson. New York: Appleton-Century-Crofts, 1957.

Ovid. *The Metamorphoses.* Translated by Horace Gregory. New York: Viking, Mentor, 1958, 1960.

Owen, D. D. R. *The Vision of Hell: Infernal Journeys in Medieval French Literature.* New York: Barnes & Noble, 1971.

Owst, G. R. *Literature and Pulpit in Medieval England: A Neglected Chapter in the History of English Letters and of the English People.* 2nd rev. edition. New York: Barnes & Noble, 1966.

Panofsky, Erwin. *Gothic Architecture and Scholasticism: The Middle Ages.* New York: New American Library, 1974.

Patch, Howard Rollin. *The Other World: According to Descriptions in Medieval Literature.* Cambridge: Harvard University Press, 1950.

Pike, E. Royston. *Encyclopedia of Religion and Religions.* New York: Meridian, 1958.

Plato. *The Dialogues of Plato.* Translated by Benjamin Jowett. New York: Random House, 1937.

Platt, Rutherford Hayes. *The Lost Books of the Bible and the Forgotten Books of Eden.* New York: New American Library, Meridian, 1974.

Praz, Mario. *The Romantic Agony.* Translated by Angus Davidson. New York: Oxford University Press, 1970.

Pritchard, James B., ed. *The Ancient Near East.* vol. I, *An Anthology of Texts and Pictures.* Princeton: Princeton University Press, 1958.

Pritchard, James B., ed. *The Ancient Near East.* vol. II, *A New Anthology of Texts and Pictures.* Princeton: Princeton University Press, 1975.

Rice, David G. and John E. Stambaugh. *Sources for the Study of Greek Religion.* New York: Scholars Press, 1979.

Robinson, James M. *et al.*, eds. *The Nag Hammadi Library in English.* 3rd ed. New York: HarperCollins, 1988.

Russell, Jeffrey Burton. *The Devil: Perceptions of Evil from Antiquity to Primitive Christianity.* Ithaca: Cornell University Press, 1977.

Russell, Jeffrey Burton. *Lucifer: The Devil in the Middle Ages.* Ithaca: Cornell University Press, 1984.

Russell, Jeffrey Burton. *Mephistopheles: The Devil in the Modern World.* Ithaca: Cornell University Press, 1986.

Russell, Jeffrey Burton. *The Prince of Darkness: Radical Evil and the Power of Good in History.* Ithaca: Cornell University Press, 1988.

Russell Jeffrey Burton. *Satan: The Early Christian Tradition.* Ithaca: Cornell University Press, 1981.

Shakespeare, William. *The Complete Works of Shakespeare.* Edited by George Lyman Kittredge. Boston, New York, Chicago: Ginn & Company, 1936.

Shelley, Percy Bysshe. *Shelley's Poetry and Prose.* Edited by Donald H. Reiman and Sharon B. Powers. New York: Norton Critical Edition, 1977.

Smith, Morton. *Jesus the Magician.* San Francisco: Harper & Row, 1978.

Snyder, James. *Medieval Art: Painting, Sculpture, Architecture, 4th–14th Centuries.* New York: Abrams, 1989.

Spenser, Edmund. *Edmund Spenser's Poetry: Authoritative Texts, Criticism.* Edited by Hugh MacLean. New York: W. W. Norton, 1982.

Sullivan, Jack, ed. *The Penguin Encyclopedia of Horror and the Supernatural.* New York: Viking, 1986.

Swedenborg, Emanuel. *Heaven and Hell.* New York: American-Swedenborg Printing & Publishing Society, 1883.

Terpening, Ronnie H. *Charon and the Crossing: Ancient, Medieval, and Renaissance Transformations of a Myth.* Lewisburg, PA: Bucknell University Press, 1985.

Tristram, Philippa. *Figures of Life and Death in Medieval English Literature.* London: Paul Elek, 1976.

Van der Meer, F. *Apocalypse: Visions from the Book of Revelation in Western Art.* New York: Alpine Fine Arts Collection, 1978.

Vasari, Giorgio. *The Lives of the Artists: A Selection.* Translated by George Bull. New York: Penguin, 1971.

254

Vatter, Hannes. *The Devil in English Literature.* Bern, Switzerland: Franke Verlag, 1978.

Vermeule, Emily. *Aspects of Death in Early Greek Art and Poetry.* Berkeley and Los Angeles: University of California Press, 1979.

Virgil. *The Aeneid.* Translated by Robert Fitzgerald. New York: Random House, 1983.

Voltaire, François Marie Arouet de. *Dictionnaire philosophique.* Paris: Garnier, 1967.

Wakefield, Walter L. and Austin P. Evans. *Heresies of the High Middle Ages.* New York: Columbia University Press, 1969. Reprint, 1991.

Walker, D. P. *The Decline of Hell: Seventeenth-Century Discussions of Eternal Torment.* Chicago: University of Chicago Press, 1964.

Warner, Marina. *Alone of All Her Sex: The Myth and Cult of the Virgin Mary.* New York: Vintage, 1983.

Weinstein, Leo. *The Metamorphoses of Don Juan.* New York: AMS Press, 1957.

Westfall, Richard S. *Science and Religion in Seventeenth-Century England.* Ann Arbor: University of Michigan, 1973.

Wolkstein, Diane and Samuel Noah Kramer. *Inanna, Queen of Heaven and Earth: Her Stories and Hymns from Sumer.* New York: Harper & Row, 1983.

Woolf, Rosemary. *The English Mystery Plays.* Berkeley and Los Angeles: University of California Press, 1972.

Young, Karl. *The Drama of the Medieval Church.* 1933. Oxford: Clarendon Press, 1967.

Photo Credits

2 Thirteenth-century Apocalypse, Ms. 422, Bibliothèque Municipal, Cambrai, Giraudon/Art Resource, New York

8 Mesopotamian statuette, Louvre, Paris, Giraudon/Art Resource, New York

8 Female figurine, Vorderasiatische Sammlungen, Berlin, Marburg/Art Resource, New York

10 Statuette from Nippur, Iraq Museum, Baghdad, Scala/Art Resource, New York

14–15 Funerary Papyrus of Princess Entiu-ny, from the tomb of Queen Meryet-Amun in Thebes. Courtesy of the Metropolitan Museum of Art, Museum Excavations, 1928–29 and Rogers Fund 1930.

17 Assyrian bronze Pazuzu, Louvre, Paris, Giraudon/Art Resource, New York

23 Athenian krater attributed to the "Persephone painter." Courtesy of the Metropolitan Museum of Art, Fletcher Fund 1928.

25 Black-figure hydria, sixth century B.C., Inv. E 701, Louvre, Paris, Photograph © by Erich Lessing/Art Resource, New York

28 Charon, sarcophagus, third century, Museo Vaticano, Photograph © by Erich Lessing/Art Resource, New York

56 *Englischer Psalter* M.835, München, Marburg/Art Resource, New York

57 *Psalter of St. Louis and Blanche of Castille*, French, 1223–1230, Ms.Lat.1186.f.171, Bibliothèque Nationale, Paris

59 N. Bataille, "The Beast of the Earth and the Beast from the Sea," Château Angers, Giraudon/Art Resource, New York

62 *Trier Apocalypse*, Carolingian copy of early Christian manuscript, Ms.31.f.37R, Trier Stadtbibliothek, Germany

64 Pantaleone, mosaic floor, twelfth century, Otranto, Photograph © by Erich Lessing/Art Resource, New York

67 *Staatsbibl Psalter*, München, 1.V.13, f.27, Marburg/Art Resource, New York

69 Andrea da Firenze, detail from *Harrowing of Hell*, Sta. Maria Novella, Florence, Alinari/Art Resource, New York

72 Twelfth-century Byzantine mosaic, Duomo, Torcello, Venice, Alinari/Art Resource, New York

75 French manuscript c. 1510, M.646.f.69, The Pierpont Morgan Library, New York, © 1993

78 "The Last Judgment," Byzantine ivory, Victoria and Albert Museum, London

81 French manuscript c. 1400–1405, "St. Augustine and the City of God," Bibliothèque Municipale, Boulogne, Giraudon/Art Resource, New York

84 Capital from St. Julien, Tours, Garanger-Giraudon/Art Resource, New York

86 Capital from St. Lazare, Autun, Lauros-Giraudon/Art Resource, New York

87 Tympanum from west facade of St. Foy, Conques, Marburg/Art Resource, New York

88 Tympanum from west facade of St. Foy, Conques, Marburg/Art Resource, New York

95 Anon. sec. XV, Loreto Aprutino, PE Sta. Maria in Piano, Scala/Art Resource, New York

96 West wall painted fresco, Church of St. Peter and St. Paul, Chaldon, Surrey. Royal Commission of the Historical Monuments of England, London.

101 *The Hours of Catherine of Cleves*, M.917 f.105v., The Pierpont Morgan Library, New York, © 1993

107 Viking stone, Statens Historiska Museet, Stockholm, Werner Forman Archive/Art Resource, New York

110 Last Judgment, Hans Memling, Marburg/Art Resource, New York

117 Elme Kathedral, Elme, Germany, Marburg/Art Resource, New York

124 Jean Colombe, Death with an Arrow, Bourges, France, M.677 f.245, The Pierpont Morgan Library, New York © 1993

124 *Three Living and the Three Dead*, M.14, f.130v–131, The Pierpont Morgan Library, New York, © 1993

130 Purgatory, M.677 f.329, The Pierpont Morgan Library, New York, © 1993

131 Hieronymus Bosch, Vision of Purgatory, Palazzo Ducale, Venice, Scala/Art Resource, New York

139 William Blake, illustration to *Divine Comedy*, Tate/Art Resource, New York

142 Giotto, detail of *Last Judgment*, Scrovegni Chapel, Padua, Alinari/Art Resource, New York

154 *The Harrowing of Hell*, c. 1550, Pieter Brueghel the Elder, Albertina, Vienna, Marburg/Art Resource, New York

155 *The Last Judgment*, 1558, Pieter Brueghel the Elder, Albertina, Vienna, Marburg/Art Resource, New York

156 *The Last Judgment*, Michelangelo, Vatican, Sistine Chapel, Scala/Art Resource, New York

164 Theophilis, *Psalter of Ingeborg of Denmark*, Musée Condé, Chantilly, Ms. G/1695 f.35v., Giraudon/Art Resource, New York

175 Giulio Romano, Nymph and Satryr, Palazzo del Te, Mantua, Photograph © by Erich Lessing/Art Resource, New York

185 After Cox, Ken Feisel

195 After Swinden, Ken Feisel

200 Joseph Thaddaeus Stammel, carved wood, Abbey Library, Admont, Austria, Photograph © by Erich Lessing/Art Resource, New York

243 Auguste Rodin, Ugolino from *Gate of Hell*, Kunstgewerbemuseum, Zurich, Photograph © by Erich Lessing/Art Resource, New York

COLOR CREDITS

PLATE 1: The Jaws of Hell Fastened by an Angel, *Psalter of Henry of Blois, Bishop of Winchester*, Bridgeman/Art Resource, New York

PLATE 2: French Beatus Apocalypse, M.644 f.152v.,f.153, Pierpont Morgan Library, New York, © 1993

PLATE 3: Limbourgs, Fall of the Rebel Angels, *Les Très Riches Heures du Duc de Berry*, Chantilly, Musée Condé, Ms.65 f.64v., Giraudon/Art Resource, New York

PLATE 4: Limbourgs, Hell, *Les Très Riches Heures du Duc de Berry*, Chantilly, Musée Condé, Ms.65 f.108, Giraudon/Art Resource, New York

PLATES 5 & 6: Collection of the J. Paul Getty Museum, Malibu, California, Simon Marmion (attrib.), *Les Visiones du Chevalier Tundal*, 1474, tempera on vellum, 36.3 × 26.2 cm. 87.MN.141 (Ms 30) f.13 v. (top), f.17 (bottom)

PLATES 7 & 8: Collection of the J. Paul Getty Museum, Malibu, California, Simon Marmion (attrib.), *Les Visiones du Chevalier Tundal*, 1474, tempera on vellum, 36.3 × 26.2 cm., 87.MN.141 (Ms 30) f.20 (top), f.24 v. (bottom)

259

PLATES 9 & 10: Collection of the J. Paul Getty Museum, Malibu, California, Simon Marmion (attrib.), *Les Visiones du Chevalier Tundal*, 1474, tempera on vellum, 36.3 × 26.2 cm., 87.MN.141 (Ms 30) f.24 v. (top), f.30 v. (bottom)

PLATE 11: Detail of Torcello mosaic, Venice, Scala/Art Resource, New York

PLATE 12: Detail of Florence baptistry, Scala/Art Resource, New York

PLATE 13: Giotto, detail of *Last Judgment,* Scrovegni Chapel, Padua, Scala/Art Resource, New York

PLATE 14: Francesco Traini, detail of *Inferno,* Camposanto, Pisa Scala/Art Resource, New York

PLATE 15: Anonymous *Last Judgment,* Pinacoteca, Bologna, Scala/Art Resource, New York

PLATES 16 & 17: Orcagna, two details of *Inferno,* Santa Maria Novella, Florence, Scala/ Art Resource, New York

PLATE 18: Luca Signorelli, detail of *The Damned in Hell,* Duomo, Orvieto, Scala/Art Resource, New York

PLATE 19: Michelangelo, detail of *Last Judgment,* Sistine Chapel, Vatican, Scala/Art Resource, New York

PLATE 20: Baciccia: *Triumph in the Name of Jesus,* Gesu Church, Rome, Scala/Art Resource, New York

PLATE 21: Jan van Eyck, *Last Judgment,* The Metropolitan Museum of Art, Fletcher Fund, 1933 (33.92b)

PLATE 22: Dieric Bouts, *Descent into Hell,* Musée des Beaux-Arts, Lille, France, Photograph © by Erich Lessing/Art Resource, New York

PLATE 23: Hans Memling, right panel, *Last Judgment,* Pomorskie Museum, Gdansk, Denmark, Scala/Art Resource, New York

PLATE 24: Hieronymus Bosch, *Inferno,* Ducal Palace, Venice, Scala/Art Resource, New York

PLATE 25: Hieronymus Bosch, right panel, *Last Judgement,* Inv. 4 D, Akademie der Bildenden Kuenste, Vienna, Photograph © by Erich Lessing/Art Resource, New York

PLATE 26: Hieronymus Bosch, right panel, *The Hay-wain,* Prado, Madrid, Scala/Art Resource, New York

PLATE 27: Hieronymus Bosch, right panel, *The Garden of Earthly Delights,* Prado, Madrid, Scala/Art Resource, New York

PLATE 28: Pieter Brueghel the Elder, *Fall of the Rebel Angels,* Royal Museum of Fine Arts, Brussels, Scala/Art Resource, New York

PLATE 29: Pieter Brueghel the Elder, *Dulle Griet,* Museum Mayer van den Bergh, Antwerp, Belgium, Photograph © by Erich Lessing/Art Resource, New York

PLATE 30: Herri met de Bles, *L'Inferno,* Palazzo Ducale, Venice, Scala/Art Resource, New York

PLATE 31: Jan Brueghel, *Orpheus in Hell,* Palatina, Florence, Art Resource, New York

PLATE 32: Peter Paul Rubens, *The Damned,* Alte Pinakothek, Munich, Giraudon/Art Resource, New York

PLATE 33: *Book of Hours of Catherine of Cleves,* M.945, f.169, Pierpont Morgan Library, © 1993

PLATES 34 & 35: "Drunkards and Lustful in Hell" and "Thieves in Hell," *Le Trésor de Sapience,* Chantilly, Musée Condé, Ms.146, Giraudon/Art Resource, New York

PLATE 36: *Hours of the Virgin* written at Rouen for Claude I Mole, M.356 f.64, Pierpont Morgan Library, © 1993

PLATE 37: William Blake: *The Simoniac Pope,* c. 1825, Tate/Art Resource, New York

PLATE 38: William Blake: *Satan Rousing the Rebel Angels,* Victoria and Albert Museum/Art Resource, New York

PLATE 39: William Blake, *The Last Judgment,* The National Trust, Petworth House, Bridgeman Art Library/Art Resource, New York

PLATE 40: William Hogarth, *Satan, Sin and Death,* Tate Gallery/Art Resource, New York

PLATE 41: John Martin, *The Fallen Angels Entering Pandemonium,* Tate Gallery/Art Resource, New York

PLATE 42: Auguste Rodin, *The Gates of Hell,* Musée d'Orsay, Paris, Giraudon/Art Resource, New York

INDEX

Pages in italics refer to illustrations.